The Firstborn of God

Resolving the contradictions in the Bible

Gail Evans

Writers Club Press

San Jose New York Lincoln Shanghai

The Firstborn of God
Resolving the contradictions in the Bible

Published by Writers Club Press
an imprint of iUniverse.com, Inc.

For information address:
iUniverse.com, Inc.
620 North 48th Street
Suite 201
Lincoln, NE 68504-3467
www.iuniverse.com

ISBN: 0-595-09695-6

Printed in the United States of America

Dedicated to Millar Burrows
A man of letters who has received the teaching of the
kingdom of heaven and is like a householder who
brings forth from his storehouse things new and old.

Matthew 13:52

Contents

Introduction vii

Chapter One.
In the Beginning 1
Chapter Two.
Origins...17
Chapter Three.
The Lost Tribes of Israel...53
Chapter Four.
The Sadducees..81
Chapter Five.
The Essenes 101
Chapter Six.
Jesus 121
Chapter Seven.
Zion 155
Chapter Eight
Sabbath 185
Chapter Nine.
The Bride..201
Chapter Ten.
The Bridegroom 237
Chapter Eleven.
Yom Kippur and the Nazarene...259

Epilogue..271
Bibliography 273

Introduction

Throughout history our religious beliefs have been instrumental in shaping our social and political structures. Whether we are devout or not, the fundamental philosophies of any given religion will dictate the way in which we interact with each other on a mental, social and political level. The Western world is no exception and has based its theology on a text known as *"The Bible."*

But what is *"The Bible?"* Is it a collection of scrolls written by a group of old men? Or is it the word of God as so many claim it to be? If the Bible really is the word of God, then it should follow that the chapters and verses will be clear cut, easily understood and lack ambiguity. But this is not the case. The Bible is ambiguous and many of its texts contradict each other which in turn implies that the scribes who wrote them had differing views on the divine word of God. Interpret the Bible one way and you get Ecclesiastes 5:3:

"For a dream cometh through the multitude of business:....."

Interpret it another way and you get Job 33:15 & 16:

"In a dream, in a vision of the night, when deep sleep falleth upon men, in slumberings upon the bed; Then he openeth the ears of men and sealeth their instruction."

Ecclesiastes regards dreams as nonsense and suggests that we pay little attention to them. Job, on the other hand, regards dreams as the vehicle through which God communicates with people. Such contradictions suggest that the Bible is not so much the hard and fast word of God, but a collection of scrolls, written by various people, who had opposing views on our relationship with the Supreme Being.

For the last two thousand years the Bible has been taken at face value and these contradictions accepted on faith. Perhaps this is due to an innate fear deep within the psyche that forbids us to question the texts in an academic or even logical way. We have this fear even though the contradictions leave democratic societies in a quandary. Do we accept Judaic/Christian theology on faith even though some of its precepts defy all logic? Or do we give the Bible a miss altogether? If theology advocates a certain philosophy, eg: sexual discrimination as advocated by Canon law which bases it's principles on the epistles of Paul and the words of Peter:

"Man only is created in the image of God, not women: therefore women shall serve him and be his hand-maid."

While our social norms advocate another, being equality between the sexes, then this poses a problem and results in a huge disparity between our social and religious ethics.

If our religious philosophy advocates servitude and slavery without due recourse to the law and basic human rights, 1 Peter 2:18 & 19:

"Servants, be subject to your masters with all fear; not only to the good and gentle, but also to the froward.

For this is thankworthy, if a man for conscience toward God endure grief and suffering wrongfully."

While our economic reforms stipulate the just and fair treatment of employees, then this results in a huge disparity between our economic and religious ethics.

I believe that it is time to challenge the texts, confront the contradictions and attempt to make sense of the Bible so that our rich religious heritage can provide a sound framework on which to ground our psychological, social and political philosophies in the future.

Societies today are a far cry from the Hebrew herdsmen who crossed into Canaan and polygamy no longer forms part of our family structures. Draconian states no longer hold sway as they did when the masses in Palestine were suppressed and finally massacred under the Roman Empire's sword. We are very different from the men and women in the Middle Ages who were burnt at the stake for daring to question the status quo or disagree with Roman Catholic doctrine. Today we cherish our hard won freedom and this in turn should enable us to use our greatest gift, the ability to think for ourselves rather than becoming brainwashed by one fundamentalistic ideology or another. By so doing, we can make up our own minds as to the validity and/or significance of a given text and we should have the right to accept or reject what the scribes wrote long ago. To quote from Qumram Text 4Q416,418, fragment 10, column 2, lines 15 & 16:

"…in the abundance of your (15) intellectual potential, investigate the Mystery of Existence." [1]

In other words, contrary to orthodox belief, I believe that it is for us to question, it is for us to undo the tangled rope of contradiction in the Bible in order to arrive at a workable religious philosophy that is not only pertinent to the modern world, but applicable for all time.

---

1. Robert Eisenman & Michael Wise. "The Dead Sea Scrolls Uncovered." Element Books Limited. 1992.

Throughout my efforts to try to resolve the contradictions, I have found that the Bible, rather than being one coherent and continuous belief system, contains two different stories, two different philosophies on life. A person or philosophy that is damned in one particular text is lauded in the next which in turn creates a contradiction. In order to resolve these contradictory beliefs, I have used the premise: democracy, equality, a justice of liberty and self empowerment in order to sift the chaff from the wheat. Only by using such a yard stick, can these ancient texts become coherent and the Bible "jig saw puzzle" falls into place.

Should you not agree with the doctrines of democracy, equality, a justice of liberty under the law and self empowerment, then in many instances you may find my conclusions to be sacrilegious. If, however, you do judge the world by these standards, and as I have stipulated, you can accept that our religious beliefs shape our social and political structures, then I hope that you will find my interpretations enlightening in the face of a new world order that desperately needs a revised religious epistemology to support it.

Chapter One.

In the Beginning

"In the beginning, God created the heaven and the earth. And the earth was without form, and void; and darkness was upon the face of the deep. And the Spirit of God moved upon the face of the waters."

So begins the first page of the Bible. This is the first story of creation. It is a Hebrew story written by what is known as *"P,"* the Priestly Author, in approximately the sixth century B.C., and is based on what is known as *"E,"* or the Elohist text which was written sometime between the eighth and tenth centuries B.C. The first name used for *"God"* in the Hebrew text is *"Elohim."* So a more accurate translation would be:

"In the beginning, Elohim created the heaven and the earth. And the earth was without form and void; and darkness was upon the face of the deep. And the Spirit of Elohim moved upon the face of the waters."

El is a masculine prefix and means *"power,"* while Ohim is a feminine suffix which is plural and duplicates the prefix El to make it *"powers,"* which implies a Supreme Being of both masculine and feminine form. With this in mind consider the Spirit that moves *"upon the face of the waters."* God does not create the Spirit, but has a Spirit. The Spirit is an inherent part of the Elohim and it's ability to duplicate, to create and

1

make more. If God is masculine, then the Spirit or Wisdom, the feminine component of the Elohim is the bride of God, as she refers to herself in Proverbs 8:22 & 23:

"The Lord possessed me in the beginning of his way, before his works of old. I was set up from everlasting, from the beginning, or ever the earth was."

Other epithets and symbols applied to the Holy Spirit are: Spirit of truth, Paraclete, Comforter, Consoler, Wisdom, Patience, Dove. The *"Holy Spirit"* equates with the Hebrew concept of the Shekinah, a divine light and is placed on Malkuth in the Kabbala.[2] Like the *"ohim"* which is a feminine suffix, the Shekinah is the feminine component of the Godhead. Some authors would go so far as to translate Elohim as a female noun translated as *"goddess."*[3] Although this may well prove to be the case, I would prefer to see it as both masculine and feminine in gender, in fact being genderless where all duality is resolved.

From the very beginning we have an active male element and a passive feminine element associated with water. We are all created when masculine and feminine join resulting in the child that is carried within the waters of the womb which duplicates. The three in one, the Holy Trinity of father, mother and the divine child. The ancient Egyptians believed in the same trinity being Amun (Amen), his wife Mut and the divine child, Khonsu. Amun and Mut together, are the equivalent of the Elohim, God and the Spirit.

---

2. Louis Jacobs. "The Jewish Religion." Oxford University Press. 1995.

3. Andrew Collins. "From the Ashes of Angels." Michael Joseph LTD. 1996.

In Genesis 1:26, 27 & 31, God and the Spirit, who were referred to as one name being Elohim, declared:

"Let us make people in our image, after our likeness...male and female...and Elohim saw all that had been made, and it was good."

Here Elohim is called *"us."* *"El"* creates through the *"Ohim,"* the Spirit, the bride, the duplicating factor. Elohim rejoices in fruitfulness and sees all under the heavens as good. It is both father and mother and we, the human race, are made in their image. The Hebrew word for *"image"* is *"selem"* and means an *"exact duplicate."*[4] Unlike religions of the time, as in Egypt and Mesopotamia, where we have a divine *"child"* which led to the belief in the divine rule of kings descended from this child, Genesis 1 speaks in terms of divine *"children"* and therefore implies that the human race as a whole is divine.

Genetically speaking, we are made up of chromosomes from both our mother and our father while psychologically, the brain is divided into left and right, each side being predisposed to male and female tendencies respectively. In such a way Genesis 1 reflects our biological and psychological make up and this religious philosophy on our origins based on divine *"children"* in turn implies equality between the sexes and all races and can be extended into the full range of the human experience, be it religious, social or political.

For those who doubt that the feminine face of God is regarded by some texts as being part and parcel of the Elohim, consider Proverbs

---

4. Michael Macrone. "Brush Up Your Bible." Harper Collins Publishers Inc., New York. 1993.

and The Wisdom of Solomon where the feminine side finds her own voice. Proverbs 8:35 & 36:

"For whoso findeth me findeth life, and shall obtain favour of the Lord. But he that sinneth against me wrongeth his own soul: all they that hate me love death."

Wisdom of Solomon 9:9 & 10:

"And wisdom was with thee, which knoweth thy works, and was present when thou madest the world, and knew what was acceptable in thy sight, and right in thy commandments...O send her out of thy holy heavens, and from the throne of thy glory, that being present she may labour with me, that I may know what is pleasing unto thee..."

As with two book ends, so the first page of the Bible is reflected in the last. The sole purpose of Revelation is to tell the story of the marriage between the Lord and Zion, the Lord and the bride which results in heaven on earth. These book ends are connected by a thread that tells the tale, in one way or another, about the separation of the unified Elohim, the separation of God and the Spirit or Wisdom, the Bride and the Bridegroom and the Lord and Zion. This separation occurs in a religious context where God is referred to as a masculine entity only and the feminine principle is derided or even totally ignored. The separation occurs in a social context where scribes such as Peter and Paul advocate the subjugation of women. The separation also occurs in an economic context where men and women are subjected to slavery for the sole purpose of benefiting a small minority such as a king and his courtiers as were the Hebrews before the Exodus. In a political context it occurs in the schism between the northern Ephraimite Kingdom of Israel and the southern Kingdom of Judah. In the last book, when heaven descends on earth, the two again become as one and are reconciled creating stability and peace:

"As it was in the beginning, is now and ever shall be...."Come!" say the Spirit and the bride. "Come!" let each hearer reply...world without end. Amen."

This story is as old as the hills. Good versus evil, freedom versus slavery. Nearly all story lines that have ever been written fall between these parameters. Running concurrent with this theme is love found, love lost and love regained. Love lost always co-insides with evil, oppression and slavery. Good and freedom are always accomplished in conjunction with love regained.

Genesis 1 describes the six steps of creation through analogy. There is a direct scientific correlation between Genesis 1, the origins of the universe and the Evolution theory. Below is a chart, mapping out their similarity.

GENESIS 1	THE ORIGINS OF THE UNIVERSE.
NO TIME	
Verses 1–2.	A pre-geometry of foamlike or
The Elohim and the	souplike space time
"Powers" that move	whose laws of physics are
across the waters.	unknown.
DAY 1.	
Verses 3–5.	Electromagnetic and weak
The powers that burst	forces that separate
forth and separate the	light and darkness, matter
universe into dark and	and antimatter. From a
light.	plasma of quarks, electrons
	and other particles. Quarks
	are able to merge to form
	protons and neutrons, the
	components of atoms.
	Particles have found substance.

DAY 2.
Verses 6–8.
From out of the waters (plasma) the firmament (stars and galaxies) are created. The basic minerals of the universe.

Clusters of matter have formed from the primordial ripples to form quasars, stars, and protogalaxies. In the interior of stars, the burning of the primordial hydrogen and helium nuclei synthesizes heavier nuclei such as carbon, nitrogen, oxygen, and iron. These are dispersed by stellar winds and supernova explosions, making new stars, planets, and life possible.

DAY 3.
Verses 9–13
The bringing forth of "seeds" that would result in life.

Chemical processes have linked atoms (seeds) together to form molecules and then complicated solids and liquids.[5]

5. George Smoot and Keay Davidson. "Wrinkles in Time. The Imprint of Creation." Little Brown & Company.1993.

DAY 4.
Verses 14–18.   Beginning of the Evolution Theory.
Our solar system begins to revolve around our sun making day and night and the Moon marks out the signs for days and for seasons.

DAY 5.

Verses 20–23
From the single celled organisms in the bottom of the oceans, fish and fowl evolve.

DAY 6.
Verses 24–31.
The evolution of mammals and then the final creation of people, resulting from a cosmic soup, the Big bang or evaporating gaseous globules throughout the universe, the waters of the void.

The above text is totally in keeping with the scientific laws that govern galaxies, the foundation of galaxies, energy and matter and is totally in keeping with the process of evolution by which all living forms came about on this planet. More importantly, God is referred to as Elohim which means *"powers"* and is called *"us,"* implying a male/female godhead which is in fact one and lacks duality. This does not mean however, that we are looking at a polytheistic philosophy, as this duality, much like the Chinese concept of Yin and Yang, is contained within one force.

The same can be said of the positive and negative electrons within an atom and left and right brain functioning. The word *"man"* in turn refers to *"them,"* being all human beings of all races and also refers to both sexes. Hence, these people are the children of God, i.e. they are all the firstborn of God, images or clones so to speak. Elohim, according to Rabbinic literature, is used in association with the world as a whole and relates to all human beings. Elohim is attributed with justice.[6]

We turn the page and come to Genesis 2 and with it, the first of many contradictions. Genesis 2 originates from what is known as the book of "J," or the "Yahwist" text, written by a scribe from the southern Kingdom of Judah somewhere between the tenth and the eighth centuries B.C. According to Rabbinic literature, Jehovah or the tetragrammatron YHVH relates only to the chosen people, his attributes being mercy.[7]

The philosophies expounded on in Genesis 2 are the exact opposite to those found in Genesis 1. There is no Spirit bride, there is no *us*, human beings are not created within the sacred six days, but after the seventh day of rest and they are not made in the image of God. There is only an all male principle being the Lord, known as Jahweh, who creates a man from the dust of the earth. This story is genetically invalid and conceptually goes against the laws of nature by precluding the bonding of male and female elements in the initiation of a life.

During this period in history however, due to ignorance, it was believed that the female role in procreation was a totally passive one and that it was the male who infused the receptacle of the womb with life giving sperm, much in the same way that the farmer sows a seed into the soil. The soil itself does not create life but only nurtures it. In many ancient religions, a God creates the universe by masturbating into his

---

6. Louis Jacobs. "The Jewish Religion." Oxford University Press. 1995.
7. Ibid.

own hand. The role of the ovum was unknown and the two female x life giving chromosomes in the ovum and sperm respectively, was completely out of the range of human knowledge at that time. Due to the biological misconception that the seed of man alone creates life, God was seen as an all male principle that infused the universe and the soil of the earth with life giving seed. Take for example a quote from the Gnostic *"Tripartite Tractate. Aenoic Emanations."*

"Rather, they only had existence in the manner of a seed, so that it has been discovered that they existed like a fetus. Like the word he begot them, subsisting spermatically, and the ones whom he was to beget had not yet come into being from him. The one who first thought of them, the Father,— not only so that they might exist for him, but also that they might exist for themselves as well, that they might then exist in [his] thought as mental substance and that they might exist for themselves too,—sowed a thought like a [spermatic] seed." [8]

I suspect that the concept of the potter Lord referred to in Genesis 2, originated in Egypt and was a counter revolutionary theory that arose at a time when the genetrix was seen as an all female principle such as the Greek concept of Gaia, the life giving mother, which in turn, during ancient times was a misconception due to the fact that it was believed that women procreated singularly. Men in society did not and do not give birth, but they could create with their hands. So a God was

---

8 .James M. Robinson. "The Nag Hammadi Library." HarperCollins. 1990.

developed who created human beings out of clay and breathed life into them. The potter Lord was a relatively new God by Egyptian standards and was not included among the descendants of Amun and Mut. He was known as Khnum, a ram-god of the sources of the Nile who made people out of clay on the potter's wheel. Gen 2:7:

"Jehovah formed Adamah [meaning red earth or clay] from the dust of the earth and breathed into his nostrils the breath of life."

After Adam is created, the biologically impossible happens. A woman is created from a man, and then the story is continued in Genesis 3 where she eats from the tree of knowledge and is punished with subjugation. Eve no longer has the right to be considered an equal partner to her husband and he is to be her *"master,"* (which translated into Hebrew is Baal) for the rest of her days. Gen. 3:16:

"....You will desire your husband, but he will be your master."

Unlike Genesis 1, the union between men and women is not looked upon as good, but as a sin and the Elohim's first commandment in Gen.1:28, *"be fruitful and increase,"* would, in Genesis 3, result in hostility between them. Gen.3:15:

"And I will put enmity between thee and the woman, and between thy seed and her seed;...."

Because Adam and Eve ate from the Tree of Knowledge, it is believed that we are all born in sin, or original sin which in turn is connected to carnal knowledge or being born through a man and a woman *"making love."* But the fact remains that Adam and Eve were not punished for sexual intercourse, but rather for disobedience, Cain and Abel being born after they left the Garden of Eden.

In Genesis 1, however, we are made in God's image, being an exact duplicate. If the concept of original sin or being born sinful due to carnal knowledge holds any water at all, which I don't believe that it does, then it must follow that God in Genesis 1:26 referred to as *"Us,"* must be sinful itself, having created exact duplicates or images of itself. If there is any sin at all in Genesis 2, then it is that one human being is subjected to slavery and subjugation by another human being, the result being that unlike Genesis 1 where there is equality and procreation is seen as good, Adam and Eve live forever in a state or disharmony and disequilibrium with enmity between them. Surely any form of disharmony is a sin against God? For harmony would typically bring with it physical, intellectual, social and political peace and prosperity.

And so love found became love lost. Eve's procreative powers, the ability to replenish the earth, did not result in the glory of creation and the joy of having a child, but would only bring her pain and agony. Gen. 3:16:

"I will greatly multiply thy sorrow and thy conception; in sorrow thou shalt bring forth children...."

This religious philosophy results in inequality between the sexes and was expanded and carried into all aspects of life, be it psychological, sexual, racial, social, economic and political. Where there was no master, now there is one, where there was no sin, now sin exists and is associated with the fruitfulness that results from a joining together of the opposites, the union of the flesh. Genesis 2 & 3 contradict Genesis 1 where the first covenant, the first law, namely to *"be fruitful and replenish the earth"* is seen as good.

The catalyst that was supposed to have caused all this pain and suffering is believed to be the apple tree, the tree of knowledge and wisdom. This is a myth, as the word *"apple"* is not mentioned once. Further on in the Old Testament texts however, the apple or apple tree is always associated with good while Israel itself is called *"the apple of mine eye."* [Deut. 32:10 and Psalms 17:8.]

Consider the fact that God in Genesis 2 is an all male principle. Consider the fact that Eve in Genesis 3 is described as the original sinner, tempted by the snake with the fruit that would give her knowledge and wisdom and that Adam is to dominate her and keep her subjected to his will. Now consider that in Proverbs 8, the feminine face of God bestows knowledge on us. verse 10:

"Receive my instruction, and not silver, and knowledge rather than choice gold."

In verse 19 she says:

"My fruit is better than gold…"

While in Proverbs 3: 16–18 it says:

"Length of days is in her right hand; and in her left hand riches and honour.
Her ways are ways of pleasantness, and all her paths are peace.
She is a tree of life to them that lay hold upon her: and happy is every one that retaineth her."

The two different texts pose a conflict of interest. In Genesis 3, the fruit plucked by the woman and the knowledge and wisdom that come with it, will result in sin and suffering. While in Proverbs 8, the fruit offered by the woman who gives us wisdom, knowledge and understanding, results in life for the receiver who will obtain favour with God. Proverbs 8: 34 & 35:

"Blessed is the man that heareth me, watching daily at my gates, waiting at the posts of my doors.
For whoso findeth me findeth life, and shall obtain favour of the Lord."

Genesis 3 advocates ignorance and slavery while the above, in conjunction with Genesis 1, advocates knowledge and self-empowerment.

The former, if taken to its logical conclusion, advocates nepotism and enslavement; the latter, democracy and equality.

Although we have been led to believe that all the prophets subscribed to Genesis 2 & 3, further examination casts doubt on that consensus. In the book of Lamentations, which was written somewhere between the sixth and seventh centuries B.C., the prophet Jeremiah deplores this religious belief when he says in Lamentations 4:2:

"The precious sons of Zion, (a feminine symbol) comparable to fine gold, now they are esteemed as earthen pitchers, the work of the hands of the potter!"

In the book of Isaiah, written somewhere between the fifth and eighth centuries B.C., this scribe appears to support Jeremiah's view. 64:7–8:

"And there is none that calleth upon thy name, that stirreth up himself to take hold of thee: for thou hast hid thy face from us, and hast destroyed us, because of our iniquities.
But now [a situation which had not gone before] we are the clay, and thou our potter; and we are the work of thy hand."

The last line sounds like a lamentation and appears to be tinged with sarcasm. Lamentations was written after the fall of the Kingdom of Israel and the Kingdom of Judah. These quotes imply that belief in the potter was a foreign concept not contained in the original texts, but something that had been inserted after 700 B.C. Taking such evidence into account, we would have to consider the fact that belief in the potter was a philosophy that the prophets, most notably Jeremiah and Isaiah, did not necessarily support. Alternatively, Isaiah 63:10 goes so far as to suggest that the feminine face of God, being the holy Spirit or Shekinah, was rejected by the populace:

"But they rebelled, and vexed his holy Spirit: therefore he was turned to be their enemy, and he fought against them."

Isaiah also suggests that when the new heavens and the new earth arrive, as in Revelation, the feminine aspect of God will be reinstated. 61:10 & 62:5:

"I will greatly rejoice in the Lord, my soul shall be joyful in my God; for he hath clothed me with the garments of salvation, he hath covered me with the robe of righteousness, as a bridegroom decketh himself with ornaments, and as a bride adorneth herself with her jewels."

"For as a young man marrieth a virgin, so shall thy sons marry thee: and as the bridegroom rejoiceth over the bride, so shall thy God rejoice over thee."

When we compare both stories we find that Genesis 1 is logical, rational and scientifically plausible. Equality, democracy and the laws of nature, including procreation and sexual intercourse, are spoken of as good and desirable. We, *"the image of God,"* are both masculine and feminine. Because we are made in the *"image"* of God and are *"exact duplicates,"* then like God, we too have everlasting life. Genesis 2 & 3 on the other hand, is not logical, rational or scientifically plausible. The story incorporates inequality, masters and myths while human procreation or sex, referred to in Genesis 1 as *replenishment,* is associated with sin and suffering. Unlike Genesis 1, the human race is made from clay and is denied immortality, the tree of everlasting life that grows in the garden of Eden.

In the Gnostic scriptures there is an interesting version on the creation story, where Elohim and Jehovah are believed to be the two sons of Eve and like the twins Jacob and Esau, have different personalities. Rather than Adam impregnating Eve, a chief archon fathers Eve's children and these children in turn, represent the two versions of God found in Genesis 1 & 2. They are then associated with Abel and Cain. In *"The Apocryphon of John"* the incredible statement is made that:

"And the chief archon seduced her and he begot in her two sons; the first and the second Elohim and Yave. Eloim has a bear-face and Yave has a cat-face. The one is righteous but the other is unrighteous. Yave he set over the fire and the wind, and Eloim he set over the water and the earth. And these he called with the names Cain and Abel with a view to deceive." [9]

The Bible, on which Western civilization is based, opens with two contradictory theories of our origins which according to the Gnostic texts, can be likened to twins, these two views running throughout the Bible and influencing it's interpretation. The one can be easily understood and accepted by most people, while the other appears to be scientifically corrupt and morally distorted. Should we seek an explanation or question the Bible's validity in light of the contradictions that it presents, then we are told to accept it on faith. There are many who can no longer do this. For those who cannot, Genesis 1 offers the opportunity to reclaim our Biblical heritage and the divine word of God, which in no way conflicts with science or with our social, economic and political values.

The choice, however, is up to each and every individual, but this choice not only paves the way for the rest of the Biblical story, but will determine our psychological, social and political bias. Genesis 2 & 3 results in the belief in mortality; left brain masculine thinking over right brain creativity; male dominance over women; social inequality based on birthright or race; and if taken to its logical conclusion,

---

9 James M.Robinson. "The Nag Hammadi Library." HarperCollins. 1990.

nepotism. Such ideologies have held sway over the human race for over three thousand years. Our societies were based on a hierarchal structure led by a single person, be he Conqueror, Emperor or King. He was bestowed with a divine right to rule, advocating his own superiority within his realm as regards nationality, race or religion. At the bottom of the ladder, women were kept in their place and considered to be the lowest of the low.

Genesis 1, on the other hand, not only offers immortality, but also a far more balanced view on life. This text, which has been overlooked in favour of Genesis 2, can finally come into it's own in the twenty first century. The old world order has fallen away and a new world order is about to replace it. Thanks to such forerunners as Freud and Jung, we have a better understanding of how our minds work. Such concepts as right and left brain functioning, conscious and subconscious mind, are embraced in the unity of a masculine/feminine Godhead called Elohim. Darwin, Einstein and Hawking have unveiled the secrets of evolution and the universe, which are poetically described in the first twenty seven verses of Genesis 1. A world grown weary of inequality, inhumane acts perpetrated on the innocent, poverty and mad men like Hitler, Idi Amin and Saddam Hussein, would surely grab the message on the first page of the Bible and ensure that these philosophies will carry us into the future.

Chapter Two.

Origins

The cradle of our present civilization as we know it, is situated in what is known today as the Middle East. This area includes Egypt, Saudi Arabia, Syria, Iran, Iraq, Turkey, Lebanon, Palestine and Israel. We do not know if the earliest people, as described in Genesis 5 & 6, came from this region. These chapters do not speak in terms of a particular geographic point, but rather in terms of the whole earth. This implies an holistic interpretation that is not based on nationality or race, but on the planet as a whole. Genesis: 6:11:

"The earth also was corrupt before God, and the earth was filled with violence."

In Genesis 2, on the other hand, a specific geographical point is identified and was known as Eden. The rivers which flowed through the garden of Eden included Pison in southern Arabia, Gihon in Ethiopia (which becomes the Nile in Egypt), Hiddekel in Assyria and the Tigris and Euphrates rivers which have their source in Turkey and their mouths in Iraq. Genesis 2: 8 & 10:

"And the Lord God planted a garden eastward in Eden;....And a river went out of Eden to water the garden:"

What the text in Genesis 3 appears to imply, is that Eden was situated in the Middle East. 3:23:

"Therefore the Lord God sent him forth from the garden of Eden, to till the ground from whence he was taken."

The generations described in Genesis 5, on the other hand, do not appear to have come from this specific point only, but were situated all over the globe.

In Genesis 5, the name Adam applies to both sexes, to all peoples and to all races. In Genesis: 5:1 & 2 we have a text that uses much the same imagery as that found in Genesis 1.

"This is the book of the generations of Adam. In the day that God created man, in the likeness of God made he him;
Male and female created he them; and blessed them, and called their name Adam, in the day when they were created."

But in the very next verse, 5: 3, we read:

"And Adam lived a hundred and thirty years and begat a son in his own likeness, after his image; and called his name Seth:"

Do we take Adam to be an individual, or has the scribe of Genesis 5 used poetic licence and reduced the *"them,"* which incorporated both sexes and all races to that of an individual for simplicities sake? Verse 2 and verse 3 contradict each other on this issue. If you advocate Genesis 1, then you will see Adam, Seth and the genealogical line down to Noah in terms of them. If you advocate Genesis 2, then you will see Adam in terms of him. The former view is an inclusive ideology that embraces both sexes and all races; the latter is an exclusive ideology that reduces itself to one genealogical family tree traced through the male line.

Verse 3 presents another dichotomy. Although the name Adam is reduced to one male entity, the verse is still a reflection of Genesis 1 in that Adam begets a child in his own image as did Elohim. In Genesis 1, Elohim created people in its own image, so people in turn, create each other in their own image and the image of God, so to speak, is perpetuated throughout time. If Adam represents all people on the planet, then up until this point, no specific geographical area has been identified, neither has a specific nationality or race group. Only when we reach the story of the great flood, do these people divide into different nations and the nation of the Hebrews takes on it's own identity.

The origins of the Hebrews can be traced to present day Turkey on the mountains of Ararat in Armenia, where Noah, the navigator, landed his ark. According to Genesis 9, Noah received the same blessings that are found in Gen.1, coupled with the seven laws. Again we are told that we are made in Elohim's image and again we are given the first covenant, to be fruitful:

9:6: *"…for in the image of God made he them."*

9:7: *"And you, be ye fruitful, and multiply; bring forth abundantly in the earth, and multiply therein."*

What the reader must note however, is that there is no mention of clay. Why does God not say in this instance, *"I made you out of clay and breathed life into your nostrils?"* The scribe of Genesis 9 was obviously sticking to the Elohist text on which Genesis 1 was based. All the descendants of Noah are blessed by the Elohim and in 10:32 we read that:

"These were the families of the children of Noah according to their genealogies, nation by nation; and from them came the separate nations on earth after the flood."

Whilst in 10:5 we read:

"From these the peoples of the coasts and islands separated into their own countries, each with their own language, family by family, nation by nation."

What the text suggests, is that all nations, countries, races and languages are from the same root and that we are all descended from the firstborn people. As such, we are the image of God in perpetuity as were the Adam people and their descendants, the people called Seth.

According to Rabbinic literature, the dividing line between other races and the *"chosen race"* begins with the sons of Noah. A *"son of Noah"* is believed to be a Gentile, who abides by the seven basic laws that govern humanity,[10] while the laws of Moses are for the *"chosen people,"* believed to be the descendants of Shem who is Israel, only. The mere fact that such a distinction is believed to exist, results in an elect rather than a universal Biblical interpretation in spite of the fact that Rabbinic belief sees this privilege as one of service rather than elitism. As I hope to make clear in the following chapters of this book, I believe that such an elect system was never intended and the term *"Israel,"* to my mind, has been grossly misinterpreted, especially when we take Isaiah 66:12 and 18 into consideration:

"Behold, I will extend peace to her like a river, and the glory of the Gentiles like a flowing stream...."

---

10. Louis Jacobs."The Jewish Religion." Oxford University Press. 1995

"…it shall come, that I will gather all nations and tongues; and they shall come, and see my glory."

From the people of Noah came the following descendants. Ham became the nations of Nubia, Ethiopia, Egypt, Arabia and Canaan. From Japheth came the isles of the Gentiles, Asia Minor and the coast of Palestine, whilst Shem remained in what is known today as Turkey. Neo Nazis claim a supremacist ideology over and above people who are not white Anglo Saxon Protestants based on the fact that Noah cursed Canaan. Canaan or the Canaanites, were a Semitic people and not of the Negroid race. What must be noted is that Noah did not curse Ham or Mizraim who established the Negroid line in north Africa nor did he curse Shem, another Semite or Japheth a Gentile. Basing racialistic or anti-Semitic policies on Genesis 9:25, is a gross misinterpretation of the texts in the interest of Arian supremacy.

Chapter 10 presents another anomaly within the given texts, as the descendants of Noah, Ham, Japheth and Shem, return to what was described as the Garden of Eden in Genesis 2, an area to which we still mistakenly believe that we have not and cannot return. There is also another unusual omission between Genesis 1 and 27. At no time does the concept of a firstborn son or a birthright handed down from father to son enter into the equation. Although the text follows the line of Shem through to Abram, there is no blessing by Noah of either Shem, Ham or Japheth as the firstborn. The reason for this omission could be that these names were the names of families rather than individuals, as Genesis 5:1 & 2 implies. Or perhaps the concept of the firstborn, or a single individual being blessed with the inheritance of the father was not custom at this time. Lastly, their beliefs could have been in accordance with Genesis 1, 5:1 & 2 and 9:6 & 7, whereby all people were created in Elohim's image and as such, there was no order of hierarchy based on the concept of a divine child which led to the political belief in the divine right to rule. But, if we look to Egypt during this same time in history, we do find the earliest form of belief in the *"firstborn"* or a *"firstborn of God."*

The firstborn in Egypt, unlike Adam in Genesis 1, was not made from clay and was born under very different circumstances. The Egyptians, according to the Greek historian Herodotus (400 B.C.), had records not only of the flood as did the Mesopotamians, but of the lost continent of Atlantis. But more important, they believed in the concept of a *"firstborn son of God"* which was based on the following story:

Thousands of years ago, the Gods walked upon the face of the earth. Two of the most renown Gods were Isis and her brother Osiris. Osiris had an evil brother called Seth who killed him, dismembered his body and scattered the fourteen parts all over the world. Isis went in search of these fourteen parts and put them back together again. She then lay on Osiris and impregnated herself, later giving birth to her son Horus. Whilst Horus was young, she hid him in an ark in the bulrushes of the Nile. When Horus grew up to be a man, he sought revenge for his father's death and killed the evil Seth. From then on, every Pharaoh who ascended the throne was considered to be Horus, the son or firstborn of the Gods and on his death, became Osiris. He was resurrected from the dead and lived on in the heavens.

Many people may regard this tale as some kind of a pagan myth. But our Biblical text states that the Gods did once walk upon the earth. In Genesis 6:2 we read:

"That the sons of God saw the daughters of men that they were fair; and they took them wives of all which they chose."

Today we are fascinated by the concept of Unidentified Flying Objects and Extra Terrestrials. Ezekiel chapter one, gives an accurate description of those flying machines found in the films *"Star Wars"* and

"Independence Day," while in 2 Kings 2:11, there is some allusion to a flying saucer picking up Elijah:

"And it came to pass, as they still went on, and talked, that, behold, there appeared a chariot of fire, and horses of fire, and parted them both asunder; and Elijah went up by a whirlwind into heaven."

Were Isis and Osiris people from another planet? Or did they come from Atlantis? Were they and their family regarded as Gods and Goddesses by the people of the Nile due to their seemingly magical abilities as have many primitive societies regarded colonialists when confronted by a more advanced civilization? Were Isis and Osiris responsible for bringing education and a civilizing process to Egypt? To date, these are questions that we cannot answer. For the moment we can only speculate as to whether there is any basis of truth, either in their story, or in Genesis 6, 2 Kings 2 or Ezekiel 1.

By the time Abram led his family into Canaan, the Egyptians were one of the most highly civilized, or the most civilized nation on earth, and their religion, unlike others in the area, was based on the concept of life after death, immortality, a belief system that was foreign to all those around them. Where they did converge with other religions was in a belief of a God and Goddess who have a holy child. In keeping with this trinity, both men and women entered religious orders. The priestesses were as entitled to study religious works as were their male counterparts. Coupled with this belief system came a stellar creed based on the belief that the Gods and Goddesses came from the heavens and were known to return there. Heaven was not just a concept, but a place that could be viewed at night when the stars moved across the sky, or heavens.

This then was the world that Abram lived in. The concept of God as an all male principle was as foreign to Abram as it was to everyone else in and around the Middle East. If anything, these early societies were based on a female dominant religion, as seen on the island of Malta (the oldest stone temples in the world dating from 5000–2500 B.C.), where a female genetrix was believed to be responsible for creating the human race.[11]

Abram is said to come from Ur of the Chaldeans, near Babylon in Mesopotamia. But what we must consider is that Terah, his father, in travelling from Ur to Canaan, stopped at Harran in Turkey and settled there. The distance from Ur (Edessa) in present day Turkey to the town of Harran, is not very far and would have been the next point of civilization from Armenia on the way to Canaan. To travel from Ur in Iraq to Harran in Turkey on the way to Canaan, just does not make sense. Looking at it logically, the travellers would not have made such a big detour by going to Harran. They would have surely turned off way before, possibly at a town called Rehoboth, then on to Tadmorr and finally Damascus where Abram made his home.

David Fasold gives an answer by interpreting the misnomer, *"Ur of the Chaldeans,"* mentioned in Genesis 11:28:

"And Harran died before his father Terah in the land of his nativity, in Ur of the Chaldees."

The Armenians referred to themselves as *"Kh(o)ai"* which means *"Ram,"* or *"People of the Ram."* They worshipped the God *"(K)Haldini"* or rather *"Khaldini"* which was the original pronunciation of *"Chaldee."* Ur of the Chaldeans is Ur of the Ram God in Armenia,[12] Turkey, not Ur in lower Mesopotamia. This would mean that Abram

---

11. Buffie Johnson. "L'ady of the Beasts. Ancient Images of the Goddess and her Sacred Animals." Harper Collins. 1990.

12. David Fasold. "Noah's Ark." Sidgwick and Jackson. 1990.

was of Armenian rather than proto-Arab descent and was part and parcel of the Hittite movement to the south.

The term *"People of the Ram,"* suggests that their belief system was based on a stellar creed. During this time in history, the constellation that would have been on the horizon at the spring equinox, was Aries, the Ram. Abram, by definition of his name, appears to have been a worshipper of Aries, the Ram. A variant of Abram is Abiramu which means, *"The Ram God is [My] Father."* [13]

In Genesis 1 the word *"God"* replaces the Hebrew word *"Elohim."* So, the Hebrew word *"Adoniram"*=Adoni meaning Lord and Ram from the constellation of Aries, has been simplistically replaced by the word *"God"* in the English translation of Job 21:22. If we read this text using the original, it means that Adoniram, or the constellation of Aries during this particular time in history when God was called Adon, was the sign of the age and held precedence over all the other Zodiac signs:

"Shall any teach Adoniram (The Ram Lord) knowledge? seeing he judgeth those that are high?"

In other words, Job speaks of the constellation of Aries, symbol a ram, which was the constellation of the time. Throughout the Christian era, the symbol of a fish has been used which relates to the constellation of Pisces. In Mesopotamia the ram was often depicted in a golden thicket while in Egypt the Ram Lord was known as Khnum, a God of the

---

13. Robert Graves. "Hebrew Myths. The Book of Genesis." 1989. Arena.

sources of the Nile who created human beings from clay on the potters wheel. Abram is named after this Ram constellation and the Armenians, the peoples of his tribe, are in turn called *"People of the Ram."*

From this evidence, we must conclude that Abram came from Anatolia where Noah landed his Ark, an area ruled by the Hittites and an area which included Armenia within its boundaries. His origins are Armenian, not Babylonian and his language was Aramaic, a precursor to what later became the Hebrew language. The Hittite influence is evident when taken against the backdrop of Abram's customs and beliefs. By comparing the two, we can discover similarities within the Biblical text.

When archaeologists compared clay tablets dating from 1600 B.C. in Boghazkoy, Turkey, with the Old Testament, it became apparent that the Armenian Abram shared many customs with his Hittite cousins. Among these are:

The sins of the father are visited upon his children.

The laws of marriage whereby it was the duty of the brother or failing him, the father, to marry a widow. (Judah and Tamar).

The ritual sacrifice whereby animals are cut in half, the pieces set opposite each other (Gen:15) [14]

The people of Anatolia, being Hittites and Armenians, migrated throughout Assyria, Mesopotamia and Canaan in search of trade and commerce. They were known as the *"People of the Ram"* and Abram, by

---

14. O.R.Gurney. "The Hittites." 1990. Penguin Books.

definition of his name, worshipped this Ram God of his Armenian descendants. Today, Turkey still has a Ram as a symbol.

Abram eventually established his home in Damascus along with other Armenians from his home territory. Old religious sights in Damascus were dedicated to the God known as Ramman and the Goddess known as *"The Queen of Heaven."*[15] She was also known as Anat, Ani or Asherah and revealed herself in a three fold manifestation of Virgin, Mother and Warrior. She was the Egyptian equivalent of Mut, or the more popular Isis. Their God head was composed of both masculine and feminine genders.

Abram, by definition of his name, appears to have been a high Priest of the Armenian God, Ramman. Sarah's name in turn, is the equivalent of the *"Queen of Heaven."* The name *"Sarah"* derives *"from an ancient Semitic noun meaning "princess"....A goddess named Sharit or Sharayat (the phonetic equivalent of Sarai) was worshipped at Bozrah in the Hauran."*[16]

Sarah as an Armenian from Harran, by definition of her name and the archaeological discoveries in Damascus, appears to have brought the belief in the Queen of Heaven with her. In all likelihood, she could have been a High Priestess of the Temple of the Goddess and changed her name from Sarai to Sarah in honour of this deity. Even today nuns and priests change their names when they are ordained. Abram and Sarah would have been a priestly class.

---

15. John Hinnells. "The Worlds Religions." 1982. Struik Christian Books. (PTY) Ltd.

16. Robert Graves. "Hebrew Myths. The Book of Genesis." 1989. Arena.

In the Old Testament we find some evidence of Sarah's possible religious ordination by comparing it with the Acadian Laws of Hammurabi which date from approximately 1700 B.C. According to these laws:

"If a man marries a priestess-natitum (a hierodule, or temple servant, forbidden to bear children) she is allowed to give her husband a bond-maid to bear children for her." [17]

Not only does Sarah give her husband a bond-maid, but so do her descendants. Both Rachel and Rebecca abided by this law that governed the High Priestesses of the Goddess. Each in turn, gave their husbands a bond-maid to bear children for them. If they were priestesses abiding by the laws mentioned above, then they were forbidden to have sexual relations with their husbands.

Here a certain amount of confusion arises as all the matriarchs mourn their infertility. But if they were living according to the laws of Hammurabi, then infertility should have been a given. The only way these woman could have sexual relations with another man, was if they were not the property of a father or a husband or if they were orphaned or widows,[18] as seen when Tamar, a widow, sits at the cross roads dressed like a concubine and sells her services to Judah. (Gen: 38:14–19.)

Throughout the Old Testament, there are many stories about whores. Our present translations have lost much of the true meaning as in Hebrew a distinction was made between whores. Not only was a

---

17. Ibid.
18. Ibid.

whore the equivalent of an orphan or widow who had no family and sometimes had to support herself through prostitution, but a whore was also the equivalent of a priestess of the Goddess. In the Hebrew a whore can be interpreted in two ways. Firstly a *"zonah"* who was seen in much the same light as a prostitute is seen today. Secondly, the sacred whores who remained chaste according to the laws of Hammurabi and these were known as the *"q'deshah."*[19] They were high priestesses or prophetesses of which there are many in the Bible. In the Old Testament, Isaiah's wife is a prophetess or q'deshah. 8:3:

"And I went unto the prophetess; and she conceived, and bare a son."

In the New Testament we find a reference to a q'deshah in Luke 2: 37:

"And she was a widow of about fourscore and four years, which departed not from the temple, but served God with fastings and prayers day and night."

In the cases of Sarah, Rebecca and Rachel, I would hazard a guess that they were q'deshah, and Rachel's story suggests that a so called *"virgin birth"* was expected. In the text Rachel's religious convictions had not come through for her. In Genesis 30:2, Jacob turns to his cousin Rachel in anger and says:

"Can I take the place of God, who has denied you children?"

---

19. Ibid.

The words *"take the place of"* infer that it was through God and not Jacob that Rachel was to conceive and it was God, not Jacob who had *"denied"* her children. From this we can gather that both Rachel and Jacob could have been awaiting a so called divine conception which did not occur. Jacob knows that he will be breaking the laws of Hammurabi if he has sexual relations with his wife as he is forbidden to take the place of God. Desperate for children, Rachel then abides by the Laws of Hammurabi and gives Jacob her bond-maid to lie with and Bilhah produces children for them both.

There are two rather strange stories told about Sarah and Rebecca. Both Abram and Isaac deny that they are married to these women and claim that they are their sisters. This would mean that they would be regarded as *"neither the property of a husband or father"*[20] and would be freed from the laws that governed a q'deshah, enabling them to have sexual relations with another man. Genesis 20:12:

"And yet indeed she is my sister: she is the daughter of my father, but not the daughter of my mother."

Why would Abram and Isaac deny that they were married to these women, women who had given them a bond-maid to lie with and women who mourned their infertility? The answer could lie in Egypt where all Pharaohs were considered to be direct descendants of the Gods. These Gods in turn, could have either been rulers of a lost

---

20. Robert Graves. "Hebrew Myths. The Book of Genesis." 1989. Arena.

generation, such as Atlantis, or as Erich van Dinekan has proposed, people from out of space who procreated with earthlings, their descendants becoming governors or rulers. In the Bible, such an incident occurs during Noah's time before the flood as we have seen in Gen 6:2. By procreating with such men, Sarah and Rebecca would have had a child of the Gods.

The story so far, is that we have a line of women who appear to be governed by the Laws of Hammurabi. All these women give their husbands a bond-maid, mourn their infertility and all these women are impregnated at an older age by apparent divine intervention as seen when the *"Lord"* visits Sarah in her old age. Genesis 21:1 & 2:

"And the Lord visited Sarah as he had said, and the Lord did unto Sarah as he had spoken. For Sarah conceived, and bare Abraham a son…."

During this period in history, Thutmosis 111 ruled from the Nile to the Euphrates River, an area that incorporated Egypt, the Sinai, Canaan, Lebanon and Assyria. The Egyptian border ended at what was then Mesopotamia. As such, Thutmosis 111 would have been regarded as *"the Lord."* Ahmed Osman[21] proposes that it was this *"Lord"* that impregnated Sarai, and by so doing, conferred the title of *"princess,"* (Sarah) upon her head. Either he conferred the title or Sarah was already an Armenian princess and priestess. By virtue of her standing in society as a q'deshah, she would only have been allowed to have a child through someone believed to be a *"God"* as the Pharaoh was considered

---

21. Ahmed Osman. "The House of the Messiah." 1992. Grafton.

to be. Sarah's marriage to Abram on the other hand, could have been a religious rather than a carnal union.

The Pharaoh's and their wives, as we have seen above, were considered to be the descendants of the Gods Isis and Osiris who walked upon the earth. As such, they were regarded as the sons and daughters of God. Therefore Sarah, as we have seen in Genesis 21:1, was impregnated by the "*Lord.*" If it was the Pharaohs who "*gave*" the matriarchs children, then Jacob would have in turn been the son of Rebecca and Amenhotep 11, whilst Joseph would have been the son of Rachel who was eventually given children by her Lord Thutmosis 1V. As Osman points out, the promised land of Canaan could have been given to Abram, due to the fact that Isaac was Thutmosis 111 son.[22] Genesis 15:18:

"In the same day the Lord made a covenant with Abram, saying, Unto thy seed have I given this land, from the river of Egypt unto the great river, the river Euphrates:"

Cuneiform tablets found at Tel-el-Armana [of which there are up to four hundred dispatches dating from 1400 B.C.] written between the Egyptian Pharaohs and the chieftains and Princes based in Canaan, give us a clearer picture of the political and religious climate of the time.[23] During this period in history, there was no separation between church and state. The Pharaoh was both the king and the high priest and his family, being his wife, daughters and sons would have been brought up

---

22. Ibid.

23. David M. Rohl. "A Test of Time." Century. 1995.

to be priestesses and priests in accordance with Egyptian belief. In other words, unlike present society where we have a separation between the church and the state, Egypt was as a theocracy. As such, any Prince ruling in a city or town of Canaan, would have been seen as both governor and as High Priest of the area and could have been referred to as the *"Lord."* In Genesis 14:18 we read:

"And Melchizedek king of Salem [of peace] brought forth bread and wine: and he was the priest of the most high God..."

The most high God at the time, was not Khnum, the Ram God potter, but Amen, the God worshipped at Karnak in Thebes who was given the added title of Ra in Heliopolis and often referred to as Amen-Ra.[24] Melchizedek, like the Pharaoh, is called a priest-king and could have been the Pharaoh himself. In 18:19 this priest-king says of Abram and his family:

"For I know him, that he will command his children and his household after him, and they will keep the way of the Lord, to do justice and judgement."

If the way of the Lord is justice, then another name for the Lord would be justice, or judgement. It comes as no surprise then to find that Melchizedek, as with all Hebrew names, has an inherent meaning and could be a Hebrew version of an Egyptian name. The Egyptian equivalent for the Hebrew word for *"king"* was *"Mose."*[25] Melchizedek means:

---

24. Egyptologists will argue that one of Amun's symbols was the Ram. It is my belief that Amun, symbolized by the Ram should be interpreted as "God manifesting itself in the age of Aries, symbol the Ram," as opposed to the Ram itself being regarded as God, as Khnum was believed to be.

25. Ahmed Osman. "The House of the Messiah." Grafton. 1992.

"My King/Mose/Melch is justice." Melchizedek is a king, a priest of the most high of justice. *"Melch"* or *"Melech"* means *"king"* in Hebrew and *"Zedek"* or *"Zadok"* means justice.[26] This will be important when we look at later texts where the priests who guarded the Ark in Judges were called priests of Zadok/Justice and even further on where the name reoccurs in *"The Dead Sea Scrolls."* What is more, it is another *"Mose"* or Mose[s]/King/*Melch* who gives us the laws of justice/*Zedek* in Exodus.

From the time that Abram crossed the Euphrates river he was guided by the Lord on numerous occasions. During his first encounter, his name changed, as often happens when one joins a religion, from Abram to Abraham and the Lord instructs him to be circumcised. Circumcision was not a custom in Armenia. In Egypt however, circumcision was practised long before Abraham entered Canaan and a high priest of the Egyptian religion, during a conversion of one of his followers, would have insisted that circumcision was adhered to.

The change in his name from Abram (Father of Ram) to Abraham, supports the premise that he was converted to the Egyptian beliefs. Abra-ham means: Ab—father; Ra—God, [the god worshipped at the ancient city of On, Heliopolis also known as the first of the Gods and another version of Amen. Sometimes called Amen-Ra where they were fused together and represented the same God;] Ham—the father of Ethiopia, Nubia and Mizraim. Abram is no longer named after the

---

26. O.Odelain and R.Seguineau. "Dictionary of Proper Names and Places in the Bible." Robert Hale Limited. 1991.

"Father God Ram" worshipped in Armenia, but the Father God, *"Amen-Ra"* of Egypt-Ham.

Soon after this incident, the Lord informs him that he will finally have a child through Sarah. The consecutive order of these two stories, Genesis 17 and 18, suggest that Sarah's conception relied on Abraham's conversion. Chapter 19 gives a brief interlude with the story of Sodom which could have been a war campaign undertaken by Thutmosis 111. In chapter 20 however, Abraham visits king Abimelech (which means *"My father is king"*)[27] and tells the truth, that Sarah is his sister. Did he presuppose that the Lord's promise entailed Sarah's pregnancy by Abimelech? This is according to the Elohist text. The Yahwist tradition on the other hand, replaces Abimelech with the Pharaoh in 12:10–20 and then tells the story again, replacing the Pharaoh with Abimelech in 26:1–11.[28] In the very beginning of chapter 21 however, Sarah is impregnated by the Lord (21:1 & 2). The same Lord who converted Abraham, who promised him the land from the Nile to the Euphrates rivers and who promised Sarah a child.

Although Sarah gives Abraham a son, it is clearly not his child but a child of the Lord who *"did unto Sarah as he had spoken."* After Isaac is weaned, Abimelech appears to regard Abraham as an equal and makes a covenant with him whereby Abraham will not deal falsely with Abimelech or with his decedents. Was this because Isaac was the son of the Lord who could possibly have been the Pharaoh himself?

---

27. O.Odelain and R. Seguineau. "Dictionary of Proper Names and Places in the Bible." Robert Hale. 1991.

28. Ibid.

In spite of Abraham's conversion, it is evident that he still worshipped other Gods. In the story of Abraham's sacrifice of Isaac found in Genesis 22, two personages are identified. One being God the tempter and the other being the angel of the Lord. During this time in history, many Gods were worshipped in Palestine, one of which was Molech who demanded sacrifice in the form of children. Throughout the Middle East, the first-born child was sacrificed in order to appease the Gods and bring abundance to the people, as seen with the Greek story of Ephigenina.

In 22:1 a God tempts Abraham to sacrifice Isaac. In the book of Joshua chapter 24, Abraham is accused of worshipping other Gods, one of which could have been the Ram, as his name before circumcision implies. I propose that the God who tempted Abraham was the *"Ram Lord"* and the angel of the Lord was an emissary of the priest-king Melchizedek who did not advocate this particular ritual. The Egyptians, to the best of my knowledge, did not sacrifice children, but held them in the highest regard. Abraham sacrifices a ram found in a thicket in place of Isaac. This *"Ram in a thicket"* could be symbolic, as idols depicting the Ram God were fashioned in thickets of gold in Mesopotamia.[29] By sacrificing this ram, Abraham has in effect made a complete break with the Ram Lord who he previously worshipped and after whom he was named.

Isaac in turn marries Abraham's great niece, Isaac's second cousin through his mother, Sarah. In 25:21, as Abraham had done before him,

---

29. Paul Hamlyn. "Art Treasures of the World." 1964. Paul Hamlyn LTD. pg. 29. Plate 3.

Isaac entreats the Lord because his wife is barren and Rebecca conceives. It is the Lord who tells her that she will have twins. Although Abraham does give Isaac all his belongings, he does not bless him as the firstborn. Was this because such a custom was not prevalent in Armenian society?

Jacob in turn also marries his cousin, the daughter of Laban, son of Nahor, Abraham's brother. Jacob, as we know, dressed himself up as Esau in order that he could wrestle the birth right away from his brother, this birth right most probably being the land from the Nile to the Euphrates river, promised to Abraham and bequeathed to Isaac, by his true father, the Lord Pharaoh. For the first time the texts speak of a father placing a blessing on a son and endowing him with the title of firstborn. Was this because Isaac was of royal Egyptian blood through the male line and therefore carried on the custom? Rebecca too interferes. She believes that Jacob should receive the blessing rather than Esau. Jacob's wife Rachel is also barren, but her words imply in 30:24, that like Sarah and Rebecca before her, it is the Lord who gives her children:

"And she called his name Joseph; and said, The Lord shall add to me another son."

The alliance between the Egyptians and the Armenians was further strengthened by the marriage between Asenath who was a priestess of On, her name meaning, *"belonging to the Goddess Neith/Isis/Anath,"*[30]

---

30. O.Odelain and R.Seguineau. "Dictionary of Proper Names and Places in the Bible." Robert Hale Limited. 1991.

and Joseph, the son of Rachel and possibly Thutmosis 1V. Ahmed Osman identifies Asenath as Tuya, a daughter of royal birth who was married to Yuya, a man who aptly fits the description of Joseph in the Bible and all the titles that were bestowed on him.[31] Yuya, in Egyptian history, was a foreigner known as an *"Ibri"* from which the word *"Hebrew"* is derived and means *"a person from beyond the Euphrates River."*[32] Yuya came to live in Egypt at about the same time that our Biblical Joseph escaped persecution from his brothers. Joseph climbed up the ranks of Egyptian society until he was only answerable to the Pharaoh himself who would have been Thutmosis 1V and thereafter Amenhotep 111. If Thutmosis 1V was his biological father, then his position within the royal family becomes perfectly understandable. Yuya held the titles of *"Prophet of Min"* and *"Overseer of the horses."*[33] Both Yuya and Tuya were held in such high esteem that they were buried in the Valley of the Kings.

Yuya (Joseph) and Tuya (Asenath) had two children; a daughter called Tiya, who became the Great Wife of Amenhotep 111, the mother of Amenhotep V1 later known as Akhenaten and the grand mother of Thutankamen; and a son called Anen, who would have been the Biblical Ephraim and became known by the title of *"Second prophet of Amen."* His son was Ay, or the Biblical Nun, husband to Thutankamen's widow Ankhsenpa-amen and father of Joshua who led the Hebrews into the New Kingdom of Israel.

---

31. Ahmed Osman. "The House of the Messiah." Grafton. 1992.

32. David M. Rohl. "A Test of Time." Century. 1995.

33. Ibid.

According to our Biblical texts which appear to be supported by Egyptian papyri, the Ibri or the Hebrews, Armenians from the mountains of Ararat, joined together in marriage and became part and parcel of the Pharaonic throne, where the Pharaoh ruled with his shepherds staff and his rod or flail and was considered to be Horus, the firstborn of the Gods. In keeping with this genealogical decent, Jacob adopted and blessed Ephraim as his firstborn and declared that his name, being *"Israel"* should be named on him. Ephraim was his grandson, the son of Joseph and Asenath. So the blessing of the firstborn was carried down from Isaac to Jacob, through Joseph to Ephraim who in turn would have inherited the land from the Nile to the Euphrates river, given to Abraham by Thutmosis 111.

Chapter 49 verse 26 implies that Joseph, as well as being regarded as a high priest and/or prophet, an interpreter of dreams, one of the righteous, the shepherd and a *"guardian of the covenant;"*[34] was also regarded as a king/Melch, or the Hebrew equivalent of the word being Moshe or Mosis due to the reference to his crown:

"...they shall be on the head of Joseph, and on the crown of the head of him that was separate from his brethren."

Or as *"The Revised English Bible"*[35] translates it:

"...on the brow of him who was prince among his brothers."

---

34. Louis Jacobs. "The Jewish Religion." Oxford University Press. 1995.

35. "The Revised English Bible." Oxford University Press. Cambridge University Press. 1989.

In other words, as the righteous, the shepherd and the prophet, a prince among his brothers, Joseph and his descendants would have been known as the priest kings of justice, *"Melchizedek,"* the eternal priesthood. Later, in the New Testament, Jesus is referred to as being of the priestly order of Melchizedek (Hebrews 7:11–19). This priesthood, according to orthodox interpretation, was believed to be the sole preserve of the tribe of Levi. But throughout Biblical texts there are references to *"the priests and the Levites,"* where a distinction is made between the two, inferring that a priest and a Levite was not necessarily considered to be one and the same person. For example, consider Isaiah 66:20 & 21:

"And they shall bring all your brethren for an offering unto the Lord out of all nations…
And I will take of them for priests and for Levites, saith the Lord."

Contrary to orthodox interpretation, I do not believe that these priests had to be descended from the tribe of Levi, but were originally from the Joseph tribes or Ephraim, and the use of the word *"levites,"* not only refers to the tribe of Levi, but also means a joiner to the order of Melchizedek, as the word levi means *"to join."*[36] These *"joiners"* in turn, could come from any nation and any tribe, including the tribe of Levi. Hence, in 1 Samuel, the judge Samuel comes from the

---

36. O.Odelain and R.Seguineau. "Dictionary of Proper Names and Places in the Bible." Robert Hale Limited. 1991.

mount of *"Ephraim"* and is associated with this tribe and is also called a *"levite/joiner."*

What Isaiah suggests in 66:20 & 21, is that all nations can become levites or *"joiners"* to his philosophy and need not necessarily have to become priests if they should choose not to do so. He implies that becoming a levite or a *"joiner,"* is not wholly and totally reliant on being born a Levite or tracing ones genealogy to the tribe of Levi, though one could of course be as such.

Contradicting my interpretation, the orthodox belief is that the priests and the Levites were considered to come from one tribe being Levi, which would in effect, make a distinction between the priests and the Levites unnecessary. The fact that there is a distinction implies that the priests and the Levites do not always come from one and the same genealogical tree. What compounds the issue is that unlike Jacob's complimentary blessing on Joseph, who is described as the *"shepherd,"* Jacob has this to say about the tribe of Levi. Gen. 49: 5 & 7:

"Simeon and Levi are brethren; instruments of cruelty are in their habitations. Cursed be their anger, for it was fierce; and their wrath, for it was cruel: I will divide them in Jacob, and scatter them in Israel."

The second contradictory view, this time surrounding a prophecy of kingship as opposed to the priesthood, lies in Genesis 49:10:

"The sceptre shall not depart from Judah, nor a lawgiver from between his feet, until Shiloh come..."

What this verse implies is that Judah, rather than Joseph, is blessed by Jacob with the title of King-Melek-Mosis due to the use of the word *"sceptre."* But the prophetic implications of the verse imply that this title shall fall away when Shiloh comes. Historically, Shiloh came when Joshua crossed into the New Kingdom of Israel, long before the reign of

David, and stored the Ark of the Covenant in *"Shiloh"* which lay within the borders of Ephraim.

There is however, another solution to this riddle. Some years ago, the archaeologist Professor Thomas Thompson from Millwakee University came to the conclusion that due to a lack archaeological of evidence, the temple in Jerusalem was not built before Ezra's time. In other words, the first temple was built after the return from exile in Babylon rather than prior to the Assyrian invasion. Subsequent to Thompson's findings, David Rohl has done extensive archaeological research in Egypt and has come to the conclusion that the reigns of David and Solomon and the books of 1 and 11 Samuel, belong prior to Joshua's entry into the New Kingdom, rather than subsequent to it.[37] In other words, a group of Hebrews ruled in north eastern Egypt whose lives reflect those of Solomon and David. Coupled with these findings, it is interesting to note that many of the verses in Psalms and Proverbs have been traced to Egyptian Wisdom religious teachings and are also dated prior to accepted Biblical chronology.[38] Such archaeological evidence would make sense of Gen. 49: 10, where the *"sceptre"* did pass from Judah when Shiloh came, which in turn would mean that Israel did not bless or sanction Judah's right to the throne in Jerusalem but instead blessed Joseph with the crown.

So far the book of Genesis not only traces the origins of the Hebrews, but tells the story of how the Ibri, or the descendants of Shem came to

---

37. David Rohl. "A Test of Time. The Bible-From Myth to History." Century. 1995.

38. Larousse. "Dictionary of Beliefs & Religions." Larousse. 1994.

live in Egypt. The saga ends with the blessing by Israel on his twelve sons, with the blessing of the firstborn being placed on Ephraim and Joseph being referred to as the shepherd and Moshe/King due to the reference to his *"crown"* and/or the fact that he was called a *"prince"* amongst his brothers. In Kabbalistic thought, this crown represents *"Kether,"* which is called the *"crown."*

From Genesis to Exodus, the Hebrews experienced a number of important changes of which are the following:

The first change was to relocate themselves and establish roots in Canaan which was then part of Egyptian territory. Due to Joseph's high position within the Pharaonic family, the Hebrews then moved closer to the Nile valley.

The second change was the link formed through the matriarchs between the families of Shem and the families Mizraim or the Egyptians. Even if we discount the possibility that the Pharaohs or the Egyptian princes fathered Sarah, Rebecca and Rachel's sons, we still have to acknowledge that the families of Shem and Ham were joined through the marriage of Joseph and Asenath.

The third change came about when Isaac gave his blessing to Jacob and thereby ensured his birthright as the firstborn. This custom, as we have seen, was not performed by any other the Biblical character until Genesis 27. The custom originated with the Pharaohs who believed themselves to be the embodiment of Horus, the firstborn, and the direct descendants of Osiris and Isis, who were either beings from outer space, or people who came from a highly civilized society that had escaped the flood and thereafter, settled in the Nile valley.

The fourth change came about through religious conversion. From belief in the Ram Lord, or the supremacy of the constellation of Aries over the other eleven constellations, Abraham and his family became circumcised and converted to belief in Amen-Ra and his wife Mut as well as the Gods and Goddesses who were believed to be their descendants.

There are many who consider the Egyptian Parthenon of Heliopolis (On) and Karnak to be pagan. But on further examination it becomes apparent that Hebrew mysticism was based on the Egyptian high Gods and Goddesses in the form of the Kabbala. The Kabbala is believed to have been given at Mount Sinai at the same time as the Torah, but was a secret teaching that was only available to a select group of people.[39] As it says in the New Testament, Luke 8: 10:

"And he said, Unto you it is given to know the mysteries of the kingdom of God: but to others in parables;"

"The Kingdom of God" was situated in the heavens, which as far as the Egyptians were concerned, was the starry night sky with it's many constellations. *"The Kingdom of Heaven"* was, as we will see below, another term for the Kabbala which in turn was based on Egyptian mysticism, hence we still use the words *"forever and ever Amen."* The Amen or Kether as it is called in the Kabbala, is made manifest through the Sephorah down to the feminine Malkuth, which is also called the *"Kingdom"* or *"Sovereignty."* In Egypt all Pharaohs ruled from the lap of Isis. In the Kabbala, divine governorship emanates from Malkuth also known as the Shekinah, the feminine aspect, and it is through Malkuth that the *"powers"* or Sephorah are made manifest in the material world.

The only major difference between the Kabbala and the Egyptian mysteries is that the former has never been immortalized in stone but has been taught as an ideology via word of mouth and a diagram

---

39. Max. I. Dimont. "Jews, God and History." Signet. 1962.

associated with the 22 letters of the Hebrew alphabet. The latter on the other hand, was given form in the many stone temples and statues that line the Nile. In other words, as God at Mount Sinai was no longer depicted in idol form but became an ideology, so the Egyptian mysteries were also no longer depicted in idol form but were an astrological blueprint or a star map.

Again, as occurs with the concept of Elohim, although the Kabbala is a duality, this duality describes the various powers within the one whole. Like Egyptian mysticism, the Sephorah, (powers of the Godhead, Elohim=powers) are divided into male and female, as seen in Genesis 1 where the Elohim is referred to as us. The right hand powers are masculine and embody divine love while the left hand feminine powers embody divine judgement,[40] as does Wisdom in Proverbs. These male and female powers were incorporated in the Temple of Solomon in the form of the great bronze pillars of Boaz and Jachin. In Egypt these pillars corresponded with the two obelisks that were erected at holy sights and believed to be necessary for the unification of upper and lower Egypt. In upper Egypt stood Queen Hatshepsut's pillar (Boaz) at the temple of Karnak whilst in lower Egypt, stood (Jachin) the obelisk found at On, or Heliopolis.

The Egyptian religion was a celestial religion based on the astronomical movement of the stars which in turn gave them a knowledge of time which was considered to be a secret science. They not only

---

40 Louis Jacobs. "The Jewish Religion." Oxford University Press. 1995.

studied earthly time, whereby it takes 365 days for our planet to revolve around the sun, but also celestial time whereby the ages are marked out by the movement of the constellations through the sky, each age appearing at the spring equinox in turn and lasting approximately 2,000 years. Each of the Gods, or the Sephorah on the Kabbala, also represent the constellations.

This religion of the Heavens was the first science developed by man and known as astronomy, the astrological blue print above being given concrete form under the titles of the Gods and Goddesses worshipped on earth below. Robert Bauval and Adrian Gilbert in *"The Orion Mystery"* have clearly explained this fact, where the pyramids of Giza and the Nile river are mirror images of Orion's belt and the Milky Way where the God Osiris is seen in the sky as Orion while the goddess Isis is the star Sirius. Robert Bauval and Graham Hancock in *"The Keeper of Genesis"* have further elaborated on this celestial belief system where they explain how the lion headed Sphinx was built in 10,000 B.C. at a time when the constellation of Leo was on the horizon at day break at the spring equinox.

The Kabbala on the other hand, took the next step, whereby the science of astrology was no longer personalized in concrete form, but became a cosmic blue print, each Sephorah representing a constellation in the night sky. Below are the parallels that I have made between the Egyptian Gods and Goddesses and the Kabbala where both follow the same paths and both are based on masculine and feminine pillars or powers of existence:

Amun(Amen)-Mut
Shu   Tefnut

(taurus)Geb (scorpio)   (aries)Nut (libra)

(gemini)Horus (sagittarius)

(leo)Seth (aquarius)　　　　(cancer)Nepthys (capricorn)

(virgo)Osiris (pisces)

Isis

KABBALA EQUIVALENT.

Kether

Binah　　　Chokmah

(taurus)Geburah (scorpio)　　　(aries)[41] Chesed (libra)

(gemini)Tiphareth (sagittarius)

(leo)Hod (aquarius)　　　(cancer)Netzach (capricorn)

(virgo)Yesod (pisces)

Malkuth

The paths along the Kabbala are also titles to the verses found in Psalm 119. Like Revelation, the last book of the Bible, this Psalm, as with the Kabbala which means *"revelation,"* is divided into 22 parts. Each part in turn has eight verses, 176 verses in all. Within the powers being the Elohim of the Kabbala, are also the powers of letters which go

---

41. As can be seen, Aries, symbol the Ram, is only one part of the whole. The same mistake has and can still be made in other ages whereby the constellation of the time is mistakenly regarded as the whole of God.

to make up words, there being 22 letters in the Hebrew alphabet. Each letter and number in turn, symbolises the vast amount of information to be found on each sephorah. The opening lines of the Gospel of John allude to this fact while the Gnostic *"The Gospel of Truth"* elaborates on their meaning:

"In the beginning was the Word, and the Word was with Elohim (powers), and the Word was Elohim (powers)."

"This is the knowledge of the living book which he revealed to the aeons, at the end, as [his letters], revealing how they are not vowels nor are they consonants, so that one might read them and think of something foolish, but they are letters of the truth which they alone speak who know them. Each letter is a complete <thought> like a complete book, since they are letters written by the Unity,[42] the Father having written them for the aeons in order that by means of his letters they should know the Father." [43]

Modern translations of the Bible do not give these titles to the verses. The poetic description of the Kabbala in Psalm 119 in the *"King James Version"*[44] is as follows:

1. Verses 1–8 are called Aleph. Aleph is the path between the powers of Kether and Chokmah.
2. Verses 9–16 are called Beth. Beth is the path between the powers of Kether and Binah.

42. "the Unity" implies something joined together.
43. James M.Robinson. "The Nag Hammadi Library." Harper Collins. 1990.
44. "Holy Bible." King James Version. William Collins Sons and Company Ltd. 1947.

3. Verses 17–24 are called Gimel. Gimel is the path between the powers of Kether and Tiphareth.

4. Verses 25–32 are called Daleth. Daleth is the path between the powers of Geburah and Chesed.

5. Verses 33–40 are called He. He is the path between the powers of Chokmah and Tiphareth.

6. Verses 41–48 are called Vau. Vau is the path between the powers of Chokmah and Chesed.

7. Verses 49–56 are called Zain. Zain is the path between the powers of Binah and Tiphareth.

8. Verses 57–64 are called Cheth. Cheth is the path between the powers of Binah and Geburah.

9. Verses 65–72 are called Teth. Teth is the path between the powers of Binah and Chokmah.

10. Verses 73–80 are called Jod. Jod is the path between the powers of Chesed and TIphareth.

11. Verses 81–88 are called Caph. Caph is the path between the powers of Chesed and Netzach.

12. Verses 89–96 are called Lamed. Lamed is the path between the powers of Geburah and Tiphareth.

13. Verses 97–104 are called Mem. Mem is the path between the powers of Geburah and Hod.

14. Verses 105–112 are called Nun. Nun is the path between the powers of Tiphareth and Netzach.

15. Verses 113–120 are called Samech. Samech is the path between the powers of Tiphareth and Yesod.

16. Verses 121–128 are called Ain. Ain is the path between the powers of Tiphareth and Hod.

17. Verses 129–136 are called Pe. Pe is the path between the powers of Hod and Netzach.

18. Verses 137–144 are called Tzaddi. Tzaddi is the path between the powers of Netzach and Yesod.

19. Verses 145–152 are called Koph. Koph is the path between the powers of Netzach and Malkuth.

20. Verses 153–160 are called Resh. Resh is the path between the powers of Hod and Yesod.

21. Verses 161–168 are called Schin. Schin is the path between the powers of Hod and Malkuth.

22. Verses 169–176 are called Tau. Tau is the path between the powers of Yesod and Malkuth.[45]

Why then, with the giving of the Torah, did these teachings become secret and only imparted to a select few? They were not secrets during the reigns of Thutmosis 111 or Thutankamen. Were they secret when the Kingdom of Israel was established by Joshua? Or did these teachings which are in accordance with the masculine/feminine Godhead in Genesis 1 become suppressed and censored at a later date?

There was another school of thought that was considered by the priests and priestesses of Amen to be a heresy. During the reign of Amenhotep IV a religious revolution took place. The Pharaoh rejected the Egyptian mysteries in favour of his new Sun God called Aten. Amenhotep changed his name to Akhenaten, meaning the *"Splendour of Aton"* or the Sun, replacing his previous name which meant *"Amen is pleased."* Amenhotep IV was the first person in history, as we know it, to advocate a monotheistic God based on a single, solar, male principle. These opposing views became entrenched in the Hebrew mind. The

45. Emily Peach. "Tarot for Tomorrow." The Aquarian Press. 1988.

latter finding expression in a monotheistic male God, the former becoming a hidden path that related to the powers of Elohim as revealed in the Kabbala and only available to initiates of a secret society, each in turn being predisposed to Gen.2 and Gen.1 respectively. If we follow the path of the Hebrews from the Exodus until the invasion of the Northern Kingdom of Ephraim by the Assyrians, I believe that we might find some answers. As always, politics raises it's head and in the wake of political bias, the concept of God is adapted to suit the rulers of the day.

Chapter Three.

The Lost Tribes of Israel

Who was Moses? The Bible describes him as a Hebrew adopted by the wife of the Pharaoh; Freud concluded that he was an Egyptian prince; Ahmed Osman believes him to have been the Pharaoh Akhenaton.[46] I believe that he was an Egyptian prince, of the royal line of the Pharaohs as well as being a Hebrew.

Until further archaeological evidence comes to light, I would like to propose that Mosis was the Egyptian Ay, in other words, the Biblical Nun, son of Ephraim, husband of Ankhsenpa-amen[47] and father of Joshua. As such he inherited all the titles bestowed upon his father and his grandfather and was of the order of Melchizedek and would have

---

46. Ahmed Osman. "The House of the Messiah." Grafton. 1993.

47. Ibid.

been known as a priest-king (Mosis), or a levite, not in the sense of the tribe, but in the sense of a *"joiner"* to justice being Zadok.

Nun-Mosis, like Horus, was placed in an ark in the reeds of the Nile to protect him from those who sought to kill him. This story could either be a retelling of the birth of Horus or an actual incident that occurred during the reign of Akhenaton. The priests of Amun were furious with the Pharaoh because of his heretical beliefs and blamed the Hebrews for his worship of the Sun God Aten. In retaliation, they sought to put all male Hebrew children to death. Nun/Ay could have been placed in an ark by his mother, Ephraim's wife, and sent down the river from Karnak to Tell el-Amarna where he was brought up in safety by the Pharaoh, his uncle Akhenaton whose mother was the Hebrew Tiya. In such a way, the *"firstborn,"* descendent of Ephraim, Joseph, Jacob and Isaac, was saved from death much in the same way that Horus had been saved from the evil Set.

After the death of Akhenaton, Thutankamen (Ay's cousin) became the Pharaoh and re-instated the belief in Amun. Today his statue as well as the statue of his wife depicted as Amun and Mut, stand outside the inner sanctum of the temple of Karnak as well as in the Temple of Luxor. After the young Pharaoh's death, Nun/Ay, who was considered to be an Egyptian prince through his grandmother Asenath and his great aunt Tiya, married Thutankamen's wife and ruled for a brief period of time.[48] His reign lasted for four years, then he mysteriously disappeared

---

48. It was not necessary for the Pharaoh to be a direct descendent of the royal line. It was, however necessary for him to marry a female of the royal line in order to become a Pharaoh.

and the military general, Horemheb took over the rulership of Egypt. Although Ay has a tomb in the Valley of the Kings, there is no evidence that he was buried in it.

I suspect that Ay/Nun became known as the Mosis of the Bible, who fled into the Sinai desert after killing an Egyptian who had been ill treating a Hebrew. Both archaeological and Biblical sources describe the Egyptians as being resentful of the Hebrews during this time in history. If, through his grandmother Asenath and his great aunt Tiya, Ay/Nun became eligible to become the Pharaoh, then it is highly likely that the Egyptians were resentful of the Hebrew infiltration into the Pharaonic family. Ay/Nun could well have killed an Egyptian for ill treating a Hebrew and civil resentment could well have erupted against him resulting in a military coup in 1320 B.C.

Ay/Nun, called Mosis or Moshe, *"the king"*—Melek by the Hebrews, could have returned to Egypt five years later during the reign of the military general Horemheb (1320–1292) who did not know Joseph and tried to get the military Pharaoh to let the Hebrews go. The killing of the firstborn on the night that the Hebrews fled could have been carried out in an attempt on Horemheb's part to completely annihilate any descendants from the *"Thut-Mosis"* line and in turn, the descendants of Joseph. The blood marks on the door could have been a sign to the would be assassins that someone had already been killed in the household. Hence, the instruction that the Hebrews should sacrifice a lamb on this night and paint it's blood on the doorway.

Ay/Nun, was not only a descendent of Thut-Mosis 111 and took on the mantle of Horus, *"the firstborn,"* he was also the son of Anen/Ephraim who was blessed by Jacob/Israel as the *"firstborn"* and inherited the title of *"prince"* and *"shepherd"* from Yuya/Joseph. Therefore, Nun-Mosis and his sons would have been regarded as the firstborn in both an Egyptian and a Hebrew sense. In response to the

Eighteenth Dynasty.

Thutmosis 111   +   Sarah
                                                    I
                                                Isaac

Amenhotep 11   +   Rebecca
                                                    I
                                                Jacob & Esau

Thutmosis 1V   +   Rachel
         I   I
         I   Asenath (Tuya) + Joseph (Yuya)
         I   I
Amenhotep 111   +   Tiya & Anen (Ephraim)
         I   I
Amenhotep V1   Ay (Nun) Mosis
         I
Thutankamen—Ankhsenpa-amen—Ay (Nun) Mosis
                    I   I
               Joshua (?)   Joshua (?)
Horemheb—Military ruler 1320-1292
                    Nineteenth Dynasty
Ramses 1 1292–1291
Seti   1291–1279
Ramses 11 1279–1213
Note: Between 1314 and 1274—The Battle of Kadesh=40 yrs

order for the slaughter, Nun-Mosis fled for his life during the night and led the Hebrews into the wilderness in approximately 1314 B.C. The *"firstborn,"* the descendants of Ephraim and the *"Mosis"* line, the believed genetic link to Osiris and Isis through Horus, remained intact.

During the reigns of Ramses 1 (1292–1291), Seti 1(1291–1279) and Ramses 11 (1279–1213) until the battle of Kadesh in 1274, the Hebrews remained in the Sinai desert. Between 1314 and 1274, which gives us forty years, Horemheb, Ramses 1, Seti 1 and Ramses 11 waged military campaigns in Canaan for the express purpose of chasing the Hittites beyond the Euphrates river. Moses could have kept his people safely hidden in the wilderness until these campaigns were over, resulting in a Canaan devoid of it's previous Hittite inhabitants. This in turn paved the way for the New Kingdom of Israel that was promised to Abraham by Thutmosis 111 and by right of the firstborn was inherited by Isaac, Jacob, Yuya/Joseph, Anen/Ephraim, Ay/Nun-Mosis and finally Joshua.

The Exodus served a number of purposes. Firstly it kept the Hebrews out of the way of the marauding Egyptian armies that swept the country from the Nile to the Euphrates river. Secondly, due to their isolation, they became united as a nation with their own identity indelibly printed for all time. Thirdly, the personification of the mysteries as seen in Amen, Mut, Khonsu, Isis, Osiris and Horus became known as the Kabbala, an ideology, the oral teachings of wisdom, or the spiritual kingdom as seen in the astronomical or celestial clock of the heavens. Fourthly, Mosis instituted a political system that had either become lost or had never been considered before. Instead of worshipping a human being in the form of a Pharaoh, regarded as Horus on earth, the divine child with a divine right to rule, the Hebrews learnt to hold the law/Zedek above that of the whims of a Pharaoh or king. In effect, the law was God as much as God was the law and there was only one law, written on clay tablets and installed in the Ark of the Covenant and later written in a text that became known as the Torah.

Moses eliminated the concept of a king who rules by divine right as a representative or the embodiment of God on earth, a king or Pharaoh who was considered to be infallible and answerable only to himself. As a result, kings were no longer considered to be the firstborn of God. Moses replaced this hierarchy with an egalitarian system that was more in keeping with the concepts of Genesis 1 by declaring that all the first-born, being divine *"children,"* no matter from which family or from which tribe, were to be considered holy unto God. Exodus 13:2:

"Sanctify unto Me all the first-born, whatsoever openeth the womb among the children of Israel, both of man and of beast it is mine."

Although these firstborn, or devoted to God, are considered by the orthodox to be male only, the original concept could have referred to both male and female, the term *"man"* being representative of the Hebrews as a whole rather than one section of it, as is inferred in Genesis 1:27. Deborah, a prophetess in Judges, was an example of a female who was *"devoted"* to God as was Adah, the only child and daughter of Jephtah. This philosophy is in keeping with Genesis 1 which is inclusive of the whole human race. In Exodus 13:15 it says:

"...the Lord slew all the firstborn of man, and the firstborn of beast: therefore I sacrifice to the Lord all that openeth the matrix, being males; but all the firstborn of my children I redeem."

Only animals were to be sacrificed, whilst the sacrifice of children, was condemned. An animal, being a lamb in the case of the passover, was sacrificed in the child's stead on the night of the Exodus. Therefore, the words *"being males"* in this quote refers to animals only, while *"the firstborn of my children"* refers to both sexes.

Because these children were holy and devoted to God, the original intention was that they should become part of the priesthood, being *"levites"* or *"joiners"* to the law, known as Zadok. Hence, it says in Exodus 19:6:

"You will be to me a kingdom of priests, my holy nation."

But not all individuals would necessarily choose to become priests, hence the concept of redemption which is still carried out by Hebrews today. Thirty-one days after a child is born, the parents, if they should choose not to devote their child to the priesthood, buy this child back, or redeem this child by paying the priest five pieces of silver, or five shekels (Numbers 18:16). [49]

But there were children who could not be redeemed or sold into the priesthood. If a child's parents were of the priesthood, then this child was automatically considered to have a priestly role, regardless of being the first, second or third born child. These children were in effect, irredeemable and unsaleable as they were considered to be part and parcel of the priesthood due to their hereditary descent.

If a person who was not the firstborn and not of a priestly family decided to join the priesthood and become devoted to God irredeemably, as were the children of the priesthood, then this person in turn, after initiation, could not be sold or redeemed. Such people became known as Nazarenes, whereby a man or a woman made a special vow of dedication. Numbers 6: 2:

"Speak unto the children of Israel, and say unto them, When either man or woman shall separate themselves to vow a vow of a Nazarite,..."

Leviticus 27: 2, 3 & 4:

---

49. Louis Jacobs. "The Jewish Religion." Oxford University Press. 1995.

"Speak unto the children of Israel, and say unto them, When a person shall make a singular vow, the persons shall be for the Lord by thy estimation.

And thy estimation shall be of the male from twenty years old even unto sixty years old, even thy estimation shall be fifty shekels of silver, after the shekel of the sanctuary.

And if it be a female, then thy estimation shall be thirty shekels."

Through this process, they were sold into the priesthood and were in turn regarded in the same light as the firstborn, the whole Nazarene ceremony being a reflection of the Passover whereby the firstborn fasts (Num. 4);[50] brings a lamb for sacrifice (Num. 12); and brings a basket of unleavened bread to the priest (Num.15). The fact that Numbers 6 states that this initiation was open to both men and women, supports the premise that the word *"man"* in Exodus 13:2 should be read as *"people."*

Isaiah takes this concept one step further whereby the belief that we are all *"firstborn"* in accordance with Genesis 1 and become *"joined"* to the law, is a concept that embraces all nations, races and sexes. 66:20 & 21:

"And they shall bring all your brethren for an offering unto the Lord out of all nations....And I will also take of them for priests and for Levites (joiners), saith the Lord."

Due to these laws that governed the firstborn, or the devoted priesthood, Mosis ensured that the vocation of priest, which entailed having a thorough knowledge of the law being Zadok and in all likelihood the

---

50. Ibid. (See under "Fast" and "Nazarene.")

Kabbala, was not just the preserve of the descendants of Joseph, (the prince, high priest, the shepherd, the righteous and keeper of the covenant) but was open to all the tribes, all classes of people, both rich and poor and was open to both sexes, as Numbers 6:2 implies.

These people became levites, the *"joiners"* to the order of Ephraim—*"the firstborn"* and therefore were blessed as such with the title *"Israel,"* as Ephraim had been, regardless of their hereditary descent. Numbers 6: 26 & 27:

> *"The Lord lift up his countenance upon thee, and give thee peace.*
>
> *And they shall put my name upon the children of Israel; and I will bless them."*

Hence, the priests and the judges rule from mount Ephraim and go to worship the Lord of hosts in Shiloh; Deborah is an Ephraimite; Ruth was married to an Ephraimite; Samuel is an Ephraimite; Ezra is a descendent of Zadok, a keeper of the law; Isaiah is named after Joshua or Hosea an Ephraimite, as the name Isaiah is a derivative of Joshua;[51] Jeremiah is from a priestly family, the high priest being Joseph; lastly Ezekiel is a descendent of Zadok, a keeper of the law.

The duties of the priests were to have a complete knowledge of the Kabbala, which as we have seen is also an astronomical blue print and the Torah, the laws of God. Rather than dictate, their duties were to arbitrate in disputes. The Hebrew priests were in effect, the first lawyers.

---

51. Ibid.

The High Priests in turn, were the *"Anointed,"* which in Hebrew is translated as *"Messiah,"*[52] and the equivalent of a judge. Leviticus 21: 10:

"He that is the high priest among his brethren, upon whose head the anointing oil was poured...."

Once a priest had reached a certain level of education and understanding, he or she became an anointed/Messiah or judge, as was Deborah. Religion and the law was intricately interwoven, the one complimenting the other. This system of governance not only gave individuals from all walks in life an opportunity to study the law and the priesthood but it also instituted the first federal democracy that united the twelve tribes into one nation. Such a philosophy is in accordance with Genesis 1 and advocates equality, democracy and a justice of liberty.

There is of course, the contradictory view. Firstly that only males be regarded as the firstborn who could be redeemed and secondly, that the priesthood was not available to both sexes and all classes of people. Unlike the comparison between Genesis 1 and 2, which is clear cut and simple, Exodus, Leviticus, Numbers and Deuteronomy are inclined to be a melting pot where opposing views are not only duplicated and recorded in one book, but sometimes, also within one chapter. This is most probably due to the fact that these works were compiled by joining together two separate documents being the *"J"* and the *"E"* texts in 500 B.C., whilst all five books, known as the Pentateuch, were finally

---

52. Ibid.

fused together in 450 B.C.[53] Human error, bias and political expediency would have played their part.

The opposing political viewpoint of a federal democracy, being an autocratic structure in line with Genesis 2, would rely on male supremacy, draconian laws and ascendancy based on hereditary blood lines. In other words, to deny the right of every individual to study the Kabbala and the law or the Torah; to prevent the populace from regarding themselves as a holy nation of priests and priestesses because this would put them on an equal footing with their leaders; and to make the majority reliant and subservient to the law as interpreted by an individual or a select group of people. Hence, we have the contradiction in Exodus 34: 20:

"….All the firstborn of thy sons thou shalt redeem."

The male in this instance, as opposed to both sexes, is clearly indicated. The next step is to make the title firstborn and/or the priesthood only available to a select group of people. Exodus 13:15 is contradicted in Numbers 3: 12, where only the Levites, from the tribe of Levi, are to be considered as the firstborn.

"And I, behold, I have taken the Levites from among the children of Israel instead of all the firstborn that openeth the matrix among the children of Israel: therefore the Levites shall be mine."

---

53. Max. I. Dimont. "Jews, God and History." Signet. 1962.

As a result, only the tribe of Levi is to be considered for the priesthood and only the children of a Levite, elevated to that of High priest. In other words, knowledge of the law and of the Torah, is now held in the hands of a select group of people. Jeremiah, on the other hand, held a very different view that was more in keeping with the idea that the Hebrews, each and every one of them, should be a holy nation of priests. 31:33 & 34:

> "...I will put my law in their inward parts, and write it in their hearts; and will be their God , and they shall be my people.
> And they shall teach no more every man his neighbour, and every man his brother, saying, Know the Lord: for they shall all know me, from the least of them unto the greatest of them..."

The final political ploy was to introduce a king with a divine right to rule, as had been the case in Egypt before the Exodus. Joshua's federal democracy whereby the twelve tribes each had self determination and were led by judges and councillors, lasted for approximately 300 years. At the close of the millennium great changes were to come about, the result being that those who believed in democracy were persecuted whilst those who believed in the divine right of a king descended from one specific blood line going back to Adam, became autonomous. The tribe of Judah, so long dormant, rose to power. This system was not sanctioned by God, or by the order of Melchizedek who were the high priests and judges. Samuel 8: 6, 7 8, 9, 14, 15, 17 & 18:

> "But the thing displeased Samuel, when they said, Give us a king to judge us. And Samuel prayed unto the Lord.
> And the Lord said unto Samuel, Harken unto the voice of the people in all that they say unto thee: for they have not rejected thee, but they have rejected me, that I should not reign over them.

According to all the works which they have done since the day that I brought them out of Egypt even unto this day, wherewith they have forsaken me, and served other gods, so do they also unto thee....

Now therefore harken unto their voice: howbeit yet protest solemnly unto them, and show them the manner of king that shall reign over them...he will take your fields, and your vineyards, and your oliveyards, even the best of them, and give them to his servants....he will take the tenth of your seed, and of your vineyards, and give to his officers, and to his servants...he will take the tenth of your sheep: and ye shall be his servants....And ye shall cry out in that day because of your king which ye shall have chosen you; and the Lord will not hear you in that day..."

Isaiah, after the fall of both kingdoms, reiterates this view and wants to see the previous system re-instated in 1:26:

"And I will restore thy judges as at the first, and thy counsellors as at the beginning: afterward thou shalt be called, The city of righteousness, the faithful city."

If our Biblical chronology is to be believed, then Judaic ascent was achieved through David, to Solomon to Rehoboam. This would of course make no sense of Genesis 49:10, where Israel decrees that sceptre shall pass from Judah when Shiloh comes. But, if David Rohl's research proves to be the more accurate,[54] then Rehoboam came to

---

54 David M. Rohl. "A Test of Time." Century. 1995.

power resting on the laurels of his ancestors who had ruled four hundred years previously in Avaris in northern Egypt and Professor Thomas Thompson is correct in his assessment that the Temple in Jerusalem was not built until after the Jews returned from Babylon in approximately 535 B.C., five hundred years later, after which the Pentateuch was compiled.

These Judaic kings in turn, became the anointed as the High priests/judges had once been and took on the title of Messiah. Unfortunately, their rise to power resulted in a split within the kingdom of Israel after the reign of Solomon (Biblical chronology), or during the reign of Rehoboam (David Rohl's chronology). In the south lay the Kingdom of Judah, which incorporated the tribes of Simeon and Benjamin. They called themselves Israelites. In the north lay the kingdom of Israel, also known as the kingdom of Ephraim and consisted of ten tribes. These people referred to themselves as Israel or Jacob and were the Hebrews. Hence, throughout the book of Isaiah, this prophet refers to both these kingdoms. The former referred to as Judah, the latter referred to as Jacob, Israel, Ephraim or Samaria. His desire for their reunification runs throughout his book. 11:13:

"...the envy also of Ephraim shall depart, and the adversaries of Judah shall be cut off: Ephraim shall not envy Judah, and Judah shall not vex Ephraim."

I have always wondered why Mosis handed over the leadership of the Hebrews to Joshua. Logic dictates that this leadership, if upheld in the orthodox line, would have fallen to the tribe of Levi or to one of the sons of Judah. But it didn't. It fell to a man called Joshua, of the tribe of Ephraim who was known as a Judge in Israel and as such a son of Zadok, being the law. Hence, he was of the order of Melchizedek, or a priest/king of justice.

The Bible does not regard Joshua as the son of Mosis, though this could be the case. Joshua could however, have been the son of Thutankamen and Ankhsenpa-amen, Mosis, the grandson of Joseph marrying the Pharaoh's widow and adopting his son, much in the same way that Joseph marries Mary in the New Testament and adopts the *"Lord's son."* In either case, Mosis laid his hands upon Joshua as Jacob had laid his hands upon Ephraim and declared him to be the *"shepherd"* of the people as Joseph had been (Num. 27:15–23). I believe that this was due to the fact that in line of the blessings, Joshua was the firstborn descended from Israel who had inherited the land from the Nile to the Euphrates river given to Abraham by Thutmosis 111. It is interesting to note that the Samaritans still living in Nabulus today, describe them-selves as direct descendants of Ephraim and Manasseh as well as of Aaron,[55] the brother of Mosis, which implies a genetic link between Aaron and Ephraim. If my theory on the line of descent is correct, that Mosis was in fact Nun-Mosis or Ay-Mosis the son of Anen-Ephraim, then It should come as no surprise then, that three hundred years later the Hebrews from the Ephraimite kingdom of Israel saw Rehoboam of the tribe of Judah as a suppressor and an upstart. 1 Kings 12:14,16 & 17:

"My father made your yoke heavy, and I will add to your yoke: my father also chastised you with whips, but I will chastise you with scorpions....
So when all Israel saw that the king harkened not unto them, the peo-ple answered the king, saying, What portion have we in David? neither

55. Steve Jones. "In the Blood. God, Genes and destiny." Harper Collins. 1996.

*have we inheritance in the son of Jesse: to your tents, O Israel: now see to
thine own house David...as for the children of Israel which dwelt
in...Judah, Rehoboam reigned over them."*

The books of Kings 1 & 2 and Chronicles, relate the stories about the
two kingdoms and the kings who ruled them. I believe that both were
guilty of idolatry for the simple reason that they had turned their backs
on the law, that it should be written in their hearts and instead had
asked for a king to judge them. This system was against the teachings of
the prophets and against the laws of Mosis as this hymn which is sometimes sung at the Passover Haggadah implies:

*"...thou art God, and except for thee we have no redeeming and saving
king, liberating and delivering, and provident and compassionate in every
time of trouble and distress. We have no king but thee, O God..."* [56]

The original intention of Mosis was to create " *a kingdom of priests..
a....holy nation."* This ideal cannot be achieved so long as there is discrimination between sexes, families or within the nation and the concept of a divine child with a divine right to rule, remains. The fact that
one of the first judges in Israel was a woman, called Deborah, should be
enough evidence to prove the point that it was not necessary to be male
or of the tribe of Levi in order to become a priest. What is more, the
judges and priests ruled from Shiloh which was within the borders of
the tribe of Ephraim and these priests of Zadok, or the order of

---

56. Nahum N. Glatzer. "The Passover Haggadah." Schocken Books Inc. 1981.

Melchizedek, were in all likelihood Ephraimites and levites, being *"join-ers"* to the priesthood from all the different tribes who guarded the ark in this town.

With the rise of the Judaic and Hebrew kings, democracy was replaced by autocracy and all power was believed to be in the hands of a king and his elect priesthood. Jeroboam however, in spite of becoming a king, did not subscribe to the latter religious view in accordance with Exodus 13:15. As a result, he was condemned by the Levites for ordaining priests from all classes of people which was in accordance with Numbers 3:12. 1 Kings 12:31:

"...and made priests of the lowest of the people, which were not of the sons of Levi."

Due to the climate of the times, the Kabbala became the secret teaching, imparted to a select few. It was dangerous knowledge in a world where women and people from other tribes other than Levi were denied entry to the priesthood. The powers of the Kabbala, or the Elohim, in accordance with Genesis 1, are both male and female in nature, the male powers being associated with the law while the female powers are associated with wisdom and the Spirit, politically expressed in democracy which ensures that draconian laws are kept at bay.

As will become evident below, the Hebrews, the northern kingdom of Ephraim never lost sight of this view. Their crime was in portraying the concept of democracy in the form of an idol, being the Ashtaroth, which later found it's way into Greece where this same ideology took the form of the Goddess Athena. Isaiah describes the suppression of this feminine concept, being the Spirit, or the Shekinah, the *"tree of life"* referred to in Proverbs which is also a symbol of the Kabbala itself in 50:1 and 63:10:

"Thus saith the Lord, Where is the bill of your mother's divorcement, whom I have put away? or which of my creditors is it to whom I have sold

you? Behold, for your iniquities have ye sold yourselves, and for your transgressions is your mother put away."

"But they rebelled, and vexed his holy Spirit: therefore he was turned to be their enemy, and he fought against them."

The Ephraimite kingdom was destroyed by Sargon at the final battle of Meddigo, Armageddon, in 722 B.C. After the fall, the most politically expedient place for the northern tribes to flee from the Assyrians, was into Judah, taking the Ark of the Covenant with them. They were not welcome and were persecuted for erecting an Ashtaroth. This was a political statement, similar to the statement made by Chinese students on June 4th 1989, when they erected a paper mache effigy of the goddess, being the Statue of Liberty in Tiananmen Square. Needless to say, the Levite priests not only condemned the idol, but the ideology as well. Again, as happened in Egypt, a man appeals to a king to *"let my people go,"* begging release from oppression. Again, the celebration of Passover had an immediate significance. Jeremiah 34:8–16:

"This is the word that came unto Jeremiah from the Lord, after that the king Zedekiah had made a covenant with all the people which were at Jerusalem, to proclaim liberty unto them.

That every man let his manservant, and every man his maidservant, being Hebrew or an Hebrewess, go free; that none should serve himself of them, to wit, of a Jew his brother.

Now when all the princes, and all the people, which had entered into the covenant, heard that every one should let his manservant, and every one his maidservant, go free, that none should serve themselves of them any more, then they obeyed, and let them go.

But afterward they turned, and caused the servants and the handmaids, whom they had let go free, to return, and brought them into subjection for servants and for handmaids.

Therefore the word of the Lord came to Jeremiah from the Lord, saying, Thus saith the Lord, the God of Israel; I made a covenant with your fathers in the day that I brought them forth out of the land of Egypt, out of the house of bondmen saying, At the end of seven years let ye every man his brother an Hebrew which hath been sold unto thee; and when he hath served thee six years, thou shalt let him go free: but your fathers harkened not unto me, neither inclined their ear.

And ye were now turned, and had done right in my sight, in proclaiming liberty every man to his neighbour, and ye had made a covenant before me in the house which is called by my name.

But ye turned and polluted my name, and caused every man his servant, and every man his handmaid, who ye had set at their pleasure, to return, and brought them into subjection, to be unto you for servants and for handmaids."

According to Graham Hancock, after the rule of Mannasseh who was put to death for worshipping the Ashtaroth, or adopting a democratic stance, the Ark is no longer mentioned in the Biblical texts and is conspicuous by it's absence. He proposes that it was at this time that the Ark was removed and taken to Egypt by the Hebrews, later known as the Lost Tribes of Israel, where it was kept on Elephantine Island near Aswan and installed in a temple resembling the temple built by Solomon in our Biblical texts.[57]

---

57. Graham Hancock. "The Sign and the Seal." Mandarin. 1993.

As the Ark was symbolic of the Bride, being democracy and the tablets were symbolic of the Lord, being the law, so their temple in this area incorporated the masculine and feminine principles of the Elohim. Papyrus texts found on this island which date to 400 B.C., refer to Hebrews settlers who had a temple there. This temple was not only dedicated to the male principle that they called *"Yaho,"* but also to the feminine principle called *"Anath"* the equivalent of the Queen of Heaven. *"Anath"* in turn, like the Ashtaroth, was as democratic symbol as was Athena who was worshipped in Greece during this same period in history. [58] These Hebrews incurred the wrath of the High Priests of the Ram God Khnum, the potter, due to the fact that the Egyptians believed that they were sacrificing their god during the Passover festivals as Abraham had done hundreds of years before.

The policies of the Ephraimites during the seventh century B.C. were simultaneously being carried out in Thebes. The Priestesses, known as the *"Adoratices of Amun"* held political power during the 25th (745–664) and 26th dynasties (664–526). [59] After the reign of Amose 11 (570–526) Egypt was invaded and became a Persian province under King Cambyses 11 in 525, whose son Daruis 1, sanctioned the building of the Temple in Jerusalem in approximately 515 B.C. when the Jews returned to Judea. The few remaining Samaritans who still lived in and around Mount Gerizim, sent a letter opposing the building of the Temple to the Persian king.[60]

---

58. Geoffrey Ashe. "The Virgin. Mary's Cult and the Re-emergence of the Goddess." 1988. Arkana.

59. Robertson McCarta. Nelles Verlag. "Egypt." 1991. Nelles Verlag.

60. "The Bible." King James Version. W.M. Collins Sons and Co. Ltd. 1947.

Louis Jacobs. "The Jewish Religion." Oxford University Press. 1995.

With the Persian invasion of Egypt, the Ark was moved yet again and the Hebrews fled from the Persian invaders, rather than seeing them as liberators. It is believed that they took the Ark to Ethiopia where there arose the legends of Prester John. The Kebra Nagast, an Ethiopian religious work, states that the Ark was brought to Ethiopia with the first-born sons of Israel.[61]

I am of the opinion that *"firstborn sons of Israel"* referred to in the Kebra Nagast refers to the Hebrews, the northern Kingdom of Israel, the tribe of Ephraim, as Ephraim, the son of Joseph, was adopted and blessed by Jacob-Israel as his firstborn. Jacob and Isaac in turn, as we have seen above, could have been born into and become part of the Moses family line, who regarded themselves as the firstborn through Menes, believed to have been a descendent of the divine child Horus, born of Isis and Osiris who was hidden in the bulrushes of the Nile. Through this lineage, the Lost Tribes are not only traced to the very beginning of Egyptian history, but by the very nature of their name, being the Ephraimite kingdom, they can also be traced to the very beginning of the Bible.

The first covenant made between the Elohim and human beings, was to be fruitful. Fruitful does not only apply to fertility, but also to constructive action. We use the word *"fruitful"* to imply, amongst other things: good results; success; maturation; adulthood; inventiveness; resourcefulness; imagination; creativity; the horn of plenty; a land flowing in milk and honey or lastly, to make the desert bloom. The

---

61. Graham Hancock. "The Sign and the Seal." 1993. Mandarin.

opposite being *"fruitless,"* is used to imply: ineffectiveness; failure; profitless; barren and useless.

Being fruitful, increasing, applies to constructive action and in Gen. 1:28 we are told to replenish the earth, refill it, renew it, but not to deplete it. Because it is a constructive requirement, it does not mean that we should breed like a bunch of rabbits. Overpopulation leads to unemployment, poverty, starvation and the depletion of the resources of the earth which in turn means that we cannot replenish, but continuously consume and make fruitless. You only have to drive through Africa or any third world country to be besieged by poverty stricken youngsters who are underfed to get the point. And yet their parents proudly announce that they have up to twelve children who they cannot afford to feed, clothe or educate.

"The Wisdom of Jesus the Son of Sirach-Ecclesiastes," found in the Apocrypha of the Catholic Bible and quoted under the name *"Ben Sira"* in the Talmud,[62] supports the premise in Genesis 1, that being fruitful and multiplying does not necessarily go hand in hand with a lack of birth control. Chapter 16:13:

"Desire not a multitude of unprofitable children, neither delight in ungodly sons. Though they multiply, rejoice not in them, except the fear of the Lord be with them. Trust not thou in their life, neither respect their multitude: for one that is just is better than a thousand."

---

62. Louis Jacobs. "The Jewish Religion." Oxford University Press. 1995

The word *"Fruitful"* when translated into Hebrew is Ephraim—Ephrathah. Therefore, the word Ephraim and it's feminine equivalent, Ephrathah, is not only the result of God and the Spirit creating as seen in Genesis 1 and thereby creation as a whole being the firstborn fruit of Elohim, but Ephraim-Ephrathah, *"be fruitful and replenish the earth,"* is in fact the first covenant itself, the first law given to human beings. As James says in 1:18:

"Of his own will begat he us with the word of truth, that we should be a kind of firstfruits of his creatures."

Although Ephraim refers to a specific tribe, it is also associated with all races and nations that were created together in the beginning. It is not exclusive or racialistic, but inclusive of all humanity as were the children of Noah and later the ideology of the federated states in Israel. Because these people did not believe in the *"mixed Marriages Act"* as advocated by Ezra in 457 B.C (9:12), which in turn is based on a blood line descended from Judah to Adam, I believe that the so called Ten Lost Tribes refers to the whole human race. Prior to the invasion by the Assyrians, the Hebrews intermarried with other peoples. Joseph married the Egyptian Asenath. Tamar, the Canaanite bore Judah's sons. Moses was married to a Cushite (black) woman. Ruth was a Moabite and David married Batsheba, a Hittite. Only when the Jews lived in exile in Babylon, did the priests forbid intermarriage with women or men from other nations and races.[63] Prior to this time and thereafter, the ten tribes intermarried frequently.

---

63. Louis Jacobs. "The Jewish Religion." Oxford University Press. 1995.

There were remnants of the lost tribes who remained in Samaria, as did some Jews remain in Judah. But most were dispersed throughout the globe. They not only went to Ethiopia, but some remained in Egypt as far north as Alexandria[64] while others were scattered around the Mediterranean. Recent research has proved that they also spread to Europe, the Far East and...the Americas![65] In other words, they have integrated with the large majority of the world's population. The Diaspora is believed to have begun in the 1st century A.D., but it is my belief that it began well before this time. It began with the Assyrian invasion itself. Steve Jones, the author of *"In the Blood. God, Genes and Destiny,"* expresses my sentiments exactly:

"The radiation of bloodlines from a centre is due to an ancient emigration from the Middle East and it's peoples assimilation of their neighbour's genes. It contains the solution to the mystery of the Lost Tribes. In fact, they never were lost: instead they live on in the inheritance of a thousand million people alive today." [66]

Steve Jones also points out that if all the descendants of the Hebrews, (who were incidently, part and parcel of *the chosen* at Mount Sinai) who had been at Megiddo (Armageddon) when the Assyrians under Sargon finally destroyed the Kingdom of Israel in 722 B.C., returned to Armageddon in the Last Days of Judgement, there would be *"ten thousand billion billion billion billion"* people at this site. Isaiah's view that

---

64. Some Samaritans remained in Egypt right up until the nineteenth century, finally returning to Israel due to persecution from Muslims.

65. Steve Jones. "In The Blood. God, Genes and Destiny." Harper Collins. 1996.

66. Ibid.

the Hebrews should be scattered to the four corners of the globe has in fact become a reality and is in keeping with his wish in 66:20:

"And they shall bring all your brethren for an offering unto the Lord out of all nations…"

What has happened is that most of the world's population now carries the genes that can connect them to the Ten Lost Tribes, the *"chosen race,"* being the Hebrews, which in turn means that we have all inherited the title *"firstborn"*[67] through the descendants of Ephraim.

In South Africa today there is a Sotho tribe who claims descent from the priestly class or Cohen from the northern Kingdom of Israel. Many of their customs are the same as those advocated by Moses in the Old Testament. In 1999 geneticists in England studied their blood lines and proved their claims to be true.

The prophet Isaiah was very even handed in his judgement of both Judah and Ephraim. In chapter seven, he speaks of the birth of a holy child called Immanuel (verse 14). Before he becomes of age and can know the difference between good and evil, the kingdom of Ephraim will have fallen to the Assyrians (verse 16). Rather than being a prediction of the future, this is a commentary on the present, whereby a remnant of Israel, being the firstborn, shall survive and flee to Egypt, as the Hebrews did, and his blood line will be saved. In chapter 11, he speaks

---

67. I believe that this will eventually be proved through genetics and will in turn substantiate my argument that ultimately, the human race is in fact one family and that racism, sexism or wars fought in the name of one specific religion or another, is self destructive to us all in the end. Hopefully, this will either be proved by "The Human Genome Diversity Project," or some other group that takes up this cause.

of a remnant of Jesse, being the house of David, who will also survive the Babylonian exile and his blood line shall also be saved.

Isaiah's ultimate aim was to see the two kingdoms united and restored under the judges and councillors that had ruled Israel at the beginning. In chapter eight he refers to his wife as a prophetess, in other words, she was a priestesses and most probably also of the order of Melchizedek, which implies that he advocated Genesis 1 over and above Genesis 2 (64:7 & 8) and believed that a woman could also join the priesthood as Deborah did.

Seven hundred years after the fall of the kingdom of Ephraim, a man called Jesus attempted to achieve the religious and political aims of Isaiah. In Mark 3:24 he says in reference to the division between Judah and Ephraim:

"And if a kingdom be divided against itself, that kingdom cannot stand."

His words were prophetic, as the Temple in Jerusalem fell in 70 A.D. In Mark 10:6,7,8 & 9 he says:

"But from the beginning of the creation God made them male and female. For this cause shall a man leave his father and mother, and cleave to his wife;

And they twain shall be one flesh: so then they are no more twain, but one flesh. What therefore God hath joined together, let no man put asunder."

His words not only refer to marriage, but to the very beginning of creation where God and the Spirit are one, referred to as *"us"* in Genesis 1. The first line is a quotation from Genesis 1:27. His words also refer to the Kabbala, where the male and female paths are interlocked within the tree of life as are the D.N.A. molecules interlocked within the body. These male and female powers in turn, must not be separated. A scientific analogy of what happens when they are, would be the splitting of the atom which results in the atomic bomb. The same can be said of the Spirit which should not be separated from God. His words in Matthew 12:31 & 32 are a reflection of Isaiah 63:10:

"Wherefore I say unto you, All manner of sin and blasphemy shall be forgiven unto men: but the blasphemy against the Holy Spirit shall not be forgiven unto men.

And whosoever speaketh against the Holy Spirit, it shall not be forgiven him, neither in this world, neither in the world to come."

"But they rebelled, and vexed his holy Spirit: therefore he was turned to be their enemy, and he fought against them."

The conflict between the tribe of Levi and the beliefs of the lost Hebrew Ephraimite Kingdom of Israel never died. Towards the close of the millennium, many Hebrews were scattered throughout the Mediterranean. From Alexandria in the west, to Assyria in the east. From Ethiopia in the south, to Gaul in the north. During the last two to three hundred years however, many Hebrews began to return, either settling in Samaria, where a small group of Hebrews still remained, to Galilee in the north or the Dead Sea in the south. By the time of the Roman invasion the division between Levitical and Hebraic thought was alive and well. Coupled with this political split was a theological split which manifested itself in two opposing religious groups known as the Sadducees and the Essenes.

Chapter Four.

The Saducees

The Saducees were a group of aristocratic priests who maintained the Temple in Jerusalem and formed part of the Levitical judicial body known as the Sanhedrin. From 17 A.D. until 36 A.D., Caiaphas, the High Priest, sat at the pinnacle of power and next to Herod Agrippa 1, held the highest office that was available under the dictates of Rome. He had almost twenty thousand people under his command, ranging from priests and acolytes, to soldiers and administrators.[68]

The Saducees did not advocate mysticism in any form, dismissing belief in life after death, the resurrection or the *"World to Come,"*[69] as well as such disciplines as the Kabbala. They advocated total adherence to every letter of the written law, upholding all the Levitical laws of

---

68. Gordon Thomas. "The Trial." Corgi. 1988.

69. Louis Jacobs. "The Jewish Religion." Oxford University Press. 1995.

purity and maintained their authority through political power. The concepts of immortality or resurrection were totally rejected by these men,[70] which is in accordance with Genesis 2 where Adam and Eve are denied the tree of everlasting life.

The Sadducees accepted Roman rule and their civic and administrative posts accommodated Rome in order that they could maintain their power and influence over the Jewish population. At times, when it suited them, they even fought on the side of the Romans in order to ensure political standing.[71]

The teachings of Jesus not only threatened the power of the High Priest, but also the Herod Kings and the powers of Rome. If we take some of the Christian messages and hold them up against a backdrop of Temple policy, the Herodian crown and the policies of the Roman Empire, it becomes blatantly obvious why early Christianity was suppressed by all three establishments.

In John 7:45–52, we have a story that exposes the totalitarian attitude of the Sadducees compared to the concept of a justice of liberty. We can gather from the script that Jesus, as a Galilean, was in favour of democracy while the Temple priests in Judea, believed themselves to be above the law:

"Then one of their number, Nicodemus (the man who once visited Jesus) intervened. "Does our law," he asked them, "permit us to pass

---

70. Michael Baigent, Richard Leigh, Henry Lincoln. "The Messianic Legacy." Corgi. 1987.
71. Ibid.

judgement on someone without first giving them a hearing and learning the facts?"

"Are you a Galilean too?" they retorted."

This simple story has clearly exposed the opposing political factions between the Galileans in the north and the High Temple Priest in Judea. The former advocated a just trial with witnesses to speak on their behalf in accordance with Mosaic law, the later believed themselves to be infallible and above this practice by exercising a trial by ordeal. When it came to religious doctrine, the High Priest believed that it had nothing to do with civil rights or the law.

The situation in Palestine during the first century A.D. was similar to the situation in Israel before the Assyrian invasion. To the south lay Judea, to the north, Samaria and Galilee. The name *"Galilee"* is reminiscent of the original concept of the kingdom of Israel as it means *"a circuit of nations."*[72] The Sadducees despised the Samaritans and the Galileans to such an extent that it says in: John 7:52:

"...Art thou also of Galilee? Search and look: for out of Galilee ariseth no prophet."

Jesus, on the other hand, who came from Galilee, clearly states what he thinks of the Sadducees in Jerusalem when he says in Matthew 16:6 & 12:

---

72. John Rogerson. "Atlas of the Bible." 1989. Phaidon Press Limited.

"...take heed and beware of the leaven of the Pharisees and of the Sadducees...

...he bade them not beware of the leaven of bread, but of the doctrine of the Pharisees and the Sadducees."

This then was one of the political implications of the Christian message which threatened not only the Temple in Jerusalem, but also King Herod Agrippa 1 who was supported by the Sadducee priesthood and the Roman Emperor, who considered himself to be the *"son of God"* and therefore to be above the law. From 59 B.C. onwards, all rulers of the Roman Empire became life dictators, most notably Augustus who proclaimed himself Emperor in 27 B.C.

In Judea, Caiaphas, as High Priest was entitled to use the term *"Messiah"* behind his name. Messiah, which means *"anointed,"*[73] was a title first used at the inauguration of the High Priests or Judges with holy oil, then used in the ceremony of kings. The word was then translated into the Greek, being *"Christos"* or *"Christ."*

Christianity derives it's name from this word. I suspect that being a *"Christian"* in the early days of the church, implied that the individual had not only received Baptism, but that the initiate had become a Nazarene, devoted and *"anointed"* into the church with holy oil. Hence they were Christians. Take for example:1 John 2:27 which implies that Christians were regarded as such because they had been anointed:

---

73. O.Odelain and R. Seguineau. "Dictionary of Proper Names and Places in the Bible." Robert Hale. 1991.

"But the anointing which ye have received of him abideth in you, and ye need not that any man teach you: but as the same anointing teacheth you of all things, and is truth, and is no lie, and even as it hath taught you, ye shall abide in him."

"The Dead Sea Scrolls":

"And they were justified, and walked according to the L[aws…anointed with the oil of the Kingship…."[74]

The Gnostic *"The Gospel Of Truth:"*

"That is why Christ was spoken of in their midst, so that those who were disturbed might receive a bringing back, and he might anoint them with ointment. The ointment is the mercy of the Father who will have mercy on them. But those whom he has anointed are the ones who have become perfect." [75]

And the Gnostic *"The Gospel of Philip:"*

"But one receives the unction of the […] of the power of the cross. This power the apostles called "the right and the left." For this person is no longer a Christian but a Christ." [76]

Spiritually, they would have attained their own *"Messiahship"* or Christ'ianty. Politically, this anointing implied self empowerment which in turn results in a democratic system. The result, both spiritually and

---

74. Robert Eisenman & Michael Wise. "The Dead Sea Scrolls Uncovered." Element. 1993. Text 4Q458. Fragment 2, column 2, lines 4 & 5.

75. James M. Robinson. "The Nag Hammadi Library." HarperCollins. 1990.

76. Ibid.

politically would be that they would not have felt obliged to bow down to a dictator either in a religious or a political context.

I suspect that the early church of Christians, or anointed, were in fact Nazarenes as Jesus had been. They became *"devoted"* by undergoing initiation as described in Numbers 6 and thereby had become *"firstborn"* of God, or Messiah the anointed, blessed with the name *"Israel"* (Num.6:27), as Jacob had blessed Ephraim before them. For example, consider this extract from *"The Dead Sea Scrolls:"*

"...By his will, devote yourself to his service, and the Wisdom of his storehouse (13)...you will advise him, and become for him a firstborn..." child. *"and he shall love you as a man loves his only child. (14)"*[77]

This is of course in direct opposition to Levitical practice whereby only the tribe of Levi were considered to be firstborn in accordance with Numbers 3: 41 and 8:18, and entitled to the priesthood.

Hence Caiaphas's anger when Jesus had the audacity to call himself *"Christ"* or *"Messiah,"* the anointed one, a child of God being the firstborn. If Jesus was to proclaim himself as Christ, or Messiah, the anointed one, in effect the firstborn, then he would be undermining the High office of Caiaphas, a Levitical priest. Jesus, as we know, was not from the tribe of Levi. For those who think that I am guilty of blasphemy when I say that we are all Christs, Messiah's and in effect, we are all the firstborn of God, consider John 10: 33–34:

---

77. Robert Eisenman & Michael Wise. "The Dead Sea Scrolls Uncovered." Element. 1993. Text 4Q416, 418, lines 13 & 14.

"'We are not stoning you for any good deed,' the Jews replied, 'but for blasphemy: you, a man, are claiming to be God.'

Jesus answered, 'Is it not written in your law, "I said: You are gods?" It is those to whom God's word[78] came who are called gods—and scripture cannot be set aside."

The implications were not only a political democracy but a moral democracy whereby everyone, through anointing, became Messiah through the Nazarene initiation and not just the High Temple Priest. If people now believed that they could have direct experience of God through the *"word,"* instead of indirect experience through the High Priest of the Temple, then the Sadducees would loose their power, their exalted status and need I add, their wealth. They would have to acknowledge enfranchisement both within the church and outside of it in the political arena.

The Levitical priesthood who sacrificed for the population and granted salvation, demanding tithe for this service, were rejected by early Christian doctrine, never more so than when Jesus entered the Temple and turned over the tables. In Matthew 23:23, he says:

"Woe unto you, scribes and Pharisees, hypocrites! for ye pay tithe of mint and anise and cummin, and have omitted the weightier matters of the law, judgement, mercy and faith."

---

78. The "word" as we have seen, relates to the 22 letters of the Hebrew alphabet which are found on 22 paths within the Kabbala and in Psalm 119.

This Christian policy that advocates a political and religious democracy of thought, speech and belief, in other words, self empowerment, is clearly spelt out in Matthew 23:8 and was ignored throughout Europe in spite of the continent adopting Christianity.

"But you must not be called Rabbi, for you are all brothers. Do not call any man on earth Father, for you have one father, and he is in heaven. Nor must you be called "master," you have one master, the Messiah." (I would translate *"Messiah"* as *"the anointing."*)

1 John 2:27:

"...ye need not that any man teach you; but as the same anointing teacheth you..."

Eisenman and Wise are of the opinion that because Josephus described the Hebrews as:

"refusing to call any man "Lord" and seem to have rallied to a cry that can be characterized by the words "no king but God," i.e. "God rules here, not man,"

which is in accordance with the Passover prayer as we have seen in the above chapter, they would also:

"...not have deigned to call any Messianic leader " Lord" either."[79]

This would imply that the concept of *"Messiah"* or anointed, was more in keeping with my interpretation of a Nazarene initiation ceremony, as opposed to the orthodox interpretation of a single saviour.

---

79. Robert Eisenman & Michael Wise. "The Dead Sea Scrolls Uncovered." Element. 1992.

Matthew 23:8 directly threatened the High Priest Caiaphas, advocating that people no longer looked to him for God consciousness, but looked to themselves. They were to look to the Messiah or Christ, the anointed one within, the light of the lamp which shone once they had been reborn through the Spirit. It also threatened the Roman Emperor who held the office of *"Father"* in the Mithraic cult of *"Sol Invictus."* Three hundred years later this quote directly threatened the power of the Emperor Constantine. I am surprised that it was not edited out along with all the other so called heresies. But then they had the teachings of Paul to uphold them.

Christian policy is largely based on the writings of Paul, a Sadducee who had Roman citizenship. Acts 22:25—28:

"And as they bound him with things, Paul said unto the centurion that stood by, Is it lawful for you to scourge a man that is a Roman, and uncondemned? When the centurion heard that, he went and told the chief captain, saying, Take heed what thou doest: for this man is a Roman. Then the chief captain came, and said unto him, Tell me, art thou a Roman? He said Yea. And the chief captain answered, With a great sum obtained I this freedom. And Paul said, But I was born free."

Paul supported the dictates of Rome and was a fervent persecutor of early Christians. The first books of the New Testament were written by Paul and are aptly called *"Romans,"* while the earliest date we can ascertain for the writing of the Gospels, is long after the disciples had died. It is doubtful that they were actually written by the original authors, but rather by their followers,[80] a view held by most theologians today.

---

80. Max. I. Dimont. "Jews, God and History." Nal Penguin. 1962.

Unlike Paul, the Apostles had taught as Jesus had taught, in the Talmudic fashion, by sermonic interpretations, committed to memory and passed on via word of mouth. This was John's *"word."* The word, the *"oral law,"* was unlike Paul's fixed and recorded decrees. More important, part and parcel of this word, was a knowledge of the Kabbala. But in order to receive this knowledge, they would have to become anointed, Christians or Nazarenes. Luke 8:10:

"....Unto you it is given to know the mysteries of the kingdom of God: but to others in parables; that seeing they might not see, and hearing they might not understand."

By comparing Paul's teachings to those of Jesus, it becomes apparent that in spite of Paul's conversion, he still supported Roman political structures. Like the Emperor Constantine,[81] he claimed a vision in order to substantiate his dictum. As an orthodox Jew and supporter of the High Temple priests, he took the side of the Sadducees and supported rule under Rome.

There is evidence to suggest that the disciples in Jerusalem under the leadership of James, were so disgruntled with Paul's version on Christianity, that they walked in his footsteps in an attempt to right the wrongs that he had wrought on early believers. Paul had tried in vain to become an apostle of James's church. If becoming an apostle entailed Nazarene initiation, then he was never anointed and did not have a

---

81. Constantine claimed to have seen the Christian cross in front of the sun, thereby amalgamating the solar cult of "Sol Invictus" with Paul's version of Christianity. The birth of the Sun was celebrated on the 25th of December and they celebrated a sacrificial meal similar to the eucharist.

knowledge of the secrets of the kingdom of heaven, being the Kabbala. Paul was rejected twice, fought with James the Righteous and then established his own sect. [82] In establishing his own sect, he believed that it was not necessary for converts to become Hebrews first, which meant that they would not practice the Sabbath, the Passover or Yom Kippur. He abandoned the dietary laws, circumcision and worst of all, the Torah, the Old Testament itself and the moral and legal codes found within it.

Many Christians are aware of the contradictions between the two teachings in the New Testament and have torn themselves to pieces in order to reconcile them. Much like the difference between Genesis 1 and Genesis 2, the choice is Jesus or Paul.

Paul's decisions still effect us today as there are hardly any Christians who acknowledge the Hebrew faith, who adhere to the Sabbath or who hold the Passover within the confines of their own homes. Both the Sabbath and the Passover encourage direct knowledge of God within the family unit as opposed to indirect knowledge of God under the leadership of a priest. The most important acts of Hebrew worship are performed in the home where the mother and the father act as priestess and priest respectively. By so doing, the children are brought up with a balance between female and male, both contributing to their spiritual welfare. As it says in Proverbs 1:8:

"Hear instruction of the father, and forsake not the law of thy mother."

---

82. Max I.Dimont. "Jews, God and History." Nal Penguin Inc.

Christianity in Ireland, as instituted by Saint Patrick, was no different to James's church and surprisingly enough, deviated from Paul's
doctrine. In Rome, the Old Testament became inconsequential and
the Mosaic law dispensable. In Ireland on the other hand, both Old
and New Testaments were regarded in an equal light while the Mosaic
law became entrenched in society. They observed both the Sabbath
and the Passover and read testaments that were considered to be heresies and forbidden by Rome. Roman policy eventually penetrated
these distant shores and in 700 A.D., at the Synod of Whitby, the
church in Ireland was pulled into line with the Church in Rome, the
result being that all Hebrew rituals were abolished, celebration of the
Sabbath was forbidden and more important, the Mosaic Code no
longer formed an integral part of Irish Christianity.[83]

Paul's version of Christianity is not just a simple question of
whether we should be circumcised or not, but is a question of politics
and political aspirations as will be discussed below. Most people
believe that Paul's words free us from the strict laws of purity found
in Leviticus, and they might well do so, but then the life of Jesus
teaches us the same. Jesus spoke out against orthodox
fundamentalism, as seen when he associated with women who he was
not afraid to touch and who he did not see as unclean. He also healed
people on the Sabbath and gathered corn on the Sabbath, thereby not
sticking to the strict orthodox rules that forbade such behaviour on
holy days. When reading Paul's words carefully, it is not the purity

---

83. Michael Baigent, Richard Leigh, Henry Lincolm. "The Messianic Legacy." Corgi 1987.

laws that he says we are freed from, but he advocates freedom from the Mosaic code, which in effect, means abandoning the concept of justice and righteousness.

Paul took his version of Jesus and what he stood for to the pagans, eventually establishing himself in Rome. Paul is given the status of a martyr who died under Nero's rule. But his writings do not imply that he was held prisoner and his death coincides with Nero's burning of Rome. It is possible that he did not die as a martyr to Christianity, but was a victim of historical circumstance.[84]

The Apocrypha and other so called *"heresies"* such as the Gnostic texts, give us a very different version of Christianity to that advocated by Paul. For example, *"The Gospel of Thomas"* advocates James, Paul's rival as the leader of the church as opposed to Peter:

"The disciples said to Jesus, "We know that you will depart from us. Who is to be our leader?"

Jesus said to them, "wherever you are, you are to go to James the righteous, for whose sake heaven and earth came into being." [85]

But it is not really necessary to go into other records for comparison as the contradictions between the teachings of Paul and the teachings of Jesus in the Bible speak for themselves. In spite of Paul's conversion to Christianity, I believe that he remained true to his Sadducee heritage and his Roman citizenship.

---

84. Michael Baigent, Richard Leigh, Henry Lincolm. "The Holy Blood and the Holy Grail." Corgi. 1990

85. James M. Robinson. "The Nag Hammadi Library." Harper Collins. 1990.

Jesus	Paul
Mat 5:17	Galatians 5:4
"Do not suppose that I Have come to abolish the law and the prophets; I did not come to abolish, but to complete. Truly I tell you: so long as heaven and earth endure, not a letter, not a dot, will disappear from the law, until all that must happen has happened. Anyone therefore who sets aside even the least of the laws demands and instructs others to do the same, will have the lowest place in the kingdom of Heaven."	*"When you seek to be justified by way of the law, you are cut off from Christ: you have put yourselves outside God's grace."* (Revised Eng. Bible.)

This whole philosophy is further elaborated on in Luke 16:31, where Jesus goes so far as to say:

"If they hear not Moses and the prophets, neither will they be persuaded, though one rose from the dead."

While in the *"Dead Sea Scrolls,"* the *"Manual of Discipline"* documents the views of the Essenes regarding a person who *"sets aside the laws demands."* Paul was rejected by James's church and the following text from the *"Manual of Discipline,"* if compared to his words in Galatians could give us the reason:

"Any of them who transgresses a word of the law of Moses overtly or with deceit shall be dismissed from the council of the community and shall not come back again." [86]

One of the basic principles of the Mosaic law was that individuals could seek justice by way of the law and have two witnesses to speak on their behalf, whereas Paul's view was in line with the Sadducees (John 7:45–52). He believed that if we should seek this justice, we would be cut off from Christ. If this was his belief, then it explains why he did not want to convert people to the Hebrew faith as James had done, and why the Mosaic law eventually played no role in Roman Christian society.

As another example, consider slavery which was rife within Roman society at the time, to the extent that the Roman's even sold their own children to make money. The slave would have referred to his or her owner as *"master"* (Baal) or *"Lord"* and was bound to him for life, unless the master decided to sell him or her. Slavery in and of itself does not offer those in bondage a right to be *"justified by way of the law."*

In 1828, the Khoisan slave in South Africa was freed from restrictions and finally granted equality before the law. With the passing of Ordinance 50, whites were not only shocked that a person of colour could take them to court, but that they could win a suit against them. Before the passing of this ordinance, slaves owners could treat their slaves badly and not be held accountable for their actions. This is in

---

86. Millar Burrows. "The Dead Sea Scrolls." Secker & Warburg. 1956.

flagrant opposition to the laws found in Exodus. The laws of Moses as well as Jeremiah 34, advocated that a slave was to be set free in the seventh year of his or her service or on the fiftieth year of jubilee. No such practice was ever carried out at the Cape of Good Hope or incidently, in the United States of America, and if such a practice had even been suggested, it would have been shot down in flames. Now take the laws of Exodus and apply them not only to the Roman Empire in the first century A.D, but apply them to South Africa and the United States of America during the 19th century. In both time periods, these laws applying to slaves would have been most unwelcome.

Exodus 21:20:"When a man strikes his slave or his slave-girl (equality between the sexes) *with a stick and the slave dies on the spot, he must be punished."*

21:26: "When a man strikes his slave or slave-girl in the eye and destroys it, he must let the slave go free in compensation for the eye."

23:6: " You must not deprive the poor man of justice in his lawsuit."

Considering that these laws were written approximately 3,000 years ago, they were advanced and humane for their time. Today, however, they have become redundant and unnecessary, as slavery, in civilized societies, has been abolished.

By contrast to these very humanitarian laws, consider the inhumane purity laws governing the High Priests in Leviticus 21:17–20:

"No man among your descendants for all time who has any physical defect is to come and present the food of his God. No man with a defect is to come, whether a blind man, a lame man, a man stunted or overgrown, a man deformed in foot or hand, or with misshapen brows…." (Revised Eng. Bible.)

Can you imagine the outcry today if a person with stunted growth was denied entry into the church? Desmond Tutu, international figure and Nobel Peace Prize winner, Archbishop of the Anglican church in

South Africa, would not have been tall enough! It was these inhumane laws of purity that Jesus rebelled against, not the Mosaic code which advocated fundamental rights within a judicious and righteous political system.

Dr. Anthony Harris points out that Jesus could well have been damned by the orthodox priesthood due to suffering from a deformity and our version of him, which is much like an Adonis figure, could be very far from the truth. He studied a work by Dr. Robert Eisler, based on material written by Josephus in 72 A.D., and published by Epaphroditus. It goes without saying that Eisler's research has not been widely accepted by other scholars as anything that does not adhere to the orthodox line is usually rejected out of hand. Eisler concluded that the following was Josephus's original description of Jesus, which was later censored and tampered with by Rome:

"Both his nature and his form were human, for he was a man of simple appearance, mature age, dark skin, sort growth, three cubits tall," (which is five feet, obviously considered to be of stunted growth) *" hunch-backed, with a long face, long nose, eyebrows meeting above the nose....with scanty hair, but having a line in the middle of the head after the fashion of the Nazarenes, and with an underdeveloped beard."* [87]

This description breaks every rule in Leviticus 21 regarding a High Priest and by virtue of this fact, if this is an accurate description, Jesus

---

87. Anthony Harris. "The Sacred Virgin and the Holy Whore." Sphere Books Limited. 1988.

would have been denied entry into the priesthood by the orthodox, Levitical Sadducees. His physical form as well as his behaviour was inconsistent with the laws of purity.

Contrary to Paul's' views on early Christian teaching, I believe that in talking about the law, Jesus was talking about the Mosaic Code. As a judicial system it advocated the basic principles of being innocent until proven guilty, an independent judiciary and that individual rights are not subordinated to those of the king, high priest or state. As Nicodemus said:

"Does our law,...permit us to pass judgement on someone without first giving them a hearing and learning the facts?"

In 1:25 & 2:12, James also advocates such a political philosophy:

"But whoso looketh into the perfect law of liberty, and continueth therein, being not a forgetful hearer, but a doer of the work, this person shall be blessed in their deed...So speak ye, and so do, as they that shall be judged by the law of liberty."

Not only did the Sadducees reject these codes but Paul advocates that early Christians do not *"seek to be justified by way of the law...,"* thereby also rejecting the very basis of the Hebrew religion. In fact, the apostles demanded that all converts to Christianity become Hebrews first, while Paul on the other hand, discouraged this policy,[88] thereby denying the converted a knowledge of the Sabbath, the Passover and the Mosaic

---

88. Ibid.

Code. In effect, he kept them in ignorance of Hebrew democracy and the law, thereby directly contradicting Jesus and safe guarding the philosophies of the Sadducee priesthood, Herod Agrippa 1 and the Roman Emperor.

Jesus	Paul
Matthew 23:9,11&12	Roman 13:1 (Revised Eng. Bible.)

"Do not call any man on earth Father, for you have one father and he is in heaven...
The greatest among you must be your servant. Whoever exalts himself will be humbled;whoever humbles himself, will be exalted."

"Everyone must submit to the authority in power, for all authority comes from God, and the existing (the Sadducees & Rome) authorities are instituted by him. Anyone who rebels against authority, is resisting a divine institution, (The Roman Empire) And those who resist have themselves to thank for the punishment they will receive.

A judicial trail is a democratic trial. The opposite is *"trial by ordeal,"* a system under which people were judged to be innocent or guilty without defence, up until the 15th century A.D. During the inquisition, heretics had to prove that they were not heretics and were not considered to be innocent until proven guilty. The church did not believe in transferring civil law to religious law and those who they believed to be propagating ideas contrary to the Roman Catholic faith were excommunicated without a just trial.

Democracy and a justice of liberty came late to Europe. The Mosaic code and the Old Testament, as well as the Greek writers who advocated democracy were rejected by the Church in Rome for hundreds of years due to the policies taken at Nicea, under the Emperor Constantine and Eusebuis, the Bishop of Caesarea, a supposed Christian who followed Pauline doctrines. As a result, Eusebuis clearly states the following political doctrine in accordance with Pauline religious philosophy:

"Monarchy excels all other kinds of constitution and government. For rather do anarchy and civil war result from the alternative, a polyarchy based on equality. For which reason there is One God, not two or three or even more."[89]

Had Eusebuis failed to read John 10: 34:?

"Is it not written in your law, 'I said ye are Gods?'"

This statement is in accordance with Genesis 1, where we are the *"image"* of God and pre-supposes a *"polyarchy based on equality."* Perhaps Eusebius had heard of that so called heresy, the Kabbala that contained the powers (Elohim) which threatened everything that Pauline doctrine stood for?

In order to discover what the apostles stood for as opposed to Paul and the Sadducees, it is necessary to look at the Essenes, a group of Hebrews whose beliefs were a mirror image of the teachings of Jesus and who were opponents of the Temple priests in Jerusalem.

---

89. Michael Baigent, Richard Leigh, Henry Lincolm. "The Messianic Legacy." Corgi. 1987.

Chapter Five.

The Essenes

Theologians have been debating whether *"The Dead Sea Scrolls"*[90] did in fact belong exclusively to the Essenes who lived at Qumram, or whether they expressed the views of all of those who lived in Judea, Galilee and Samaria during the first century A.D. Parts of the Scrolls appear to be Zealot, Pharisee as well as Sadducee. The Sadducees in turn, appear to have divided into two groups, those who believed in an eschatological philosophy of death and resurrection based on Gen.1. and were known as the sons of Zadok, and those who didn't, basing their beliefs on Gen.2. and who appeared to maintain the temple in Jerusalem. I am inclined to support Norman Golb, who has hypothesised that the *"Dead Sea Scrolls"* came from all sectors of the community and express

90. Religious texts, dating from between 200 B.C. and 70 A.D., found in caves at Qumram in 1947. A large proportion of these texts have not been published or made available to the world.

various opposing points of view just as the Bible expresses various opposing points of view.

Both the descendants of Judah and the descendants of Joseph were practising a form of religion known as Essene, two hundred years before the birth of Jesus. The Essene faith, as we shall see, encompassed both the paradigms of the individual dynamic and the group dynamic, the laws and the mystical teachings, right and left brain functioning. In effect, the Essenes laid the foundations for the emergence of what was to later be known as the Christian faith.[91]

Their social and economic lives also adhered to two principles. On the one hand they advocated communal living, in a group dynamic, as is done today on a Kibbutz in Israel, but they also encouraged individual enterprise in the commercial centres, utilizing both forms to their benefit.[92] Within their order, socialism and capitalism were linked.

On the one hand, they believed in peace and in being pacifists and yet, evidence at Masada, associates them with some of the toughest opponents to the Roman invasion. Excavations at Masada in the 1960's turned up manuscripts that were exactly the same as the manuscripts found amongst the Dead Sea Scrolls. This appears to imply that the Essenes who had lived next to the Dead Sea were prepared to fight alongside troops who were opposing the Roman army at Masada, and successfully at that. They held out against these legions for two years before their stronghold finally fell in 73 A.D.[93]

91. Max.I.Dimont. "Jews, God and History." Nal. Penguin. Inc. 1962.

92. Ibid.

93. Michael, Baigent, Richard Leigh, Henry Lincoln. "The Messianic Legacy." Corgi. 1987.

In a democratic structure, not all individuals believe in the same things. In fact, this is the very nature of a democracy, where differences of opinion as relates to religion, sex, race, language and social custom are tolerated as opposed to being discriminated against. This appears to have been the case amongst the Essenes except for one important fact. The only thing that they had in common was the belief in direct knowledge of God. This resulted in a philosophy whereby the individual attempted to obtain personal salvation as opposed to going through a priest as intermediary. In other words, enfranchisement within the church as well as out of it, thereby taking away the power and control that the established priesthood had over the people.[94] As a result, the Essenes were totally opposed to the Temple in Jerusalem[95] and everything that it stood for. As we have seen in chapter 4, Jesus advocated this philosophy and in keeping with this philosophy, was actively hostile towards the Sadducees and the Pharisees.

This did not mean however, that the Essenes were opposed to the Mosaic Code and the Law. According to the Edmond Szekely's translation of the Essene version of the Ten Commandments, God was the Law:

"I am the Law, thy God, which hath brought thee out from the depths of the bondage of darkness. Thou shalt have no other Laws before me."[96]

The Essenes not only adhered to the law as laid down by Moses, but they also had a mystical orientation, believing in the souls resurrection,

---

94. Ibid.

95. Louis Jacobs. "The Jewish Religion." Oxford University Press. 1995.

96. Edmond Bordeaux Szekely. "The Gospel of the Essenes." 6th Impression. C.W.Daniel. Co. LTD. 1988.

rebirth through baptism, astrology, numerology and the Kabbala.[97] All these beliefs were rejected by the Sadducees and the Pharisees and the last three are still rejected by orthodox religion today. These mystical teachings, found in the Kabbala, or what is referred to in the New Testament texts as the *"Kingdom of Heaven,"* incorporated the constellations in the night sky:

"(1) Adar On the first and the second Aries. On the third and the fourth Taurus. On the fif[th, sixth and seventh Gemini]. (2) On the eighth (and) ninth Canc[er. On the tenth and eleventh L]eo. On the...." and so on.[98]

In other words, the Essenes studied the movement of the constellations in the heavens, which in turn was a study of the celestial clock as it moves from one age to another. As we have already seen, the Sephorah on the Kabbala relate to these constellations. During the first century A.D., the celestial clock was moving from the age of Aries into the age of Pisces. The Essenes also embraced the solar calender as opposed to the lunar calender adopted by the orthodox priesthood and were criticized for it.

As far as numerology goes, each and every letter in the Hebrew alphabet is attributed to a Sephorah on the Kabbala as well as ascribed a certain number. A numeric record, if translated, can become a written record and visa versa. Hence we have John's reference to 666 in Revelation which translates into *"tav-resh-samekh-vav."*[99] When adding

---

97. Max. I. Dimont. "Jews, God and History." Nal. Penguin. Inc. 1962.

98 Robert Eisenman & Michael Wise. "The Dead Sea Scrolls Uncovered." Element. 1993. Text 4Q318. Brontologion. Fragment 2, column 2.

99. Louis Jacobs. "The Jewish Religion." Oxford University Press. 1995. see under "Alphabet, Hebrew."

the vowels to the consonants, this word means innocence, gullibility, naivete and ignorance. In other words, a lack of Gnosis, knowledge, wisdom, understanding and education. Or rather, choosing to be ignorant, choosing not to embrace knowledge, wisdom and understanding of all things in life, whether it be psychological, social, economic, political, scientific, medical or even theological. Every great discoverer, scientist, medical practitioner, artist or even philosopher has come up against this attitude before his or her discoveries have been accepted by the general population. Take for example, the Gnostic *"The Gospel of Philip"*:

"...let each one of us dig down after the root of evil.....if we are ignorant of it, it takes root in us... While [it exists] it is active. Ignorance is the mother of [all evil.] Ignorance will result in [death because] those that come from [ignorance] neither were nor [are] nor shall be...For truth is like ignorance: while it is hidden it rests in itself, but when it is revealed and is recognized, it is praised inasmuch as it is stronger than ignorance and error. It gives freedom. The word said, "If you (pl.) know the truth, the truth will make you free" (Jn 8:32)" [100]

As all religions have a prophet who is the personification of the belief system, so did the Essenes. He was known as the *"Teacher of Righteousness."* He preached humility and poverty as did Jesus; observance of the Law but the law completed due to his revelations as did Jesus; was believed to be a Messiah and a redeemer, as was Jesus; and he was condemned by the Sadducees as was Jesus.[101]

---

100. James M.Robinson. "The Nag Hammadi Library." Harper Collins. 1990.

101. Max .I. Dimont. "Jews, God and History." Nal Penguin. 1962.

There are approximately forty six references to Righteousness in the Old Testament and forty one in the New. But what is meant by a Teacher of Righteousness? The Essenes spoke of:

""the Perfect of the Way, or "the way of Righteousness"—"way" meaning "the work of the Law," or "the way in which the Law functions."" [102]

Which implies that The Teacher of Righteousness was the teacher or holder of the Law, the Covenant. As it says in Psalms 11:7 and 96:10:

".....the righteous Lord loveth righteousness..."

"...thou shalt judge the people righteously...."

In other words, you will judge the people within the Law and not by a trial by ordeal or have detention without trial. Isaiah prophecies that the Law, the Covenant, *"Righteousness"* will become a world wide institution in 26:9

"....inhabitants of the world will learn righteousness...."

In the New Testament, Jesus says in the Beatitudes:

"....that except your righteousness shall exceed the righteousness of the scribes and the Pharisees, ye shall not enter the kingdom of heaven."

Here Jesus advises people to uphold righteousness, the Law, in a personal capacity that is greater than the scribes and the Pharisees, who were referred to as *"vipers and hypocrites."* Jesus also infers that we

102. Michael Baigent & Richard Leigh. "The Dead Sea Scrolls Deception." Corgi. 1992.

should make these laws our own and not rely on a leader or a scribe to hold sway over us. This is in fulfilment of Jeremiah 31:33–34:

"But this shall be the covenant that I will make with the house of Israel; After those days, saith the Lord, I will put my law in their inward parts, and write it in their hearts; and I will be their God, and they shall be my people.

And they shall teach no more every man his neighbour, and every man his brother saying, Know the Lord: for they shall all know me, from the least of them unto the greatest of them, saith the Lord: for I will forgive their iniquity, and remember their sin no more."

In other words, all individuals, from the richest to the poorest, the highest to the lowest, will be educated, have knowledge and understanding and know their rights under the law; that they are innocent until proven guilty and allowed to have witnesses to speak on their behalf. By so doing, they would not worship the beast of ignorance being 666. In other words, they were to eat from the tree of knowledge, or the Kabbala which according to Proverbs, was the Holy Spirit or Wisdom. 19:8 & 3:18 & 19:

"He that getteth wisdom loveth his own soul: he that keepth understanding shall find good."

"She is a tree of life to them that lay hold upon her: and happy is every one that retaineth her.

The Lord by wisdom hath founded the earth: by understanding hath he established the heavens."

The opposite of Jeremiah's vision is an arbitrary form of justice, eg: the French Inquisition; Nazi Germany; the pogroms held under Joseph Stalin; the apartheid regime in South Africa; and the death camps imprisoning Muslims in Bosnia. The result of righteousness becoming a world wide institution, is that arbitrary forms of justice will be abolished and draconian laws will all fall away. These same sentiments are

expressed in the New Testament in conjunction with Isaiah's desire to
see Israel and Judah reconciled: Hebrews 8:8–11:

"*....Behold, the days come, saith the Lord, when I will make a new
covenant with the house of Israel and with the house of Judah: Not according to the covenant that I made with their fathers in the day when I took
them by the hand to lead them out of the land of Egypt; because they continued not in my covenant, and I regarded them not, saith the Lord. For this
is the covenant that I will make with the house of Israel[103] after those days,
saith the Lord; I will put my laws into their mind, and write them in their
hearts: and I will be to them a God, and they shall be to me a people. And
they shall not teach every man his neighbour, and every man his brother,
saying, Know the Lord: for all shall know me, from the least to the greatest.*"*

Paul on the other hand, states in Romans 10:4:

"*....Christ is the end of the Law of Righteousness...* "

How so, when Jesus clearly stated that our righteousness should
exceed that of the leaders? There was and is a difference between equal
justice for all and the laws of purity which are bigoted and intolerant of
the differences between people. It is clear from the Gospels that Jesus
advocated the former and rejected the latter. Paul on the other hand,
rejected both.

Further examination of the word righteousness reveals that it was
not an exclusive title applicable to one person, but that it was associated

---

103. The descendants of the Lost Tribes of Israel, being the whole human race.

with a number of people, i.e. heterogeneous, a group dynamic. In 2 Peter 2: 5 Noah is referred to as:

"...a preacher of righteousness..."

In Matthew 21:32:

"John the Baptist came in the way of righteousness."

James, the brother of Jesus, is also referred to as *"the Righteous"* (Just) by Clement who was the Bishop of Alexandria in the late half of the second century and by Josephus who states that:

"...these things happened to the Jews in requital for James the Righteous,...for though he was the most righteous man, the Jews put him to death."[104]

When Isaiah talks about the Righteous one being put to death, who is he talking about? The Teacher of Righteousness spoken of in the Dead Sea Scrolls? John the Baptist who was also put to death? Jesus who was a Teacher of Righteousness? Or James, the Just, the Righteous? All of these people were persecuted for their faith. Is Isaiah perhaps referring to a sect within Israel instead of an individual whereby all who *"walk in the path of righteousness for his names sake"* will suffer persecution at the hands of those who seek not to make the law available to all? Persecution from those who seek to impose an authoritarian, draconian, dictator state?

---

104. Michael Baigent & Richard Leigh. "The Dead Sea Scrolls Deception." Corgi. 1992.

This appears to be the case when we consider that within the Essene community, after a probation period of three years, students were admitted to the religious order by an anointing,[105] they became the anointed, the Messiah's, the Nazarene Christ-ians, who *"walked in the path of righteousness"* for the Law's sake and were then allowed to preach to the people. In effect, they all became Teachers of Righteousness. They were *"anointed with the oil"* and became *"a firstborn."*[106] For Example, consider Isaiah 61: 1–3, 6, 8 & 11:

"The Spirit of the Lord God is upon me; because the Lord hath anointed me to preach good tidings unto the meek; he hath sent me to bind up the brokenhearted, to proclaim liberty to the captives, and the opening of the prison to them that are bound. To proclaim the acceptable year of the Lord, and the day of vengeance of our God; to comfort all that mourn. To appoint unto them that mourn in Zion, to give unto them beauty for ashes, the oil of joy for mourning, the garment of praise for the spirit of heaviness; that they might be called trees of righteousness, the planting of the Lord, that he might be glorified…But ye shall be named the Priests of the Lord: men shall call you the Ministers of our God:…For I the Lord love judgment, I hate robbery for burnt offering; and I will direct their work in truth, and I will make an everlasting covenant with them…so the Lord God will cause righteousness and praise to spring forth before all nations."

---

105. Barbara Thiering. "Jesus the Man." Doubleday Publishers. 1992.

106. Robert Eisenman & Michael Wise. "The Dead Sea Scrolls Uncovered." Element 1993. Text 4Q458, fragment 2, column 2, lines 4 & 5. Text 4Q416, 418, lines 13 & 14.

Followers of this faith, the *"Messiahs"* who followed instruction from their anointing, who refused to turn their back on their God, their Law and acknowledge the Roman Emperor as Lord, as the Sun and the Son of God, his representative on earth, turned their backs on an autocratic dictatorship state and were put to death, as Isaiah prophesied the Righteous would be, en mass by the Romans in 70 A.D.

Not only does Essene belief reflect Christianity in the story of the Teacher of Righteousness, but also in the basic tenets of their belief system. The Essenes believed in a messianic religion, giving birth to the ideas which were to play a dominant role in the lives of John the Baptist and Jesus.[107] What is more, it is clear from the Gospels that the followers of Jesus already believed in resurrection, rebirth and immortality of the soul, an eschatological philosophy, as did the Essenes prior to the Biblical resurrection in accordance with Genesis 1 where we are made in the image of God, and as *"exact duplicates,"* we are immortal as is God. The Gospel of Mark makes reference to it in 12:18, at the very beginning of his ministry:

"Then came unto him the Sadducees, which say there is no resurrection."

As does Luke in 20:27:

"Then came to him certain of the Sadducees, which deny that there is any resurrection;..."

---

107. Max. I. Dimont. "Jews, God and History." Nal Penguin Inc. 1962.

Resurrection was seen as a fundamental spiritual belief by the Essenes, as opposed to the Sadducees who believed that we are mortal, that we only pass through this life time once and when we die, that is the end of us. Coupled with the belief in resurrection was Baptism, a vocation to which John dedicated his life's work. John appears to have been an Essene. He lived in the area where they had a monastery and where a large Essene community flourished.[108] The Essenes did not hold much store by the *"leaven of the Sadducees"* and neither did Jesus, both were opposed to the established priesthood in Jerusalem. By this very act Jesus encouraged direct, first hand knowledge of God as did the Essenes, and discouraged the practice whereby the High Priest acts as intermediary between God and Man. [109]

The Essene doctrine not only precedes the ministry of Jesus, but the life of the Teacher of Righteousness parallels the very basis of the Christian faith. These factors can be undermining to Christianity unless we have missed some vital link, some vital piece of information that would make sense of it all.

The story of the Teacher of Righteousness appears to have been superimposed over the story of Jesus or visa versa and could have been a Greek translation from the original scripts kept at Qumram. If Jesus was of the Essene faith, as the evidence suggests, then it would be a logical assumption to presume that the teachings of Jesus were Essene teachings that had already gained a foothold for two hundred years.

---

108. Max.I.Dimont. "Jews, God and History." Nal Penguin Ic. 1962.

109. Michael Baigent, Richard Leigh, Henry Lincolm. "The Messianic Legacy." Corgi. 1987.

When the Dead Sea Scrolls were first discovered it was believed that the Teacher of Righteousness had been alive in approximately 60 B.C. But since this time, scholars are beginning to think that the texts are in fact concurrent with the 1st century A.D. Either they relate to a specific person, or as I suspect, they relate to a number of people, and the personification of an individual within the texts in fact embraces an overall concept, one which can be traced throughout the Old Testament texts. The reference to *"the prophets"* in the New Testament who were put to death on numerous occasions, (Zechariah in Chronicles 24 and the Zechariah mentioned in Luke 11:51) could be a reference to these *"Teachers (plural) of Righteousness"* who were persecuted. The Hebrew *"prophets"* in turn, were seen as just that. In the *"Manual of Discipline"* found amongst the Dead Sea Scrolls it states:

"....until there shall come a prophet and the Messiahs of Aaron and Israel."[110]

Rather than having a *"Messiah"* singular, we have *"Messiahs"* plural and a prophet, rather than a saviour or a king, who will come to restore order to Israel. I suspect that the New Testament is possibly a portrait of a number of people. They have been superimposed over each other and the stories have been interwoven together. Unfortunately, the original intent has been lost and the clearly defined edges of each have blurred one into the other. Whether this was done on purpose or not, I do not

---

110. Millar Burrows. "The Dead Sea Scrolls." Secker & Warburg. 1956.

know. But one thing stands out in my mind. A large proportion of the
New Testament Gospels are allegorical metaphors, their comparisons
being found in Old Testament texts. The orthodox story line is well
known by many making an assessment unnecessary. I believe that this
was the story of a Teacher or Teachers of Righteousness as recorded by
the Essenes, who taught Christian principles and were put to death by
the Sanhedrin with the support of the Roman procurators. His or their
lives and the principles that the Essenes upheld were later translated into
Greek where they were given the embodiment of an individual symbolized by the name Jesus. This had after all, been done before, as we have
seen in Genesis 5:2 where *"Adam"* refers to a group of people and then
in 5:3, where *"Adam"* suddenly becomes an individual.

Due to Roman interference with it's renunciation of the Old
Testament and coupled with Paul's anti-Semitic doctrine, our Latin Jesus
was given a decidedly Adonis flavour by the Emperor Constantine who
was the designated *"Father"* of the Mithraic cult of the sun and who
claimed a vision where the cross of Christianity was seen superimposed
over the sun. In other words, Constantine superimposed Jesus with
Mithras or Adonis. This old Canaanite God, whose rites and rituals were
similar to Mithras, was believed to be an immaculate conception by his
mother Myrna; he was considered *"the son of God"* by direct intervention as were all the Roman *"saviour deities;"* and his sacrificial death was
witnessed by women followed by his resurrection that was greeted by
women. The Adonis rituals of drinking the blood and the flesh promised
redemption from sins through this sacrifice.

Coupled with the rise of Adonis, was the abolition of Goddess worship in all it's forms, inaccurately described as the abolition of religious
prostitution. Prostitution, as we have seen, has remained and become
an integral part of society as it was when Judah picked up Tamar at the
cross roads. The worship of the Goddess on the other hand, who stood
for democracy, has been forgotten. Socially women lost all their rights,
amongst which was the right to own and control money and property

which remained hers even after marriage and was hers to leave, as she so chose, after death. The high status of women in Egypt and the written laws pertaining to women in the code of Hammurabi (1700 B.C.) have taken almost 2,700 years to regain. It has also taken over three thousand years to re-instate democracy as well as the right of a woman to become a priestess, or in a biblical context, a lawyer and a judge.

By 300 A.D. Rome had weeded out any *"Christian"* texts that did not concur with their social, economic and political structures which were based on a patriarchal hierarchy, and texts such as the Gnostic scriptures and those from the Ebionites were considered to be heresies. Take for example, this quote from the Gnostic scriptures:

"The Son of Man", replies the Christ, "joined with Sophia his companion and produced a great androgyne light: the masculine name of it is 'Saviour generator of all things'; its feminine name is 'Sophia, universal genetrix', who by some is called 'Pistis'. "[111]

This quote can be compared to and is compatible with Isaiah 61:10:

"...for he hath clothed me with the garments of salvation, he hath covered me with the robe of righteousness, as a bridegroom decketh himself with ornaments, and as a bride adorneth herself with jewels."

And is also compatible with the Gnostic *"The Gospel of Thomas:"*

"Jesus said to them, "When you make the two one, and when you make the inside like the outside and the outside like the inside, and the above

---

111. Jean Doresse. "The Secret Books of the Egyptian Gnostics." Inner Traditions Limited. 1986.

like the below, and when you make the male and female one and the same, so that the male not be male nor the female female...then you will enter [the kingdom]."" [112]

How could there be a feminine face to God when the church had already decided that only men were made in the image of God, whilst women were not, and were to be the servant and the handmaid of their husbands? Politically speaking, democracy, self-empowerment and self-determination was definitely not on the cards. Unbeknown to them, a time bomb lay hidden at Qumram and two thousand years later it emerged, creating in-fighting throughout theological establishments the world over.

I believe that within the Gospels there is another story, a story which fascinates me and whose shadowy forms show through the fading canvas of orthodox Christian belief. I believe that it is totally in keeping with Israel's origins, history and law, but we need to become familiar with her customs in order to understand the actions, time periods and yearly rituals that are very briefly alluded to in the New Testament texts.

Most Christians do not know about or understand the Sabbath, Pentecost, Yom Kippur or the feast of Tabernacles and I include myself in this group. We pay no attention whatsoever to the fact that our religious beliefs have a Hebrew heritage making a very clear division between an Aryan type son of God and a Hebrew man whose teachings

---

112. James M.Robinson. "The Nag Hammadi Library." HarperCollins. 1990.

still effect the world today. I believe that this Hebrew heritage must be included in our analysis, as it is the basis from which our Christian faith emerged, whilst an anti-Semitic outlook can only obscure the truth behind the texts.

One man seemed to have adopted both Ephraimite and Essene tendencies, fully understanding Jesus's message. This was Rabbi Johanan ben Zakkai, a pacifist who took no part in the war. In 68 A.D. he escaped besieged Jerusalem in a coffin, a remarkable symbol of death and resurrection. In exchange for prophesying that the Roman Commander Vespian would become Emperor, he was permitted to establish an academy of learning in Jabneh, north of Jerusalem. Like Jesus, Johanan be Zakkai set in motion laws which were to safeguard the *"liberal tradition of the Oral Law,"*[113] the *"word,"* the *"mysteries of the kingdom of heaven,"* being the Kabbala, which is open to argument and individual interpretation as a counterweight to the Mosaic Code.

Zakkai and his descendants formulated a *"Talmudic Code,"* which was conveyed to the Hebrews via emissaries known as Responsa.[114] Among the Laws which reflect the teachings found in the New Testament and which orthodox Christianity, to this day has still not managed to come to terms with, are the following:

1. The reader of the Torah no longer had to be a specialist, but could be anyone from the congregation. They were in effect, ordaining priests from all classes of people.

---

113. Max.I.Dimont. "Jews, God and History." Nal Penguin. 1962.
114. Ibid.

2. Every Hebrew was his brother's keeper. As Jesus said, we are all brothers. *"Do unto others as you would have done unto yourself."*

3. Education could not be denied to any girl who wanted to continue schooling. This meant that a woman was entitled to become a student of the Law, the Talmud and the Torah, as Hebrew education at the time revolved around these studies. Like Deborah in Judges, Zakkai was advocating that a woman could become Judge and Prophetess also, in other words, a priestess. Jesus did not turn away women from his ministry.

4. Hebrew physicians were to administer to Hebrews and non-Hebrews alike, not charging the poor for their services. Jesus healed Hebrews and non-Hebrews alike.

5. Charity was to be provided for Hebrews and non-Hebrews alike. Jesus gave to Hebrews and non-Hebrews alike. [115]

These laws, in and of themselves break the laws of purity but still uphold the Mosaic code. In Johanan ben Zakkai, the *"word that was with God,"* in the Talmudic tradition of Jesus and the Apostles was carried on through history and did not advocate draconian type laws.

Since the fall of the temple in 70 A.D., the Hebrew nation has had no king, no temple, no high priest and no country. In other words, every single form of institution and the individuals who represent it, who could be idolised in one way or another, have been removed. The Law, as given by God, has been seen as the highest authority above all institutions, high priests, kings and Empires. Through the Hebrews, *"nations of the world"* have learned righteousness, in other words, a system of governance led by

---

115. Ibid.

councillors and judges where individual rights are not subordinated to those of the high priest, king or the state. In a sense the Hebrews have been the Teachers of Righteousness and now that their mission has been fulfilled, they are returning to the promised land, Samaritans and Felasha's alike.

The story of Johanan ben Zakkai does not, however, solve the duality of The Teacher of Righteousness and Jesus. It still leaves us wondering who Jesus was. What I hope to do below is find one thread in order to clarify the religious teachings while at the same time I have tried to keep within historical accuracy in order to identify a man called Jesus. If I have failed in the latter, then I still believe that the political, spiritual and religious thread of self empowerment is still valid, as ultimately, this was and is the whole purpose of the exercise.

Chapter Six.

Jesus

In order to find out who Jesus was, let us first look at his name. *"Jesus"* is a Greek translation of the Hebrew, *"Yeshu"* or *"Yeshua,"* better known in English translations as Joshu or Joshua.[116] People are often named after descendants or historical characters in the hope that some measure of an ancestor's past history and accomplishments will rub off on the new generation. Joshua in the New Testament was named after Joshua in the Old Testament, the son of Nun of the tribe of Ephraim who led the Hebrews into the promised land.

At every crucial point in Exodus, Moses was accompanied by Joshua. Joshua ascended Mount Sinai for forty days and forty nights

---

116. O.Odelain & R.Seguineau. "Dictionary of Proper Names and Places in the Bible." Robert Hale. 1991.

(Ex. 24:13), the same amount of time that Jesus spent in the wilderness. Joshua bore witness to the Ten Commandments which he in turn wrote on stones at Mount Ebal (Joshua 8: 32). Joshua was there when instruction was given for the building of the Ark of the Covenant. Joshua never left the tent of meeting, but guarded the Ark with his life (Ex. 33:11). Whenever Moses received an instruction from the Lord, Joshua was there beside him, but remained hidden in the tent when Moses gave these instructions to the people. Lastly, it was Joshua who led the people across the river Jordan into the *"New Kingdom,"* a term often used in the New Testament, and it was Joshua who buried his grandfather Joseph, at his great grandfather Jacob's tomb at the foot of Mount Gerizim in Samaria. Exodus 13:19 & Joshua 24:32:

"Moses took the bones of Joseph with him: For he had straightly sworn the children of Israel saying, "God will surely visit you; and ye shall carry up my bones away hence with you."

"And the bones of Joseph, which the children of Israel brought up out of Egypt, buried they in Shechem...."

Joshua established the New Kingdom of Israel in the promised land, but his kingdom is not of this world, meaning that he did not become a king to the Hebrews. Rather his kingdom was in the abstract, it was of the law, Zedek/Justice which incorporated the twelve tribes in a federal democracy, these groups in turn being *"the trees of righteousness"* (Isaiah 61:3 & Proverbs 2:18), the Asherah or Ashertaroth which was symbolized by the tree of life and taught in the form of the Kabbala. *"The Damascus Document"* V11:

"But David did not read the sealed book of the law which was in the ark; for it was not opened in Israel from the day of the death of Eleazer and Joshua and the elders who served the Ashtaroth, but was hidden and not disclosed until Zadok arose."[117]

The name Joshua-Jesus in the 1st century A.D. is symbolic and carries the weight of Joshua in the Old Testament behind it, implying a desire to return Israel to it's former unified glory under judges and councillors as had been the situation in the past. As the turn of the century approached, prophets and saviours of all descriptions arose throughout Judea, Samaria and Galilee, preaching one form of liberation or another in order to achieve freedom from slavery under Rome, self determination and rule under the laws of Moses. But why, at this particular point in history, was there such religious and political fervour? Those with a mystical knowledge, or a knowledge of astronomy and the Kabbala, as the Essenes did have, could have initiated the idea that radicle changes were to come about with the dawn of the new age of Pisces, much in the same way that the end of the 20th century brought about predications of the end of the world and the new world to come.

Today our age is symbolized by Aquarius, the water carrier. In the first century A.D., the age changed from Aries to the constellation of Pisces, the fishes. When asked for a *"sign,"* Jesus says that the only

---

117. Millar Burrows. "The Dead Sea Scrolls." Secker & Warburg. 1956.

sign that will be given is the sign of Jonah which was a fish. Matthew 12:39 & 40:

"But he answered and said unto them, An evil and adulterous genera-tion seeketh after a sign; and there shall no sign be given to it, but the sign of the prophet Jonah:
For as Jonah was three days and three nights in the whales's belly; so shall the Son of man be three days and three nights in the heart of the earth."

The age of Pisces occurs in spring in the northern hemisphere, and so the age of Pisces represents a rebirth of the earth itself. The sign of a fish is *"Dagim"* in Hebrew. In the Kabbala, the month of Adar is the Sephorah of Yesod and the constellation of Pisces, the fish. As there are twelve hours in a day and twelve months in the year, so there were twelve tribes of Israel and twelve constellations in astronomy. The tribe of Joseph repre-sents Adar, which is Yesod, the fish-Nun and the sign dagim.[118]

Kabbalistically speaking, at the beginning of the first century A.D. we are looking at Yesod, Pisces and Joseph. Yesod on the Kabbala is shared with the opposite and ideal marriage partner to Pisces, which is Virgo, the sign of the Virgin, known to us as Mary. Hence, the beginning of the Gospels could be a Kabbalistic parable explaining the celestial clock as it moves through the ages. The Archangel of Yesod is Gabriel and the symbols of the path are perfume and sandals. The God name is El

---

118. Dr. Philip S. Berg. "The Kabbalah Connection." Research Centre of Kabbalah. 1985.

Shaddai. In Yesod, both masculine and feminine are in balance as with all Kabbalistic paths.

During the month of Adar, the Jews celebrate Purim when Esther, who was married to the King Ahasuerus, saved them from persecution. The Arcadian translation of Esther is *"Ishtar,"*[119] a goddess of love, worshipped in Ninevah, where Jonah was sent by God. She was also known as *"The Queen of Heaven."* Esther means *"star"*[120] and astrologically, is the planet Venus which rises in the east at the dawn of a new day and is the first star seen at night.

By superimposing astronomy or Kabbalistic teachings over the Gospels, we have Joseph and the Virgin; the angel Gabriel; the star or Esther who saves in the month of Adar; and the sign of the fish which are all mentioned in the Biblical texts and interwoven with the history of the time. The star, the planet Venus forms the geometric symbol of a pentagon as it travels across our sky. As Jesus said, all these things are done in parables, or simple stories to protect spiritual knowledge from the profane.

As can be seen from the diagram below, each Sephorah is attributed with two constellations, two symbols, two tribes and two months of the year. Kether, Chokmah, Binah and Malkuth are excluded. Kether above is the masculine crown. Malkuth below is the feminine kingdom. Binah to the left is the feminine pillar and Chokmah to the right is the

---

119. O.Odelain and R. Seguineau. "Dictionary of Proper Names and Places in the Bible." Robert Hale Limited. 1991.

120. Ibid.

masculine pillar. If we had to join these four points, we would get the Christian cross.

KABBALA

KETHER

BINAH　　　　　　　　　　　　　　CHOKMAH

ox-GEBURAH-eagle　　　　　　　lamb-CHESED-scales
Simeon/Dan　　　　　　　　　　　Reuben / Benjamin
Taurus/Scorpio　　　　　　　　　Aries/ Libra
Iyar/Marhesvon　　　　　　　　　Nisan/ Tishrei

twins-TIPHARETH-rainbow
Levi/ Naphtali
Gemini/Sagittarius
Sivan/Kislev

lion-HOD-vessel　　　　　　　　　crab-NETZACH-goat
Issachar/ Asher　　　　　　　　　Judah/ Gad
Leo/ Aquarius　　　　　　　　　　Cancer/ Capricorn
Av/ Shevat　　　　　　　　　　　　Tamuz/ Tevet

virgin-YESOD-fish
Zebulun/ Joseph
Virgo/ Pisces
Adar/Elul

MALKUTH

If *"The Kingdom of Heaven"* and it's secrets were the Kabbala which forms a cross by joining Kether to Malkuth above and below, and Binah to Chokmah to the left and the right, this would make sense of the Gnostic *"The Gospel of Philip"* where it says:

"But one receives the unction of the [...] of the power of the cross. This power the apostles called "the right and the left." For this person is no longer a Christian but a Christ." [121]

Were Joseph, Mary and Gabriel real personalities or not? Perhaps. Perhaps real people took on these names, people who were educated into the mysteries of *"the kingdom of heaven"* or the night sky and astronomy, and taught their knowledge against a back drop of the Kabbala. *"Mary"* in turn is a Greek translation of the Hebrew *"Mizraim,"* which means Egypt.[122] So another interpretation could be that Joseph married Egypt being Asenath, or the religious equivalent of Isis, being the Queen of Heaven, a title under which Mary often goes, who gives birth to the divine child, Horus who was Ephraim, the firstborn. This in turn parallels the prophecy found in Matthew 2:15:

"....Out of Egypt (Mizraim-Mary) have I called my son."

If there were a number of anointed, as *"The Dead Sea Scrolls"* suggest, then this was the dawn of the *"Messianic age,"* as had been prophesied. Coupled with these symbols is the belief in resurrection as acted out by the Egyptian priests and priestess who practised a living resurrection at their initiation ceremonies in remembrance of Osiris who was raised from the dead.

In Egypt, only the Pharaoh was considered to be the son of God, in the guise of Horus. But according to Mosaic law, all children that open

---

121. James M.Robinson. "The Nag Hammadi Library." Harper Collins. 1990.

122. O.Odelain and R. Seguineau. "Dictionary of Proper Names and Places in the Bible." Robert Hale Limited. 1991.

the womb, no matter from which tribe, were considered to be a child of/or belonging to God. Exodus 13:2:

"Sanctify unto me all the firstborn, whatsoever openeth the womb among the children of Israel, both of man and of beast: it is mine."

What this Mosaic law implies, is that there was no *"virgin birth"* as we have been led to believe. The mention of a *"virgin"* refers to the constellation of Virgo represented by Mary, the opposite constellation to Pisces represented by Joseph, and to the planet Venus which is both the morning and the evening star. Rather than Jesus being born intactus, he was born in accordance with Mosaic law and as the child that opens the womb, was considered to be sanctified, devoted and holy unto God. The reference to his mother being a Virgin is a Kabbalistic interpretation rather than a physical fact. Throughout the Gospels, Jesus refers to himself as *"the son of man,"* and the title *"Son of God,"* implies being a firstborn who according to Exodus, was automatically considered to be devoted to God due to Mosaic law. The Gospel of Luke says as much of Jesus's birth in 2:23:

"As it is written in the law of the Lord, Every child that openeth the womb shall be called holy to the Lord;"

But who was this *"holy child?"* The name Joshua in turn, could have been symbolic and incorporated the works of a number of people born in the new age of Pisces, symbolized by Joseph and the Virgin Mary. The same holds true of the term *"The Teacher of Righteousness"* mentioned in *"The Dead Sea Scrolls."* These people came from all the tribes, Judah included. To quote Millar Burrows:

"The identification of these individuals and groups is something like the solution of a picture puzzle. The problem is to fit what the commentary says about the characters into what is known of Jewish history. The various

characters interact in such a way that they cannot be separately identified and placed in different historical periods or situations."[123]

According to Barbara Thiering, the titles *"Jacob," "Joseph," "Mary," "Miriam," "Hannah,"* and I would like to add one other, *"Joshua,"* were all used in Essene religious initiation.[124] This poses the possibility that any number of people who had reached the same level at any one or different times could have been known by these names. In other words, these names were symbolic religious titles used by a number of people.

An interesting point made by Ahmed Osman, is that Philo Judaens called the Essenes *"Essaens"* from the Arabic *"Essa,"* which is their name for Jesus. The plural, *"Essaioi"* in turn means *"a follower of Essa,"*[125] or in Hebrew, *"a follower of Joshua."*

In those days it would have been easier to convey a concept by reducing it to personification within an individual than to teach a political ideology to the masses. Much like the concept of democracy, the people of the time needed tangible evidence. Hence, democracy, or the Ashtaroth, became a Goddess immortalized in the form of a statue, much like the *"Statue of Liberty"* is today. Many people in the modern world still pray before statues, light candles, burn incense and bring flowers for these concrete manifestations of their beliefs in the hope that their prayers will be answered. According to Mosaic law, this is idolatry, in the same way that worshipping a statue of Zeus was idolatry. The individual *"Jesus"* in turn, came to symbolize Joshua's federal

---

123. Millar Burrows. "The Dead Sea Scrolls." Secker & Warburg. 1956.

124. Barbara Thiering. "Jesus the Man." Doubleday. 1992.

125. Ahmed Osman. "The House of the Messiah." Grafton. 1993.

democracy. Today, educated societies can conceive of an abstract idea without reducing it to a concrete form or personalizing it.

The name Joshua not only refers to the Essenes as a group, the word Essene having it's roots in the Arabic for Jesus, but it is also associated with Joshua in the Old Testament and his genealogical descent going back through Nun, to Ephraim, to Joseph and to Israel. The name Joshua was in fact a common one, referring not only to the Essenes in the first century A.D., but also to a number of individuals. This name was also a religious one, which as the Gospels tell us, was given to Jesus when he was circumcised. Luke 2:21:

"Eight days later the time came to circumcise him, and he was given the name Jesus."

Today, a religious name is still given to a baby boy when he is circumcised. This is the name by which Hebrews are called when it is time for their Bar Mitzvah [son of the commandment] and when they read from the Torah in the synagogue for the first time. It is not the name by which they are commonly known. Today, women also celebrate their Bat Mitzvah [daughter of the commandment], their Hebrew name being given on the Sabbath after their birth. In Reform Judaism, they not only sit side by side their male counterparts, but they also read from the Torah. Hence it states in the Gnostic *"The Gospel of Philip:"*

""Jesus" is a hidden name, "Christ" is a revealed name."

A person or persons, given the name Joshua at circumcision during Biblical times would have been called Joshua when reading from the Torah in the synagogue or giving a sermon, such as The Sermon on the Mount. Religious writers would have referred to them by their mitzvah name, in this case, the Greek known as Jesus when relating the words of a teacher of Righteousness, who was most probably an *"Essaioi,"* or a follower of Joshua. Historical writers would have referred to them by their common name used in daily life. Perhaps this is why historians have found it so difficult to track down this individual called Jesus in any historical account. One such historian from which we get most of our information about the 1st century A.D. was Josephus.

Josephus was a Jew from Galilee who after the fall of the Temple in 70 A.D., became a Roman citizen and wrote a history of the Jews. In *"Josephus Wars,"* the writer mentions such characters as James the Righteous, the Baptist, Theudas and James Zebedee. But scholars now agree that the reference made to a man called Jesus in Josephus's account, was a later insertion and not part of the original document.[126] If this assessment is accurate, then his omission of a man called Jesus must strike both historians and Biblical scholars alike, as odd. Unless, as I believe, there were a number of Teachers of Righteousness who were given the name Joshua at circumcision and were called by this name when reading from the Torah, or, all these Joshua's were in fact the Essenes themselves, as Ahmed Osman proposes.

The Apocryphal *"The Wisdom of Solomon"* suggests that this was the case where the author refers to the Righteous in the plural. These righteous judge the nations and are given immortality. *"The Wisdom of Solomon"* is believed to have been written in the 1st century B.C by an unknown Alexandrian Jew[127] who could possibly have been the Jewish philosopher Philo of Alexandria who died in 50 A.D. His writings form part of the wisdom literature, a counterweight to the law.

---

126. Robin Lane Fox. "The Unauthorized Version." Penguin. 1992.

127. Larousse. "Dictionary of Beliefs and Religions." Larousse. 1994.

"*The Wisdom of Solomon*" is not accepted as part of Jewish and Protestant Bibles, though it is however, accepted in the Old Testament of Catholic Bibles.[128] The reference to the righteous is as follows. 3:18 and 5:15 & 16:

"*But the souls of the righteous are in the hand of God, and there shall no torment touch them. In the sight of the unwise they seemed to die: and their departure is taken for misery. And their going from us to be utter destruction: but they are in peace. For though they be punished in the sight of men, yet is their hope full of immortality. And having been a little chastised, they shall be greatly rewarded: for God proved them, and found them worthy for himself. As gold in the furnace hath he tried them, and received them as a burnt offering. And in the time of their visitation they shall shine, and run to and fro like sparks among the stubble. They shall judge the nations, and have dominion over the people, and their Lord shall reign for ever.*"

"*But the righteous live forever more; their reward also is with the Lord, and the care of them is with the most High.*
Therefore shall they receive a glorious kingdom, and a beautiful crown from the Lords hand: for with his right hand shall he cover them, and with his arm shall he protect them."

In chapter two of this work, the author describes what has happened to the righteous in the singular. The verses are an uncanny repetition of

---

128. Ibid.

the Gospel story as well as the story of the Teacher of Righteousness in *"The Dead Sea Scrolls."* Like Jesus, the righteous is accused of calling himself the son of God; like Jesus he is called meek; like Jesus he is tortured; and like Jesus he is challenged to call down God to defend him and deliver him from his enemies:

"Let us oppress the poor righteous man; let us not spare the widow, nor revenge the ancient grey hairs of the aged. Let our strength be the law of justice: for that which is feeble is found to be worth nothing. Therefore let us lie in wait for the righteous; because he is not for our run, and he is clean contrary to our doings: he upbraideth us with our offending the law, and objecteth to our infamy the transgressions of our education. He professeth to have the knowledge of God; and he calleth himself the son of God. He was made to reprove our thoughts. He is grievous unto us even to behold: for his life is not like other mens, his ways are of another fashion. We are esteemed of him as counterfeits: he abstaineth from our ways as from filthiness: he pronounceth the end of the just to be blessed, and maketh his boast that God is his father. Let us see if his words be true, and let us prove what shall happen in the end of him. For if the just man be the son of God, he will help him, and deliver him from his enemies. Let us examine him with despitefulness and torture, that we may know his meekness, and prove his patience. Let us condemn him with a shameful death: for by his own saying he shall be respected.

Such things they did imagine, and were deceived: for their own wickedness hath blinded them. As for the mysteries of God they knew them not: neither hoped they for the wages of righteousness, nor discerned a reward for blameless souls. For God created man to be immortal, and made him to be an image of his own eternity. Nevertheless, through envy of the devil came death into the world: and they that do hold of his side do find it."

Chapters two and three again suggest that there were many who went under the title of Righteous; who claimed to be the son of God; exercised a living resurrection; preached immortality; saw themselves as made in the image of God; and were persecuted for their beliefs. I believe that we can, in the end, identify a central character whose life epitomises the Biblical Jesus who was Teacher of Righteousness, which I will explore below. But what is of importance at this point, is to understand the political implications of a group of people who were advocating Essene philosophies, or in other words, the philosophies of Joshua. I believe that they were attempting to bring about the re-unification of Judah and Israel under councillors and judges, as Isaiah and Jeremiah had prophesied, which in turn implied self empowerment in the religious arena by regarding themselves as the children of God, the image of God and immortal, and in the political arena where they would have self determination. Both ideologies were no doubt, rejected by the orthodox Levitical priesthood, the Herod Kings and the Roman Empire.

The next question we must ask is this: Can we, in all objectivity, believe that Joshua in the New Testament advocated the return of a Davidic Messiah king? He may well have come from the tribe of Judah through the paternal line, but it is evident that he was an Essene, or largely influenced by the Essenes and became a Nazarene initiate. According to "*The Damascus Document. History and Exhortation V11,*" David was not considered to be one of the Righteousness due to the fact that he had more than one wife. Noah, who was referred to as one of the Righteousness only had one wife, as did Joseph:

"*...they will be caught in two nets: in fornication by taking two wives during their life-time, whereas the foundation of creation is, "male and female he created them;" and those who went into the ark, "Two by two they went into the ark." And concerning the prince it is written, "He shall* *not multiply wives for himself." But David did not read the sealed book of the law..."*[129]

According to the *"Habakkuk"* text, the Essenes were also totally against the concept of Judaic domination under a Davidic King who they believed would subject the Hebrews to slavery as they had done in the past as seen in Jeremiah 34:

"(17)...for Lebanon is the council of the community, and the beasts are the simple ones of Judah, the doers of the law...this means the city, that is Jerusalem, in which the wicked priest wrought abominable works and defiled God's sanctuary; and violence to a land, these are the cities of Judah, because he plundered the wealth of the poor."[130]

On the other hand, they believed that there was salvation for Judah, providing that it adopted Essene religious and political philosophies as can be seen in *"The Habakkuk"* commentary (4) where Judah gains salvation:

"This means all the doers of the law in the house of Judah, whom God will rescue from the house of judgement because of their labour and their faith in the teacher of Righteousness."[131]

In Matthew 10:5 & 6, Jesus says something similar. If Lebanon was *"the council of the community,"* then the Habakkuk text is referring to the council being in the north, as opposed to in Judea in the south. Mount Lebanon, during the time of the Kingdom of Israel, was it's

129. Millar Burrows. "The Dead Sea Scrolls." Secker & Warburg. 1956.

130. Ibid.

131. Ibid.

northern most border as it was the northern most border of Galilee in
the first century A.D:

*"...Go not into the way of the Gentiles, and into any city of the
Samaritans enter ye not: But go rather to the lost sheep of the house of Israel."*

I suspect that the *"lost sheep"* in this instance, rather than Samaria
and Galilee, refers to Judah as it does in the Habakkuk text and that the
Teacher of Righteousness was not from the tribe of Judah. In the
Gnostic *"The Tripartite Tractate"* it states:

*"Also, other men of the Hebrew race, of whom we already spoke, namely
the righteous ones and the prophets....By interpreting them they established many heresies which exist to the present among the Jews."* [132]

But what about the Gospels, and do they in turn clearly identify Jesus
as a Davidic Messiah king? The genealogies going back to king David
and in turn Abraham given in Matthew contradict the genealogies given
in Luke which go back to David, Abraham and in turn Adam. Luke goes
so far as to add in brackets, 3: 23:

"...being (as supposed) the son of Joseph, which was the son of Heli."

His words, *"as supposed"* imply that this genealogy was conjecture, an
imagined guess. Matthew traces this genealogy to Rehoboam, Solomon
and then David, while Luke traces it back to Nathan, David and Jesse
without mentioning Solomon. According to Levitical law at the time

---

132. James M.Robinson. "The Nag Hammadi Library." Harper Collins. 1990.

which was based on Ezra, a person would not have been considered a Jew, ie. of the tribe of Judah, if their mother was not a Jew. Even today, a person can only rightfully claim to be Jewish if their mother is a Jew. If their mother is not a Jew, then they are not considered to be as such, even though their father may be Jewish. [133]

Mary's lineage is not given in the Gospels, though the Apocrypha does describe her as being of a priestly family. She is also described as having danced in the Temple like Miriam, the sister of Moses and automatically had a priestly role due to her genealogy, as did many women before the fall of the northern kingdom of Israel.[134] I believe that the mother of Jesus was a Samaritan, who in turn would have been a descendent of Rachel, and an Ephraimite due to the following passages in the Gospels.

In the second chapter of Matthew there is an interesting quote, which if it had been inserted in full, would nullify the Judaic genealogy found in Matthew 1 especially if the line of descent was considered to be carried through the maternal rather than the paternal line. If the mother of Jesus was not a Jew, the word Jew deriving from the Hebrew *"Yehudi"* which means *"from the tribe of Judah,"*[135] but was instead descended from Joseph, the son of Rachel, then in spite of his father's Judaic lineage, which is contradictory and tenuous anyway, Jesus would not have been considered a Jew by the orthodox priesthood in Jerusalem. Consider these two verses which hang precariously between the story of Herod:

---

133. Louis Jacobs. "The Jewish Religion." Oxford University Press. 1995.

134. Book of James. The Apocryphal New Testament Oxford. 1926.

135. Louis Jacobs. "The Jewish Religion." Oxford University Press. 1995.

"Then was fulfilled that which was spoken by Jeremiah the prophet, saying,

In Rama was there a voice heard, lamentation, and weeping, and great mourning, Rachel weeping for her children, and would not be comforted, because they are not."

Rachel was the mother of Joseph and Benjamin. The territory of Benjamin once included Jerusalem, but was then taken over by the tribe of Judah. The tribe of Benjamin, per say, disappeared completely, though it is believed that it was absorbed by Judah. The tribe of Joseph, as we have seen, became the Lost Tribes in 722 A.D. and were referred to as the Samaritans and Galileans by 1 A.D. In the above verse Rachel mourns the fact that both Joseph and Benjamin *"are not."* What are these verses doing in the middle of Matthew 2?

Between 70 A.D. and 300 A.D., the Gospels went through many editors, the story being adapted and changed through the centuries. According to Burton Mack in *"The Lost Gospel Of Q,"* the original Gospels consisted of sayings and quotes from a person called Jesus as well as quotes from the Old Testament. But these quotes did not include an historical or biographical account of the life of Jesus. Many of these sayings, written in a similar fashion to the Gnostic Scriptures, were preceded by a question which was followed by the words, *"Jesus said:..."*[136] The reference to *"Jesus said..."* in turn, might not necessarily have

---

136. Burton L. Mack. "The Lost Gospel. The Book of Q & Christian Origins." Harper Collins. 1994.

referred to the present, but could have been a quote from a text written by Joshua in the Old Testament, or from Isaiah, whose name in turn is a derivative of Joshua.[137] These sayings were interwoven with an historical account at a later date and interspersed with mystical analogies, as we have seen above in the Kabbalistic parable of Joseph and the Virgin in the age of Pisces.

Verse 18 in Matthew 2 is an Old Testament quote that implies that the northern tribes are no longer and will never be re-instated. But what if this verse was part of the original Gospels and the full quote was censored, whilst Matthew 1 on the other hand, being part of a biographical account, was a later insertion? Matthew 18 is an extract from Jeremiah 31, which if read in it's entirety, changes the implications of the Gospel story completely and implies the return of the Joseph tribes, or Israel to their own land:

15, 16 & 17: *"Thus saith the Lord; A voice was heard in Ramah, lamentation and bitter weeping; Rachel weeping for her children, refused to be comforted for her children, because they were not.*

Thus saith the Lord; Refrain thy voice from weeping, and thine eyes from tears: for thy work shall be rewarded, saith the Lord; and they shall come again from the land of the enemy.

And there is hope in thine end, saith the Lord, that thy children shall come again to their own border."

---

137. O.Odelain and R. Seguineau. "Dictionary of Proper Names and Places in the Bible." Robert Hale Limited. 1991.

I believe that Matthew 2:18 was cut because Matthew 2:17 states that Jeremiah's prophecy would be fulfilled. But what exactly was fulfilled by the words of the prophet Jeremiah referred to in Matthew 2:17? Throughout chapter 31, Jeremiah speaks of a re-unification of Israel and Judah under the laws of the prophets. Much like Isaiah, he longed for the kingdom of Israel to be re-established under the councillors and the judges as it had been in Joshua's time. In John chapter four, Jesus went to Sychar, a town between Mount Ebal and Mount Gerizim, an area where Jacob, Joseph and Joshua had been buried. There he met a Samaritan woman at Rachel's well. His words to the woman reflect the philosophies of both Isaiah and Jeremiah. 4:20:

"Our fathers worshipped on this mountain, but the Jews say that the place where God must be worshipped is in Jerusalem.

"Jesus replied, the time is coming when you will worship the Father neither on this mountain nor in Jerusalem....God is spirit, and those who worship him must worship in Spirit and truth."

Jesus was no doubt aware of Isaiah and Jeremiah's views, as were the Essenes. But the most telling verse in Jeremiah 31 which Matthew 2:18 says will be fulfilled (Matthew 2:17) is as follows:

9: *"They shall come with weeping, and with supplications will I lead them: I will cause them to walk by the rivers of waters in a straight way, wherein they shall not stumble: for I am a father to Israel, and Ephraim is my firstborn."*

12:*"Therefore they shall come and sing in the height of Zion, and shall flow together to the goodness of the Lord, for wheat, and for wine, and for oil, and for the young of the flock and of the herd: and their soul shall be as a watered garden: and they shall not sorrow any more at all."*

If these verses had been included in their entirety, then the Judaic line found in Matthew chapter 1, would be an anomaly and a direct contradiction of the quote found in Matthew chapter 2. Jeremiah 31 suggests that the firstborn is not a Levitical priest or a Davidic Messiah king, but Ephraim and his descendants being the kingdom of Israel. Hence it says in Luke 2:32:

"A light to lighten the Gentiles, and the glory of thy people Israel."

The Jesus in our Gospels might well have come from the tribe of Judah through the paternal line, but in keeping with the *"Habakkuk Commentary"* 17, quoted above, he had faith in the teachers of Righteousness and therefore followed the Essene line where anyone, from any tribe, could become a priest, or Messiah as mentioned in *"The Dead Sea Scrolls,"* and not necessarily be from the tribe of Levi or a Davidic king. The Gospels imply as much in Matthew 22:42 & 45:

"...What think ye of Christ? whose son is he?
They say unto him, The Son of David.
He saith unto them....."If then David calls him "Lord," how then can he be David's son?'

While in Luke 20:41-44 it says:

"And he said unto them, How say they that Christ is David's son? And David himself saith in the book of Psalms (110), The Lord said unto my Lord, Sit thou on my right hand. Till I make thine enemies thy footstool. If David therefore calleth him Lord, how is he then his son?"

Matthew 22:45 refers to Psalms 110 where Melchizedek blessed the bread and wine in Genesis. Melchizedek pre-empts the carrying out of this ritual by Jesus and he is mentioned only once in the Old Testament long before David was born. As discussed above, in the second chapter on *"Origins,"* Melchizedek was the Priest-King of Peace(Salem) and justice as Jesus was believed to be. In Psalm 110:4 it states:

"...Thou art a priest for ever after the order of Melchizedek."

What this verse implies, if taken in conjunction with Matthew 22: 45, is that the Christ/Anointed/Messiah is not the son of David, but a priest, and due to the words *"after the order of Melchizedek,"* this priest or Christ/Anointed/Messiah is one of many within the *"order."* Such a philosophy is totally in keeping with *"The Dead Sea Scrolls"* that speak of the Messiah, the Christ, the Teacher of Righteousness or the anointed ones in the plural.[138]

In Hebrews chapter 7, the authors speak of Jesus as being of the tribe of Judah through the paternal line as well as being of the order of Melchizedek, and also refer to the Levitical priesthood as being superceeded by this order. Verses 11–15:

"If therefore perfection were by the Levitical priesthood, (for under it the people received the law,) what further need was there that another priest should rise after the order of Melchizedek, and not be called after the order of Aaron?

For the priesthood being changed, there is made of necessity a change also of the law. For he whom these things are spoken pertaineth to another tribe, of which no man gave attendance at the altar.

For it is evident that our Lord sprang out of Juda; of which tribe Moses spake nothing concerning priesthood. And it is yet far more evident: for that after the similitude of Melchizedek there aristh another priest."

What we must now ask is, who would David and Matthew call Lord in both time periods? Obviously someone who through descent was

---

138. See Dead Sea Scrolls: Manual of Discipline. "…until there shall come the Messiahs of Aaron and Israel."

considered by Hebrew standards, not Levite or Aryan, to be superior to him. In Luke 20: 17 & 18, we find a possible answer:

"And he beheld them, and said, What is this then that is written, The stone which the builders rejected, the same is become the head of the corner?

Whosoever shall fall upon that stone shall be broken; but on whomsoever it shall fall, it will grind him to powder."

The Sadducees knew exactly what Jesus was referring to in this quote and tried to get him arrested in order to hand him over to the governor because of the political undertones in his words which threatened the Levitical priesthood. Jesus in Christianity, is associated with this *"stone"* and this stone in turn, is not only associated with the Messiah, but is also a reference to Joseph, the shepherd, the Prince and the crown and to Joshua and Mount Gerizim in Samaria, which was rejected when the Temple was built in Jerusalem in approximately 521 B.C. The Samaritans felt so strongly at the time, that they wrote a letter of protest to the Persian King.[139] Genesis 49:24 refers to Joseph as the *"stone"* and the *"shepherd,"* as Joshua (Num. 27:15–33) and Jesus were believed to be, while in Joshua 24:26, Joshua places a *"stone"* at Mount Gerizim as a symbol of Israel's dedication to the law:

Gen. 49:24:

---

139. Louis Jacobs. "The Jewish Religion." Oxford University Press. 1995.

"But his bow abode in strength, and the arms of his hands were made strong by the hands of the mighty God of Jacob; from thence is the shepherd, the stone of Israel: "

Numbers 27: 18 & 17:
"And the Lord said unto Moses, Take thee Joshua the son of Nun, a man in whom is the spirit, and lay thine hand upon him...that the congregation of the Lord be not as sheep which have no shepherd..."

Joshua 24:26:
"And Joshua wrote these words in the book of the law of God, and took a great stone, and set it up there under a great oak, that was by the sanctuary of the Lord."

There could be only one person or persons who would possibly fit this mould and that would be an Ephraimite and direct descendent of Joshua, or a Nazarene initiate from any one of the twelve tribes being a levite or *"joiner,"* who was or had become a *"firstborn"* through the anointing, a prophet, a judge, a holder of the law and a Teacher of Righteousness.[140] As in the name Melchizedek, he, she, or they would have been seen as a king [Melch] of justice [zedek], or in the feminine a queen [Bithiah] of justice[zedek.]

Being aware of scripture, the Sadducees would have also read Zechariah, who was murdered between the sanctuary and the altar. He writes in a similar vein, calling Joshua the high priest, the *"stone"* as was

---

140. Qumram text 4Q416, 418, lines 13 & 14:"...By his will, devote yourself to his service, and the Wisdom of his storehouse(13)...you will advise him, and become for him a firstborn...and he shall love you as a man loves his only child." Qumram text 4Q458. Fragment 2, column 2, lines 4 & 5. "And they were justified, and walked according to the L[aws...anointed with the oil of the kingship of..."

Joseph, and what is more important, the *"branch"* from which the Messiah comes, which is a reference to Joseph in Genesis 49:22:

"Joseph is a fruitful bough, even a fruitful bough by a well; whose branches run over the wall:"

Zechariah 3:8–10:

"Hear now, O Joshua the high priest, thou, and thy fellows that sit before thee: for they are people wondered at: for, behold, I will bring forth my servant the BRANCH .

For behold the stone that I have laid before Joshua; upon one stone shall be seven eyes: behold, I will engrave the graving thereof, (Joshua 8: 32) saith the Lord of hosts, and I will remove iniquity of that land in one day.

In that day, saith the Lord of hosts, shall ye call every man his neighbour under the vine and under the fig tree."

The root, as we have been led to believe, is supposedly from Jesse, son of Judah and father of David. But there is a difference between *"Israel"* both as a name for the Hebrew people and as a geographical area. In Jeremiah 31, the prophet differentiates between Judah and *"Israel"* which is associated with the Joseph tribes and Ephraim in 31:27 as does Isaiah in 5:7:

"Behold, the days come saith the Lord, that I will sow the house of Israel and the house of Judah with the seed of man, and with the seed of beast."

"For the vineyard of the Lord of hosts is Israel, and the men of Judah his pleasant plant."

The *"Damascus Document, History and Exhortation 1,"* in turn, makes no mention of Judah at all and instead implies that the root of the Messiah comes from Israel and Aaron, who as we have seen above, referred to the Joseph tribes and the northern kingdom of Ephraim.

"...he visited them and caused to sprout from Israel and Aaron a root of planting to inherit his land." [141]

Jesus in our Gospels might well have been the firstborn child as Luke claims he was, and therefore, according to Exodus, regarded as sanctified, devoted and holy to God. But in Judea only the Levites were considered to be the firstborn and of the priesthood, whilst in Qumram, the priestly class was of Israel and Aaron. If Jesus was not born into the Levite priesthood through the paternal line; was not considered to be a firstborn and devoted to God according to Levitical practice (Num.3:12); was not descended from Israel through the paternal line but rather through the maternal line, then he would have had to be initiated into the priesthood, in other words, become a *"joiner"* and a Nazarene. This in turn means that if his father came from the tribe of Judah and his mother from the tribe of Joseph, then Jesus was the genetic embodiment of Isaiah and Jeremiah's wish to see the two kingdoms re-united.

The evidence in support of Joshua as High Priest and Judge, descended from the tribe of Ephraim or an Essene initiate, in accordance with the time period prior to the Davidic kings, is substantiated through the words and actions of a Jesus found in the Gospels, as well as the fact that he was known as a Nazarene where during his final ordination he was blessed with Israel's name and became the firstborn of

---

141. Millar Burrows. "The Dead Sea Scrolls." Secker & Warburg. 1956.

God under the order of Ephraim, as the *"Habakkuk Commentary 17"* and Qumram text 4Q416, 418, lines 13 & 14 imply.

1. We have his own words in Matthew 22:43 and Luke 20:41:

"If then David calls him lord, how then can he be David's son?"

2. He tells us that his kingdom is not of this world, which logically speaking would mean that is was of the Kabbala and the law as it was in the Kingdom of Israel prior to Saul's anointing in approximately 1037 B.C...

3. We have him running away from the crowds when they want to make him king, a concept he would have abhorred if he was a descendent of Joshua and Samuel. John 6:15:

"When Jesus therefore perceived that they would come and take him by force, to make him a king, he departed again into a mountain himself alone."

4. When the Jews accuse him of being possessed and of being a Samaritan, which he would have been due to his mother's lineage going back to Joseph and to Rachel (Luke 2:32), he denies the former and in defence of the latter says that he went to honour his father, who would have been Joseph (both past and present) and in turn Jacob, who are buried at Mount Gerizim in Samaria. John 8:48 & 49:

"Then answered the Jews, and said unto him, Say we not well that thou art a Samaritan, and hast a devil?

Jesus answered, I have not a devil; but I honour my Father, and ye do dishonour me."

The Samaritans were and are descendants of Ephraim, and in turn Joseph and Jacob, a fact which will be elaborated on below. In the 1st century A.D., these Hebrews were despised and considered untouchable by the Jews. Nicodemus is disparagingly accused of being a Galilean by the Sadducees whilst Jesus goes so far as to tell the story of the Good

Samaritan and holds a discourse with a Samaritan woman at a well. His actions are in flagrant opposition to Levitical practice at the time.

At this point I would like to make it very clear that this author is not anti-semitic or rather anti-Jewish. The fact of the matter is that the Hebrews themselves became divided as a nation, rather than this author setting out to divide them. The term *"Jew"* in the 1st century A.D., as we have seen above, referred to those who were born from the tribe of Judah through the maternal line. Since this time, however, the term *"Jew"* has become a more encompassing title, referring to the Hebrews as a whole, including Samaritan and Felasha Jews. Many Jews today still retain surnames such as Ephraim, Asher, Benjamin and Joseph, which suggests that the northern tribes still exist amongst the *Jews* themselves.

Throughout John's Gospel a distinction is made between the followers of Jesus and the Jews, who on numerous occasions cross question him and try to stone him. Jesus also says, *"the Jews say....but I tell you."* The implication being that Jesus is not from the tribe of Judah, but a Hebrew from the north.

5. Before entering Jerusalem on a donkey, he retires to the borders of Ephraim, which implies that he had strong links with this tribe. When he rides into Jerusalem on a donkey, we have another contradiction between the synoptic gospels and the Gospel of John. Matt. 21:9 and Mark 11:9 both refer to him as *"the king, son of David,"* a title which he later refutes in Matt. 25:25 and Luke 20:41. Luke in 19:38 on the other hand, although calling him a *"King,"* does not identify him as a descendent of David, implying in 2:32 that he is a king of Israel being the northern kingdom of Samaria and Galilee while John in 1:49 & 12:13 states:

"...Rabbi, thou art the Son of God; thou art the King of Israel...." (compare with Jeremiah 31)

"Blessed is the King of Israel that cometh in the name of the Lord."

If John is accurate, and if this is what was said about a Jesus when he entered Jerusalem, then this was the equivalent of throwing the cat amongst the pigeons, to put it *very* mildly. Nobody in their right mind, during this period in history, nobody from the northern kingdom any-way, would have had the audacity to enter into a Judaic city and pro-claim themselves the *"King of Israel,"* which implied being from the northern kingdom of Israel being Samaria and Galilee, and the original kingdom of all twelve tribes in the time of Joshua. Or did they? And was this title of *"King"* in keeping with the order of Melchizedek, where the meaning is a priest-king of justice, being a teacher of Righteousness blessed with the name *Israel*?

6.Throughout all four Gospels, Jesus admits to being the firstborn of God, which according to Exodus 13:2 and Luke 2:33 is a child that first opens the womb. While the firstborn in Genesis 48:15–20 and Jeremiah 31:9, is Ephraim. As such, he is an anointed priest. The Essene priests were anointed, being Christs or Messiahs, in the same manner that the priests were anointed in the Old Testament before this ritual was used for the inauguration of kings. During the 1st century A.D., however, only the high priest of the temple was allowed to use the title Messiah after his name. According to John, Jesus could have been a *"king of Israel,"* *"the priesthood being changed...after the similitude of Melchizedek,"* suggesting a descent from Ephraim the firstborn and Joseph, the shepherd, the prince and the keeper of the covenant. Jesus's priestly anointing had nothing whatsoever to do with being a *"king of the Jews,"* and therefore he denies this accusation. His answer to Pilate is, *"the words are yours,"* implying that they are not his at all. (Matt. 27:11, Mark 15:2, Luke 23:3, & John 18:37.)

"'Are you the king of the Jews?' the governor asked him. 'The words are yours,' said Jesus."

Taking the above factors into account, it appears that Joshua in the New Testament, much like Joshua in the Old, is the anointed Messiah as seen in a judge descended from Ephraim through the maternal line and is a Teacher of Righteousness. He is not the anointed Messiah as seen in a Davidic King, as his kingdom was not of this world, but was in the abstract, being justice and righteousness and the Kabbala/Ashertaroth as it was in Joshua's time.

What is more, the name Jesus could apply to a number of historical characters who were Essenes or given the Mitzvah name Joshua. If, through Nazarene initiation, these people were blessed with Israel's name, then they could have either in a religious sense, or in a common sense, have also used the name Jacob.

The New testament was first written in Greek and the Greek translation for Jacob is James.[142] We have two characters in the Gospels with this name. Firstly, James the son of Zebedee and brother of John, who joined the group when widowed and in middle age. Zebedee is a derivative of Zabad, who was an Ephraimite.[143] James Zebedee was crucified by Herod Agrippa 1 in 44 A.D. [144]

The second is James the Righteous, described as the brother of Jesus and not a disciple, who was born in 1 A.D., a date from which we now take our calendars.[145] James was stoned to death in 62 A.D. If the words, *"If you have seen me then you have seen the Father"* refer to the name Jacob/Israel, then the sentence makes sense and pertains to inheritance

---

142. O.Odelain and R. Seguineau. "Dictionary of Proper Names and Places in the Bible." Robert Hale Limited. 1991.

143. Ibid.

144. Larousse. "Dictionary of Beliefs & Religions."Larousse. 1994.

145. Robin Lane Fox. "The Unauthorized Version." Penguin. 1992.

or to religious titles, meaning that James Zebedee and James the Righteous could both have been seen as *"Israel."* Hence we have the *"living God,"* who John refers to in Revelation as the person *"who was, and is and is yet to come,"* the title itself believed to be everlasting in the immediate present and perhaps not necessarily reliant on a specific genealogy. To quote from the Gospels and take the concept one step further as Luke does in 3:8:

"God is able of these stones to raise up children unto Abraham."

Another illusive character was Theudas, who was not an apostle, who is mentioned only once in the Gospels, and whose life in this verse directly parallels the life of Jesus. Acts 5:36

"For before these days rose up Theudas, boasting himself to be some-body; to whom a number of men, about four hundred, joined themselves: who was slain; and all, as many as obeyed him, were scattered, and brought to nought."

Theudas, as we shall see later, was a more central character than our Gospels have led us to believe. He was the head of the Egyptian Therapeutae, in other words he *"came from out of Egypt,"* was of the order of Ephraim[146] and was crucified in by Herod Agrippa 1 in 44 A.D.

Lastly we have a character called Judas from Galilee, who could have been either Judas, described as the brother of Jesus and a disciple, Judas Iscariot, or both. Acts. 5:37:

---

146. Barbara Thiering. "Jesus The Man." Doubleday. 1992.

"After this rose up Judas of Galilee in the days of the taxing, and drew away as many people after him: he also perished; and all, even as many as obeyed him, were dispersed."

All four men, whether of the tribe of Ephraim or not, could have been given the religious name Jesus, or Joshua in keeping with Hebrew circumcision customs and used this name when reading from the Torah in the synagogue or giving a sermon. They could also have been referred to as *"Joshuas"* or Essenes, being advocates of the philosophies of the Old Testament Joshua as well as Isaiah, whose name is a derivative of Joshua.

The lives of James, James Zebedee, Theudas, Judas the brother of Jesus and/or Iscariot are the same as the life of a Jesus found in the Gospels, the Teacher of Righteousness in the Qumram texts and the righteous mentioned in the *"Wisdom of Solomon"* chapters 2 & 3. These people entered the priesthood; established a new church; taught what is known today as Christian principles or Reform Judaism; and were judged and put to death for their beliefs, either by crucifixion or by stoning.

The political implications of the disparity between the Davidic Judaic line and an Essene, or Joshua initiate, is that by giving Joshua a Judaic, Davidic descent, which he certainly did not have in the Old Testament, both Matthew and Luke have kept their Gospels in line with Paul's ideology of an autocratic state led by a high priest, king or emperor who upheld draconian laws as opposed to Joshua's federal democracy upheld by a supreme court led by judges and councillors, where the law was tempered with mercy and a justice of liberty in the promised land of Israel.

If we take Burton Mack's view that the Gospels originally consisted of sayings and Old Testament quotes, and we keep in mind that *"The Dead Sea Scrolls"* spoke of the teacher of Righteousness who came from the root of Israel and Aaron as opposed to the tribe of Judah or the Levitical priesthood, then we must consider the fact that the historical and biographical account was inserted at a later date, and in turn, upheld the bias of it's authors. It is obvious that *"The Dead Sea Scrolls"* contributed to the Gospels in one way or another and we must consider the following facts when interpreting the Gospel accounts:

1. The Dead Sea Scrolls were in the cave at Qumram when the Temple fell in 70 A.D.

2. Many of the teachings found in the texts are part of Jewish, Christian and Gnostic faith.

3. James Zebedee and Theudas were put to death by crucifixion in the early forties whilst James the Righteous was stoned in 62 A.D. All three could have been referred to as Teachers of Righteousness, or the anointed Messiahs, and in keeping with the texts, would have been called Messiahs of Israel and Aaron.

4. All the characters in the Gospels could have either written the texts or read the texts. They were most certainly aware of them as the parallels in the Gospels suggest as much.

Chapter Seven.

Zion

Lamentations 4:2,7 & 8:

"The precious children of Zion, comparable to fine gold, now regarded as earthen pitchers, the work of the hands of the potter.

Her Nazarites were purer than snow, they were whiter then milk, they were more ruddy in body than rubies, their polishing was of sapphire:

Their visage is now blacker than coal; they are not known in the streets: their skin cleaveth to their bones; it is withered, it is become like a stick."

There are four pivots on which Christianity basis itself. These are:

1. The belief in the concept of a *"child"* or a *"son of God,"* who according to this author was a Nazarene initiate, male or female, an *"anointed/ Messiah/Christian"* and a teacher of righteousness blessed with the name Israel who was *"devoted"* to God, of which there were many;

2. the teachings which advocate democratic thought through the laws of Moses, being justice and righteousness and to love our neighbours as ourselves, whether they be Judeans, Galileans, Samaritans, Gentiles or any other nationality or race group;

3. an unjust trial and death sentence of a teacher or teachers of Righteousness;

4. and lastly the concept of life after death.

There is however, one other which we all tend to ignore. This is the triumphant ride into Jerusalem on a donkey where the daughter of Zion is embraced by the Lord. Matthew 21:5:

"Tell ye the daughter of Zion, Behold thy King [Mose/Melech] cometh unto thee, meek and sitting upon an ass, and a colt the foal of an ass."

John 12:15:

"Fear no more, daughter of Zion; see, your king [Moses/Melech] is coming, mounted on a donkey's colt."

Both these extracts, in conjunction with Lamentations 4:2, 7 & 8 quoted above, refer to *"Zion,"* whose children are Nazarenes, comparable to *"finest gold,"* who have been ignominiously called *"earthen pitchers,"* a philosophy which they did not support in accordance with Gen.1. Zion in turn is a feminine symbol which means *"holy mountain"* in Hebrew. Before the last journey into Jerusalem where a Jesus comes to embrace Zion, he withdraws to Ephraim, on the borders of Judah in the northern country of Samaria. John 11:54:

"Jesus therefore walked no more openly among the Jews; but went thence unto a country near to the wilderness, into a city called Ephraim, and there continued with his disciples."

Thereafter, the judge, the priest-*"king of Israel"* (John 12:13), a precious son of Zion and a Nazarene of the order of Melchizedek, Joshua mitzvah name, from Ephraim, enters Jerusalem on a donkey where there is a gathering of people who witness his entry into the city. This event parallels Genesis 49:10 & 11, where *"Shiloh"* rides on an ass, or the foal of an ass amidst a gathering of people. Politically speaking, when "*Shiloh*" comes, as prophesied in Genesis 49:10 & 11, and the leader of "*Shiloh*" tethers his donkey to the vine or Zion, the sceptre will pass from Judah as it had done in the Old Testament with the establishment of the Kingdom of Israel by Joshua.

"*The sceptre shall not depart from Judah, nor a lawgiver from beneath his feet, until Shiloh come; and unto him [Shiloh] shall the gathering of the people be.*

Binding his foal unto the vine, and his asses colt unto the choice vine; he washed his garments in wine, and his clothes in the blood of grapes:'

"*Shiloh*" is a reference to a town in Ephraim where Joshua, an Ephraimite, kept the Ark of the Covenant. Shiloh means "*a conduit for water.*" [147] Spiritually, this infers that we embrace the Holy Spirit, while politically we embrace democratic principles. eg: Proverbs 18:4:

"*....the well spring of wisdom is a flowing brook.*"

The vine in turn, is spoken of in Ezekiel 19:10 as the Mother of all Israel and as such, equates with Zion:

"*Thy mother is a vine in thy blood, planted by the waters: she was fruitful [Ephraim] and full of branches [Joseph-Genesis 49:22] by reason of many waters [Shiloh].*"

---

147. O.Odelain and R.Seguineau. "Dictionary of Proper Names and Places in the Bible." Robert Hale Limited. 1991.

I believe that as the Lost Tribes of Israel worshipped the feminine principle in Elephantine[148] after escaping persecution from the Assyrians, so did our Joshua in both the Old and the New Testaments under the name of *"Zion,"* who was considered to be the mother of all Israel sometimes referred to as the Ashtaroth as *"The Dead Sea Scrolls"* imply in the *"Damascus Document. History and Exhortation. V11:"* [149]

This feminine principle was not only a concept, but was immortalised in the form of female Nazarenes. After leaving Ephraim and before entering Jerusalem, Jesus went to Bethany. The town of Bethany was situated on the slopes of the Mount of Olives where a grove of trees, an *"Asherah"*[150] grew in the garden of Gethsemane. Bethany or Beth-Anoth, means *"The house of the Goddess Anath."* [151] Asenath, the mother of Ephraim, as we have seen in chapter 2, means *"belonging to the Goddess Neith/Isis/Anath."* [152]

In this house Jesus was anointed by a woman called Mary. Mary in turn means a *"Seeress"* or prophetess.[153] In *"the house of the Goddess Anath"* Joshua was anointed by a High Priestess of a religious order, as was Asenath in the Old Testament and Ankhsenpa-amen who anointed Thutankamen, before going into Jerusalem to embrace a daughter of Zion, who was to become the bride of the Lord. This was the sacred and holy marriage written about in Revelation. This *"Mary"* who anoints him with oil, is not kneeling before him in submission, but is rather acting as a conduit for the Holy Spirit, which she symbolises and embodies as a Nazarene priestess. This anointing by a woman was carried out

148. Geoffrey Ashe. "The Virgin. Mary's Cult and the Reemergence of the Goddess." Arkana. 1988.

149. Millar Burrows. "The Dead Sea Scrolls." Secker and Warburg. 1956.

150. Michael Jordan. "Gods of the Earth." Bantam Press. 1992.

151. O.Odelain and R. Seguineau. "Dictionary of Proper Names and Places in the Bible." Robert Hale Limited. 1991.

152. Ibid.

153. Ibid.

in Egypt by the wives of the Pharaohs, which suggests that this *"Mary"* in turn, was his wife who performed a ritual that is alluded to in *"The Dead Sea Scrolls."*

"Jacob (8)…and all of His Holy implements (9)…and all her anointed ones (10)…" [154]

One of the last parables that Jesus gave to the multitudes in the Temple, was the parable of the marriage feast in Matthew 22: 2:

"And Jesus answered and spake unto them again by parables, and said, The kingdom of Heaven is like unto a certain king, which made a marriage for his son…"

This parable was not only about his own marriage, which I suspect was to a daughter of Zion, but was also of the religious joining together of Zion to the Lord, God and the Spirit. As Jesus said, he did not come to abolish the laws of the prophets and of Mosis, but to complete. By completing, he taught the Wisdom teachings (fem.) which complement the laws (mas.) For example:

"Thou shalt not bare false witness,"

is complemented by the Wisdom teachings in Proverbs 12:20:

"Deceit is in the heart of them that imagine evil: but to the councillors of peace is joy."

---

154. Robert Eisenman and Michael Wise. "The Dead Sea Scrolls Uncovered." Element. 1992.

This wedding ceremony, to which we are all invited, is pertinent to each and everyone of us who takes on the role of bride or bridegroom, or who unite these two forces, being the Elohim within us. The Elohim relates to left and right, conscious and subconscious minds. For example, if Revelation 18:23 is written in the positive voice instead of the negative, due to righteousness being achieved, as it is with the marriage of the Lord and Zion, it would state:

"And the light of a candle shall shine in thee; and the voice of the bridegroom and of the bride shall be heard in thee..."

This ideology is paralled in the Gnostic *"The Gospel of Philip"* where part of the initiation ceremony is *"the bridal chamber:"*

"The lord [did] everything in a mystery, a baptism and a chrism and a eucharist and a redemption and a bridal chamber." 155

And in the Gnostic *"The Gospel of Thomas"* which reflects John's view in Revelation:

"...and when you make the male and the female one and the same....then you will enter [the kingdom]."

Politically, the parable of the marriage feast fulfils Isaiah's prophecy where the Lord embraces his wife, Israel's mother, being Zion, who he had previously put away. Isaiah 62:15:

---

155. James M.Robinson. "The Nag Hammadi Library." Harper Collins. 1990.

"For Zion's sake will I not hold my peace, and for Jerusalem's sake I will not rest, until the righteousness thereof go forth as brightness, and the salvation thereof as a lamp that burneth.

And the Gentiles shall see thy righteousness, and all the kings thy glory: and thou shalt be called by a new name, which the mouth of the Lord shall name.

Thou shalt also be a crown of glory in the hand of the Lord, and a royal diadem in the hand of thy God.

Thou shalt no more be termed Forsaken; neither shall thy land any more be termed Desolate: but thou shalt be called Hephzibah, my delight is in her, and thy land Beulah: for thy Lord delighteth in thee, and thy land shall be married.

For as a young man marrieth a virgin, so shall thy sons marry thee: and as a bridegroom rejoiceth over the bride, so shall God rejoice over thee."

A wedding is the most important ceremony commemorated by the Samaritans today. The celebrations last for a week, beginning and ending on the Sabbath. The actual wedding takes place on the fourth day after the first Sabbath. The Samaritans believe that they are directly descended from Ephraim, the son of Joseph and also claim a priesthood directly descended from Aaron.[156] By comparing their customs which stem from Biblical times, it is possible to make sense of the Gospels.

---

156. Lonely Planet. "Israel." Lonely Planet Publications. 1992.

In the texts, Jesus celebrated the first Sabbath in Bethany and announced the beginning of the wedding celebration. A woman anointed him with oil, in accordance with *"The Song of Songs"* which was sung at weddings; *"The Dead Sea Scrolls;"* and his wedding and anointing as High Priest and Judge in accordance with Leviticus 21:10 & 13:

Song of Songs 4:10:

"How fair is thy love, my sister, my spouse, how much better is thy love than wine and the smell of thine ointments than all spices."

"Dead Sea Scrolls:" ,

"...and all her anointed ones...." [157]

Leviticus:

"And he that is the high priest among his brethren, upon whose head the anointing oil was poured,...And he shall take a wife in her virginity..."

The next day saw his ride into Jerusalem on a donkey, after which he again returned to Bethany. On the fourth day, the actual wedding took place to a woman from his own family, being a cousin, who was most probably an Ephraimite-Samaritan Nazarene woman of priestly descent. Hence we have the story of the wedding feast in the Gospels on this day. This marriage was in all likelihood, a union between a priestess representing the Spirit, the vine, the mother, Zion and her

157. Robert Eisenman and Michael Wise. "The Dead Sea Scrolls Uncovered. Element. 1992.

cousin, a priest-king as had occurred between Abraham and Sarah, Isaac and Rebecca, Jacob and Rachel and Joseph and Asenath. The laws of marriage do not prevent a man marrying his mothers, cousin's daughter.

Throughout the Gospels, there are many, many Mary's who travelled with the Apostles throughout Galilee and Judea. Dr. Barbara Thiering points out that there was an Essene woman's *"Order of Asher"* at Bethany beyond the Jordan near Qumram.[158] I cannot think of a more pertinent name, for the Order of Asher, meant the order of the *"grove,"*[159] one of their places of worship most probably being at Bethany on the slope of the Mount of Olives in the Ashertaroth of Gethsemane.

As with their male counterparts, these Nazarene women studied and perfected holy scripture and after being ordained, travelled around the countryside administering to the poor and the needy. Their religious names were in relation to a sequence of initiation and at certain times they could be known as a *"virgin," "Mary," Martha," "Miriam,"* or *"Anna/Hannah"* the Bishopess,[160] in remembrance of Hannah of the tribe of Ephraim who gave her firstborn, Samuel, to God. The titles can be confusing for as seen with the religious titles *"Teacher of Righteousness," "Joseph,"* and *"Jacob,"* we cannot know for certain which character is which as the names were changed at various times. Someone referred to as a *"virgin"* in one part of the story might have

---

158. Barbara Thiering. "Jesus the Man." Doubleday. 1992.

159. Michael Jordan. "Gods of the Earth." Bantam Press. 1992.

160. Barbara Thiering. "Jesus the Man." Doubleday.1992.

become a *"Mary," "Miriam," or "Martha"* at another, and then a *"Hannah"* at yet another.

Some of the women who travelled with the Apostles were widows referred to as whores. They were in fact priestesses, independent women not subservient to men and conducted themselves as their ancestress Miriam, the sister of Moses and Deborah the judge had done before them. The Levitical priests would have regarded them as prostitutes, zonah as opposed to q'deshah and would have been violently opposed to their singing in the Temple as Miriam did or becoming anointed judges as Deborah and all Nazarene women were considered to be. Women within the Gospels play an unconventionally high role compared to the Orthodox Judaism of the time and Jesus was known to associate with and touch women who were seen as unclean by Levitical standards of purity.

Jesus's mother was in all probability ordained into the order of Asher at an early age. According to the Book of St. James, the Protevangelium V, 2, Mary's birth is described thus:

"...And her months were fulfilled, and in the ninth month Anna brought forth, and she said unto the midwife: What have I brought forth? And she said: a female. And Anna said, My soul is magnified this day...and she gave suck to the child and called her name Mary." [161]

As with the mitzvah name Jesus, so the name Mary is a religious mitzvah title given on the first Sabbath of her birth and is not her

---

161. Lawrence Durdin Robertson. "The Year of the Goddess." Thorsons. 1990.

common name. Mary's birth is almost an exact copy of the birth of Jesus in our Gospels as well as the birth of Samuel by his mother, another Anna or Hannah.

If this was part and parcel of the ceremonies within the Essene order of Asher, then it is possible that the term *"Mary"* used in these documents might not only have referred to the mother of a *"Jesus,"* but also to other *"Marys"* ordained into the order who were called *"virgins"* after the constellation *"Virgo."* As such they were *"daughters"* of Zion. Because the name Anna or Hannah referred to the religious name of the Bishopess of the order of Asher, we have no way of knowing Anna's public name or Mary's or the Magdalene's for that matter. Later it was said of Mary:

"And when the child was three years old, Joachim said, "Let us invite the daughters of Israel, and they shall take each a taper or a lamp, and attend on her." And having come to the temple, they placed her on the first step, and she ascended alone all the steps of the altar: and the high priest received her there, kissed her. And being placed before the altar, she danced with her feet, so that all the house of Israel rejoiced with her, and loved her."[162]

The fact that she is described as being of *"the house of Israel"* rather than of Judah, implies that she was an Ephraimite or Samaritan. This record of her dancing in the Temple is reminiscent of Jeremiah 31:13

---

162. Ibid.

which could be a Kabbalistic interpretation based on the constellation of Virgo, the opposite and ideal partner to Pisces.

"Then shall the virgin rejoice in the dance, both young men and old together: for I will turn their mourning into joy, and will comfort them, and make them rejoice from their sorrow."

Because Mary enters the Holy of Holies, she is the physical symbol of the Ark itself and this particular extract implies that she became a priestess. The ceremony was obviously part of an age old tradition, as we find parallels in Exodus where Miriam dances with a sistrum, in the Song of Songs where the bride is attended on by maidens and in Jeremiah, while the connection between the Ark and a woman from heaven is spoken about in Revelation 11:19 and 12:1 & 2 where it says:

"God's sanctuary in heaven was opened, and within his sanctuary was seen the ark of his covenant. After that there appeared a great sign in heaven: a woman robed with the sun, beneath her feet the moon, and on her head a crown of twelve stars. She was about to bare a child...."

As such, all the Ephraimites or the brotherhood of the Essenes, would have been regarded as the sons of the Ark, or Aaron. *"Aaron"* in the Ethiopian *"Kebra Nagast,"* which is kept by the descendants of the Lost Tribes in Ethiopia, is translated by them as *"Ark."* [163] So therefore, when we read the words *"Israel and Aaron,"* they might not refer to Israel and the tribe of Levi as Aaron was believed to have been, (though

---

163. Graham Hancock. "The Sign and the Seal." Mandarin. 1993.

I see Aaron as a *"joiner;"* but to *"Israel and the Ark,"* which was a feminine symbol to the extent that the Ark had two female angels on the lid.[164] The Ark itself, embraces both the masculine and the feminine by virtue of the fact that the laws are the masculine symbol while the Ark, as a container, is a feminine symbol.

In the Gospels, Mary took her new born baby to the temple where he was blessed not only by Simeon, but by a widow, q'deshah, a prophetess/priestess Anna (Hannah), of the tribe of Asher. Luke 2:36 & 37:

"And there was Anna, a prophetess, the daughter of Phanuel, of the tribe of Asher: she was of a great age, and had lived with an husband seven years from her virginity. And she was a widow of about fourscore and four years, which departed not from the temple, but served God with fastings (Nazarene) and prayers day and night."

Taking Barbara Thiering's research into account, the baby was most probably blessed by the Bishopess of the Essene order of Asher, of the grove, who changed her name on ordination and became known as the Anna or Hannah. The temple to which Mary takes her child was occupied by both a man and a woman who are ordained into the priesthood as were male and female Nazarenes in Numbers 6. This concurs with archaeological discoveries at Qumram. At first it was believed that the community who lived next to the Dead Sea was a celibate, male, monastic order. But the grave site in the vicinity of

---

164. Ibid.

Qumram tells a different story. Here men, women and children are buried, suggesting a family orientated community which is totally in keeping with Hebrew traditions that denounce celibacy as a sin against God.

By the time Jesus had entered the Essene order, Joseph was dead, leaving Mary a widow. This meant that as a prophetess or q'deshah, of the Essene order of Asher, with her children now fully grown, she would have been free to go throughout the countryside administering to the poor and needy as no doubt many Nazarene women did, travelling with her son, who would have been known as *"the son of a widow"* as he went about a similar mission.

It was and is an on going process applying to specific people as well as to the whole group. In other words, those who were initiated into the mysteries, rather than worshipping a *"Joshua," "Mary" or a "Hannah"* in the past tense as we do today, became these people through their religious beliefs in the immediate present. It was a *"now"* event, where titles such as *"the righteous," "the shepherd," "Miriam"* and *"the vine"* were passed on from one century to another and from one generation to another. For those who followed these teachings, the kingdom, rather than being something that would happen in the future, was forever *"at hand"* to those who were willing to take responsibility for it in the here and now.

Isaiah 8:3 and 9:6 suggests that what had occurred in the 1st A.D., had also occurred in Isaiah's time.

"And I went unto the prophetess and she conceived, and bore a son….For unto us a child is born, unto us a son is given: and the government shall be upon his shoulder: and his name shall be called Wonderful, Counsellor, The Mighty God, The Everlasting Father, The Prince of Peace."

This child in the past, the present and in the future is directly connected with Shiloh, politically and in a religious context, where the waters of Shiloh refer to democracy and to Baptism. 8:6:

"Because this nation has rejected the waters of Shiloh..."

He will bring light to the world, 9:1-2:

"Formerly the lands of Zebulun and Naphtali were lightly regarded, but afterwards honour was bestowed on Galilee of the Nations on the road beyond Jordan to the sea.[165] *The people that walked in darkness have seen a great light; on those who lived in a land as dark as death a light has dawned."*

Again we see a prediction based on Cabalistic studies where Zebulun-Galilee, represents Yesod and the sign of Virgo and it's opposite sign being Pisces, who are the Joseph tribes of Ephraim and Manasseh-Samaria, joined to it in marriage.

After being Baptised, Jesus spent a three year period on probation, a period which is regarded by the orthodox line as being the time during which he carried out his missionary service. But according to Barbara Thiering, this missionary service where the Essenes were allowed to go out and preach, only occurred *after* their anointing.[166] As I hope to prove below, Jesus only started his ministry *after* his anointing and *after* the Last Supper. Coupled with this fact was that he had married a *"Mary,"* a daughter of Zion, a prophetess of the Essene order of Asher,

---

165. Isaiah makes reference to both Galilee and beyond Jordan to the sea, which would be in the vicinity of the Qumram community. Perhaps this community was already being established in 500 B.C.?

166. Barbara Thiering. "Jesus the Man." Doubleday. 1992.

who lived on the Mount of Olives, in Beth-any or Beth-Anath. The implications were that he had made a social, religious and political statement in accordance with the prophecies found in Genesis (49:10), Isaiah, Jeremiah and Zechariah 3 which were in accordance with his initiation and anointing as a priest after the order of Melchizedek.

The crowds sings the Hallel (Hallelujah) whilst he tells the daughter of Zion, the daughter of the Ark, to fear no more, for he is coming to embrace her. I believe that the Mary who was to become the bride of the Lord would have been his cousin. Through this union, all prophecies come to pass in the immediate present as they had done in the past and as they continued to do in the future with other Essene initiates as we have seen in Isaiah 62 quoted above, Revelation 19 and Jeremiah 31:

"Let us be glad and rejoice...for the marriage of the Lamb is come, and his wife hath made herself ready...."

"Again I will build thee, and thou shalt be built, O virgin Israel...For there shall be a day, that the watchmen upon mount Ephraim shall cry, Arise ye, and let us go up to Zion unto the Lord our God...Behold, I will bring them from the north country, and gather them from the coasts of the earth...I will cause them to walk by the rivers of waters in a straight way wherein they shall not stumble: for I am a father to Israel, and Ephraim is my firstborn...he that scattered Israel will gather them, and keep them, as a shepherd doth his flock....For the Lord hath redeemed Jacob....Therefore they shall come and sing in the height of Zion, and shall flow together to the goodness of the Lord...then shall the virgin rejoice in the dance...A voice was heard in Ramah, lamentation, and bitter weeping, Rachel weeping for her children, refused to be comforted for her children....And there is hope in thine end, saith the Lord, that thy children shall come again to their own border....Lord bless thee, O habitation of justice and mountain of holiness."

Zion, as a *"holy mountain"* in this instance, is referred to in relation to the holy mountain of Ephraim, which was mount Gerizim in Samaria. Much like the differentiation between the *"priests and the levites,"* *"Israel and Judah,"* so a similar differentiation exists between *"Zion and Jerusalem."* Because there is a differentiation, they are not one and the same thing. *"Zion"* refers to the holy mountain in the north, being Mount Gerizim, whilst Jerusalem refers to the city in the south, both of which were eventually destroyed by the Assyrians. Jerusalem in turn, being one twelfth part of Israel, is referred to as a daughter of Zion, in other words, a daughter of Israel. Isaiah 52:2 & 4:

"Shake thyself from the dust; arise, and sit down, O Jerusalem: loose thyself from the bands of thy neck, O daughter of Zion....For thus saith the Lord God. My people went down aforetime into Egypt to sojourn there; and the Assyrian oppressed them without cause."

The *"watchtower"* mentioned in relation to mount Ephraim (Zion) on which the *"watchmen"* stand in Jeremiah 31, is further elaborated on in the *"Damascus Document. History and Exhortation. V1."* where is states:

"...they shall no more join themselves to the house of Judah, but every one must stand up on his watchtower...."[167]

Which again suggests that the Essenes were in favour of Joshua's philosophies as opposed to Judaic domination under a Davidic King.

---

167. Millar Burrows. "The Dead Sea Scrolls." Secker and Warburg. 1956.

I suspect that the Hebrew view, whereby Zion was seen as Mount Gerizim, became obscured after the Jews returned from exile in Babylon. They rejected the notion that this mountain had a role to play in their religious, social or political lives, to the extent that they believed that Jacob and Joseph were buried in Hebron, as opposed to Schechem. They had after all, been divided from Israel for over 200 years and by this time they would not have felt any affiliation towards Schechem whatsoever.

The Hebrews or the Samaritans did not hold the view that Zion was a hill in Jerusalem, in the same way that they did not hold the view that Jacob and Joseph were buried in Hebron. They held to the old religious custom where the celebration of Pentecost was a celebration of the *"holy mountain"* in Samaria where Israel became rededicated to the law.

The Pentecost festival, *Shavuot* in Hebrew, which celebrates the giving of the Torah at Mount Sinai held fifty two days (seven weeks) after the Passover,[168] was, in Biblical times prior to the Assyrian invasion, held at Mount Gerizim in Samaria, regarded as the new *"Mount Sinai,"* the *"Holy Mountain"* in the promised land, due to the fact that Joshua had engraved the laws of God on stones in this area. eg: compare Isaiah 4:5 with Exodus 19:18

"And the Lord will create upon every dwelling place a mount Zion, and upon her assemblies, a cloud and smoke by day, and the shining of a flaming fire by night: for upon all the glory shall be a defence."

---

168. Louis Jacobs. "The Jewish Religion." Oxford University Press. 1995.

"And mount Sinai was altogether on a smoke, because the Lord descended upon it in fire: and the smoke thereof ascended as the smoke of a furnace..."

Shavuot or Pentecost, came to symbolize a rebirth, resurrection or rededication to the law due to the fact that Joshua in chapter 24, after crossing into the promised land, rededicated the Hebrews to the law at Mount Gerizim near Schechem where Jacob and Joseph are buried. He swore the people to the laws of Moses and laid a foundation stone, a corner stone under the oak tree, thereby establishing the New Kingdom under judges and councillors. This was the main corner stone that the builders rejected when they built the temple in Jerusalem. Joshua 24: 1, 25, 26, 27, 30 & 32:

"And Joshua gathered all the tribes of Israel to Shechem, and called for the elders of Israel, and for their heads, and for their judges, and for their officers; and they presented themselves before God....So Joshua wrote these words in the book of the law of God, and took a great stone, and set it up there under an oak, that was by the sanctuary of the Lord...And Joshua said unto all the people, Behold, this stone shall be a witness unto us; for it hath heard all the words of the Lord which he spake unto us: it shall be therefore a witness unto you, lest ye deny your God...And it came to pass after these things, that Joshua the son of Nun, the servant of the Lord died, being a hundred and ten years old. And they buried him in the border of his inheritance in Timnathserah, which is in mount Ephraim, on the north side of the hill of Gaash....And the bones of Joseph, which the children of Israel brought up out of Egypt, buried they in Schechem, in a parcel of ground which Jacob bought...."

This stone in turn came to symbolize Mount Sinai, Zion, Mount Gerizim, the *"holy mountain."* In the days of Israel, all celebrations connected with mount Sinai were held at Mount Gerizim, one of which was the festival of Tabernacles, *"Sukkot"* in Hebrew, where the people remembered how God had provided for them in the wilderness of the

Sinai desert. They built shelters of branches and lived under them for a week. In Luke 9:28 & 33, it is apparent the Jesus celebrated the festival of Tabernacles, at Mount Gerizim, the new *"Mount Sinai."*

"...and went up into a mountain to pray. And as he prayed, the fashion of his countenance was altered, and his raiment was white and glistening. And behold, there walked with him two men, which were Moses and Elias....it is good for us to be here: and let us make three tabernacles..."

The actions of a Jesus and his disciples were totally in accordance with the Old Testament where it says in Nehemiah 8:14, 15 & 17:

"And they found written in the law which the Lord had commanded by Moses, that the children of Israel should dwell in booths in the feast of the seventh month: And that they should publish and proclaim in all their cities and in Jerusalem, saying, Go forth unto the mount, and fetch olive branches and pine branches, and myrtle branches, and palm branches, and branches of thick trees, to make booths as it is written...And all the congregation of them that were come again out of captivity made booths and sat under the booths: for since the days of Joshua the son of Nun unto that day had not the children of Israel done so. And there was very great gladness."

If we compare Nehemiah 8 with Luke 9 and John 4:20 where the Hebrews still attached significance to the *"Holy Mount"* in Samaria in 1 A.D, it becomes evident that Jesus as a Hebrew and a Samaritan/Galilean practised Hebrew traditions, although he does prophecy in John 4:20, that there will come a time when worship at the Temple in Jerusalem and the mountain at Schechem, will no longer be possible.

Joshua 24, Nehemiah 8, Luke 9 and John 4:20, all suggest that Zion was Mount Gerizim, also referred to as *"Tabbur Haerez"* the *"navel of the earth,"* while Jerusalem is a city in Judah often referred to as a *"daughter of Zion."* The feminine symbolism not only referred to Zion, Wisdom, the Holy Spirit, the northern Ephraimite kingdom, which in effect would make it the bride, but to the embodiment of these symbols in the form of female Nazarene initiates; just as male Nazarene initiates embodied the Lord, righteousness, the laws of God and the southern kingdom of Judah. Hence, when Isaiah and John in Revelation talk about the bridegroom and the bride, they are in effect, from a political standpoint, referring to the re-unification of both kingdoms into the New Kingdom of Israel led by judges and councillors. From a religious standpoint, Jesus embraces Zion and by so doing, embraces the Holy Spirit, Wisdom and the female embodiment of this symbolism in the form of a *"daughter of Zion."*

If we ignore the feminine in any way and advocate Genesis 2 over Genesis 1, then from a religious, social and political standpoint, we are in effect denouncing the Holy Spirit, equality and democracy respectively.

Both Peter and Paul on the other hand, supported Genesis 2 and the social and political implications which follow on from it. The first time original sin and the inferior status of Eve is mentioned in the New Testament, is by Paul who as we saw above, did not believe that we were entitled to be *"justified by way of the law,"* an essential and inherent part of an equitable and democratic system. Hence, the term *"Holy Spirit"* was given a masculine connotation and instead referred to as the *"Holy Ghost."* In order for their religious beliefs to justify their political bias, both Paul and Peter would have had to advocate Gen. 2 and denounce Gen. 1 and Proverbs. Peter 3:1:

"In the same way you women must submit to your husbands, so that if there are any of them who disbelieve the gospel they may be won over without a word being said."

Corinthians 11:8 & 9:

"For man is not of the woman; but the woman of the man. Neither was the man created for the woman; but the woman for the man."

We all know that Genesis 2 is a scientific impossibility. As far as our genetic structure goes, creation is dependent on the joining together of two female x chromosomes from the sperm and ovum respectively in order for life to be possible. The extra x or y chromosomes in the sperm determine sexuality not life, when added to the extra x in the ovum. So therefore we have either a female child being x [life]+x [sex]; or a male child being x [life] + y [sex]. What is more, genetic inheritance is passed on through the mitochondria, the energy giving part of the cell which is only inherited from the mother. Even genetic engineering is reliant on an egg or ovum for a carbon copy or clone to be possible.

Jesus, in the Gospels, never once mentions original sin, the fall, Eve made from Adam's rib, Adam eating from the tree of knowledge or expulsion from the Garden of Eden. The only time that he ever makes mention or quotes from the creation stories is in Matthew 19:4 where he refers to Genesis 1:

"…he which made them at the beginning made them male and female."

Genesis 1:27:

"….male and female created he them."

Later in this chapter, he refers to the man and woman becoming one flesh. Men and women become one flesh in the sexual act and hence cleave to each other. As the Elohim is one in God and the Spirit or the Lord and Zion, so we become one symbolically through the sanctity of marriage. Through this act we are able to carry out the first command-ment, to replenish the earth. There is no *"sin"* implied in these words.

In the book of Jeremiah, where he prophecies the coming of Jacob-Israel from the north to embrace Zion, it says: 31:21:

"Build cairns to mark your way, set up signposts; make sure of the road, the path which you will tread. Come back, virgin Israel, come back to your

cities and towns. How long will you waver, my wayward child? For the Lord has created a new thing in the earth: a woman will play a man's part."

By playing *"a man's part,"* women in general have not only become lawyers, judges or priestesses again as Asenath, Miriam and Deborah were, but bake the two loaves of the Sabbath (Proverbs 9:5), for it is their bread and their body, their blood of the vine[169] that ensures the continuation of the first covenant Ephraim—Ephrathah, *"be fruitful and increase," "the firstborn of God."* Matthew 13:33:

"The kingdom of heaven is like unto leaven, which a woman took, and hid in three measures of meal, til the whole was leavened."

Today Christian women do not celebrate the Sabbath on a Friday evening as Hebrew women do and as early Christians did in Palestine, in Ireland and in the south of France. The inquisition during the middle ages was one of the biggest anti-Semitic and sexist drives in history. The holocaust over a period of two hundred years put to death close on nine million women who were shaved, made to walk naked through the streets and courts, raped, tortured and burnt at the stake as witches for celebrating Sabbath over a twenty-four hour period between Friday and Saturday evening.

The suppression of women and the denial of their right to Biblical study upheld a political motivation based on authority under a king, autocrat or dictator, which in turn advocates sacrificing the individual

---

169. The vineyard in Proverbs 31 is theirs as is the vineyard the bride's in "The Song of Songs"

for the benefit of the state. By subjugating women, the egalitarian concept of democracy itself was subjugated as symbolized by the *"daughter of Zion"* and a political philosophy of a *"polyarchy based on equality"* was regarded as a subversive movement that contradicted the church's teaching against women priests and in turn, the rights of the individual within the community. The law without democracy becomes an autocracy. Democracy without the law becomes anarchy. The one cannot exist without the other just as the laws of the prophets cannot exist without the Wisdom teachings. Due to this philosophy, the *"Holy Spirit,"* rather than being seen as a feminine concept, became the masculine *"Holy Ghost,"* a theory that not all early Christians agreed with, as seen in the Gnostic *"The Gospel of Philip"*:

"Some said, "Mary conceived by the holy spirit." They are in error. They do not know what they are saying. When did a woman ever conceive by a woman?" [170]

On closer examination, one thing stands out very clearly in the New Testament. Both the teachings of the Baptist and a Joshua are of the Holy Spirit, being the bride as symbolized by the Holy Spirit, Wisdom or Zion, and correspond to the teachings found in the Old Testament texts. Here are a few examples, the contradiction lying in the fact that the Old Testament is written in the feminine voice while the New Testament, in accordance with the male concept of a *"Holy Ghost,"* is

---

170. James M.Robinson. "The Nag Hammadi Library." HarperCollins. 1990.

written in the masculine voice. I would suggest that the New Testament quotes which so closely resemble the Old, were either the Wisdom teachings quoted by a male Nazarene, or were the Wisdom teachings taught by a female Nazarene herself.

OLD TESTAMENT:
Gen 1:2:
"And the earth was without form and void; and darkness was upon the face of the deep. And the Spirit of God moved upon the face of the waters."

Proverbs 8:22 & 30:
"The Lord possessed me in the beginning, or ever the earth was...Then I was by him, as one brought up with him...."

Wisdom of Solomon 9:1,2,9 & 18:
"O God of my father, and Lord of Mercy, who hast made all things with thy Word and ordained people through thy Wisdom...and Wisdom was with thee; which knoweth thy works, and was present when thou madest the world...and [we] were saved through Wisdom."

NEW TESTAMENT:
John 1:1, 8:42, 17:21:
"In the beginning was the word[171] *and the Word was with God and the Word was God."*
"...If God were your Father, ye would love me: for I proceedeth forth and came from God...."

---

171. The "word" in this instance being the Sophia, or word of Wisdom.

"I am come forth from the Father and am come into the world: again I leave the world, and go to the Father."

OLD TESTAMENT:
Proverbs 5:1:
"My son, attend to my wisdom, and bow thine ear to my understanding."

NEW TESTAMENT:
James 1:4 & 5:
"But let Patience have her perfect work, that ye may be perfect and entire, wanting nothing. If any of you lack Wisdom, let him ask of God, that giveth to all liberally, and upbraideth not; and it shall be given."

Luke 7:35, 11:13:
"But Wisdom is justified of all her children....If ye then, being evil, know how to give gifts unto your children: how much more shall your heavenly Father give the Holy Spirit to them that ask him?"

OLD TESTAMENT:
Proverbs 1:20 & 23:
"Wisdom crieth without, she uttereth her voice in the streets....behold, I will pour out my Spirit unto you, I will make know my Word unto you."

NEW TESTAMENT:
John 15:26
"But when the Comforter is come, whom I will send unto you from the Father, even the Spirit of truth, which proceedeth from the Father, shall testify of me."

John 17:17:
"Thy Word is Truth."

John 15:3:

"Now ye are clean through the word which I have spoken unto you."

OLD TESTAMENT:
Proverbs 3:1 & 8:7 & 8:
"My son, forget not my law; but let thine heart keep my commandments.
For my mouth shall speak Truth...all the words of my mouth are in
Righteousness..."

NEW TESTAMENT:
John 14 & 16, 8:31 & 32, 8:45 & 46.
"I am the way, the Truth, and the life;"
"If ye continue in my Word, then are ye my disciples indeed; And ye
shall know the Truth, and the Truth shall make you free."
"....And because I tell you the Truth, ye believe me not....And if I say
the Truth, why do ye not believe me?..."

OLD TESTAMENT:
Proverbs 23:9:
"Speak not in the ears of a fool; for he will despise the wisdom of thy
words."

NEW TESTAMENT:
Matthew 7:6:
"Give not that which is holy unto the dogs, neither cast ye your pearls
before swine, lest they trample them under their feet, and turn again and
rend you."

OLD TESTAMENT:
Proverbs 8:35 & 9:5:
"For who so findeth me findeth life."
"Come, eat of my bread, and drink of the wine which I have mingled."

NEW TESTAMENT:
John 5:24, 6:47, 6:54 & 14:6:

"In very truth I tell you, whoever heeds what I say and puts his trust in him who sent me has eternal life."

"Verily, verily, I say unto you, He that believeth on me hath everlasting life."

"Whoever eats my flesh and drinks my blood has eternal life."

"I am the way and the truth and the life; no one comes to the Father except by me."

OLD TESTAMENT:
Proverbs 8:36:
"But he that sinneth against me wrongeth his won soul: all they that hate me love death."

NEW TESTAMENT:
John 15:18:
"If the world hates you, it hated me first, as you know well."

John 16:25:
"These things have I spoken unto you in Proverbs: but the time cometh, when I shall no more speak unto you in Proverbs, but I shall show you plainly of the Father."

Acts 2:1,2,3 & 4:
"And when the day of Pentecost was fully come, they were all with one accord in one place. And suddenly there came a sound from heaven as of a rushing wind, and it filled all the house where they were sitting. And there appeared unto them tongues like as of fire and it sat upon each of them. And they were all filled with the Holy Spirit, and began to speak with other tongues, as the Spirit gave them utterance."

OLD TESTAMENT:
Wisdom of Solomon 10:21:
"For Wisdom openeth the mouth of the dumb, and made the tongues of them that cannot speak eloquent."

Proverbs. 1:23:

"...I will make known my word unto you."

It appears that the deeper meaning behind Christian teachings is that of the Gospel of the Holy Spirit, the bride of the Lord being Zion, which is sent to guide us in righteousness and justice as She does in Proverbs and the Wisdom of Solomon 9:10:

"O send her out of thy holy heavens, and from the throne of thy glory, that being present She may labour with, that I may know what is pleasing unto thee."

The fact that the disciples have a revelation of the Holy Spirit at Pentecost, is totally in keeping with Hebrew belief. The Samaritans ascend Mount Gerizim-Zion at Pentecost and celebrate the giving of the law, whilst it is Wisdom, Zion, the bride of the Lord who leads us in righteousness and justice in Proverbs. As such, she is democracy itself, the container of the law, the Ark. Proverbs 4:8 & 9:

"Exalt her, and she shall promote thee: she shall bring thee to honour, when thou dost embrace her. She shall give to thine head an ornament of grace: a crown of glory shall she deliver to thee."

Isaiah 62:3 & 5:

"Thou shalt also be a crown of glory in the hand of the Lord, and a royal diadem in the hand of thy God....For as a young man marrieth a virgin, so shall thy sons marry thee: and as the bridegroom rejoiceth over the bride, so shall God rejoice over thee."

The comparison between the Old Testament and the New Testament texts suggest that the Wisdom teachings, symbolised by Mount Gerizim in a geographical sense and the bride of God, being the Holy Spirit, Zion or Shekinah in a spiritual sense, formed the basis of early Christianity, as taught by the Nazarenes, both male and female within the Essene order. The Shekinah in turn, plays an integral part within the Sabbath, and it is to the celebration of the Sabbath, which is so similar to the Gospel story of the Last Supper, that we shall now turn.

Chapter Eight

Sabbath

I suspect that the death of Jesus as we know it, is a hodge podge of edited works that incorporate Yom Kippur, the Sabbath, the Passover, Pentecost as well as the Holy Marriage and the deaths of the Baptist, Theudas, James Zebedee, James the righteous and Judas, all of which have been superimposed over each other. But for the moment, we will look at the Last Supper, which I believe was the Sabbath held during the Passover week and the conclusion of the wedding ceremony as is Samaritan practice to this day.

The Passover is a celebration in every generation where each and every individual experiences liberation from slavery and is saved, or redeemed, as the Passover represents a night of redemption from oppression. From midday on the eve of the Passover being the 14th of Nisan, all leven is removed from the house. During Biblical times, the *"Hallel,"* which is an abbreviation of the word *"Hallelujah,"* was sung an hour or two after midday on the 14th of Nisan.[172] Today the

---

172. "Holy Bible." King James Version.

"*Hallel*" forms part of the Passover "*Haggadah*" sung after sunset on the 14th.

> "*...I will give thanks unto Thee, for Thou hast answered me,*
> *And art become my salvation.*
> *The stone which the builders rejected / Is become the chief corner-stone.*
> *This is the Lord's doing; / It is marvellous in our eyes...*
> *Blessed be he that cometh in the name of the Lord; / We bless you out of the house of the Lord.*" [173]

The "*Hallel*" is a quote from Psalms 113–118. 118:26:

> "*Blessed is he that cometh in the name of the Lord....*"

According to all four Gospels, the "*Hallel*" quoted from Psalm 118:26 which is sung on the 14th of Nisan after midday, was sung when Jesus rode into Jerusalem on a donkey on the first day of the week, known to Christians as "*palm Sunday.*" This means that according to Hebrew traditions, the Passover with the eating of the sacrificial lamb did not occur on the night of the Last Supper, but six days *before* and also implies that the "*Hallel*" was most probably not sung to a specific individual called Jesus, but was part and parcel of the Passover festival being held in Jerusalem at that time. Matthew 21:9, Mark 11:9, Luke 19:38 & John 12:13:

> "*Blessed is he who comes in the name of the Lord!...*"

---

173. Nahum. N. Glatzer. "The Passover Haggadah." Schocken Books. 1981.

During the Temple period, animal sacrifices were carried out at the Temple continually, from the 15th of Nisan, known as the day of *"holy convocation,"* and during the whole week of the Passover which lasts for seven days.[174] In preparation for these sacrifices, vendors sat in the temple selling animals for sacrifice, which would be bought by those who came to Jerusalem for the Passover and given to the High Priest in the hope that their sins would be forgiven and they would be redeemed. In such a way, the wealth of the poor was plundered in the interests of religion. Any person who expected to find peace and prayer within the house of God would have been shocked to find that the Temple had been turned into a market with all the dirt, noise and bustle of money changing hands, the equivalent of Notre Dame Cathedral being filled with sheep, goats and doves and all their excrement scattered over the church floor. Matthew 21:12 & 13:

"And Jesus went into the temple of God, and cast out all them that sold and bought in the temple, and overthrew the tables of the moneychangers, and the seats of them that sold doves. And said unto them, It is written, My house shall be called the house of prayer; but ye have made it a den of thieves."

On the Passover evening, being Sunday the 14th of Nisan, Jesus returned to Bethany for the Passover meal where a lamb was slain at sunset and whatever was not eaten was consumed by fire. I suspect that

---

174. Ibid.

the Passover prayers known as the *"Haggadah"* could have possibly have been included in this Gospel at one time, but have since been edited out. Matthew 21:17

"And he left them, and went out of the city into Bethany; and he lodged there."

Matthew 21:18 then goes on to relate the events of the following day, after the *"Hallel"* was sung, which would bring us to Monday, the 15th Nisan.

"Now in the morning he returned into the city…"

In John 12:24 we have a reference to the feast of firstfruits, when the harvest sheaf, the *"Omer,"* is waved and this occurred on Tuesday, the 16th of Nisan, which again suggests that the Passover with the singing of the *"Hallel"* and the *"sacrificial lamb"* had occurred two days before as it still does today:

"Except a corn of wheat fall into the ground and die, it abideth alone: but if it die, it bringeth forth much fruit."

In Matthew 22:1–10 there is a reference to the marriage feast, which according to Samaritan custom, would have occurred on the fourth day after the first Sabbath, which brings us to Wednesday, the 17th of Nisan:

"Go ye therefore into the highways, and as many as ye find, bid to marriage…"

In Matthew 26:6 Jesus again returns to Bethany, to the house of Simon the leper, which brings us to Thursday evening, the 18th of Nisan:

"Now when Jesus was in Bethany, in the house of Simon the leper…"

The next day, in Matthew 26:17, the disciples go to prepare a place to eat which brings us to Friday, the 19th of Nisan. Although verse 17 suggests that this was the Passover meal, Matthew 21:9 contradicts this view where the Passover had already occurred in accordance with Hebrew customs where the *"Hallel"* is sung after midday on the eve of the Passover being the 14th of Nisan.

"Now when the even was come, he sat down with the twelve..."

On the 19th and 20th of Nisan, the Sabbath, which takes place during a twenty four hour period, was celebrated. On the eve of Friday the 19th we have the blessing of the bread and the wine, during the early hours of the morning we have the prayers in the Garden of Gethsemane whilst during the last hours of Saturday the 20th of Nisan Hebrews say a prayer in honour of the hour of the death of Moses. It appears that the Last Supper, although taking place during the Passover week where unleavened bread would have still been eaten for seven days, did not take place on the 14th of Nisan when the sacrificial lamb was eaten but on the 19th of Nisan. This would in turn, from a symbolic point of view, associate the Last Supper with the deeper meaning behind Sabbath, where the Shekinah, a feminine symbol, is invited into the house, as opposed to the symbolism of the sacrificial lamb. This would mean that the Last Supper was not a cannibalistic rite, eating the flesh and drinking the blood of a firstborn, but a celebration of the bride of God. The Shekinah is believed to be the *"in-dwelling presence of God,"* a divine light,[175] or as this author would put it, the Spirit of God being the Holy Spirit.

---

175. Louis Jacobs. "The Jewish Religion." Oxford University Press. 1995.

Central to the Last Supper, is the bread and wine, two elements that are necessary in a Hebrew Sabbath. The sacrificial lamb of the Passover is noticeably absent from the meal, suggesting that the night on which the Last Supper occurred, was the Friday evening with the beginning of the Sabbath at sunset. Because Paul eliminated all the Hebrew elements in early Christianity, the Sabbath being one of them, and because the Church in Rome followed his teachings and banned all Hebrew traditions, as they did in Ireland, the Gospels that we have today follow the Adonis line where it is the Father of the Temple rather than the bride or mother of the house who leads us into the Sabbath and the welcoming of the Shekinah into the house.

Hebrew Sabbath consists of the following:

1. The Mother Lights the two candles representing God and the Spirit or the Shekinah. The menorah, the seven branched candle stick relates to the seven days of creation, the seven days in a lunar cycle, the seven seals spoken of in Revelation, the seven chakras, the seven colours in a rainbow and the seven emanations or steps which resulted from the Spirit/Shekinah moving over the face of the waters. Proverbs 9:1:

"Wisdom hath builded her house, she hath hewn out her seven pillars."

2. On the Sabbath the Hebrews advocate peace-Salem. The day of rest is a day of peace, known as *"menhuah."* We make peace with our fellow man. In Biblical times it was the one day where the servant was considered equal to the master, where everyone was royalty and everyone was equal. Jesus washes the disciples feet and today we say *"peace be with you"* as a Christian greeting. It is the equivalent of the Hebrew Shalom and the Arabic Salaam. (Compare with Revelation 19:10 & John 13:14)

3. After lighting the candles, the father of the house blesses 2 loaves of bread made by plating 2 pieces of dough interwoven together as

well as the wine, both of which are made and prepared by his wife. Central to the Last Supper, is the blessing of the bread and the wine. Proverbs 9:3 & 5:

"She hath sent forth her maidens, she crieth upon the highest place of the city…come, eat of my bread, and drink of the wine which I have mingled."

Today, the cup that was used at the Last Supper is believed to be the Holy Grail. This grail is supposed to carry the *"blood"* of Christ, or the anointed. I believe that this *"blood"* is symbolic of a *"bloodline."* In Genesis, Joseph was a cup bearer to the Pharaoh and possesses a silver cup of his own. The bloodline that the cup holds, goes from Joseph, to Nun, to Ephraim and to Joshua, both in the Old and the New Testaments. Genesis 44:2:

"…And put my cup, the silver cup, in the sacks mouth of the youngest…."

4. The father of the household then reads from Proverbs 31 and praises his wife. [As a Christian woman I would love to see the day…] The central core of Proverbs is about Wisdom, the bride of the Lord, equated with the Christian Holy Spirit. Proverbs 1:20 & 23:

"Wisdom crieth without: she uttereth her voice in the streets…behold, I will pour out my Spirit unto you, I will make known my words to you."

The Sabbath not only symbolizes the seven days of creation, but celebrates the Holy Marriage of God and the Spirit. Friday night is considered to be a representation of the consecration of the marriage between the Lord and Zion.[176] Hence, in the Gospels we have that illusive *"beloved"* who lay on the breast of Jesus.

---

176. Pinchas H.Peli. "The Jewish Sabbath." Schocken Books. 1988.

5. Before sunrise, worshippers enter a garden and recite Solomon's Song of Songs. In the Gospels, the disciples enter the Garden of Gethsemane. On the Sabbath morning which represents part of the Holy marriage, the Lord or the lover, gives Zion, or the beloved gifts.[177] From the Eve of the Sabbath until sunrise, all prayers deal with creation, where God and the Spirit are one. Hence the reciting of the Song of Songs which deals with the bridegroom and the bride. Proverbs 8:1,2 & 23:

"Doth not wisdom cry? and understanding put forth her voice? She standeth in the top of high places by the way in the places of paths:...the Lord possessed me in the beginning of his way, before his works of old."

6. After sunrise, Hebrews go to the synagogue where they recite the Pentateuch-the Law. The Sabbath afternoon service which is part of the Holy Marriage, represents the union of the Lord and Zion, or the lover and the beloved.[178] Proverbs 8:3,4, & 20:

"She crieth at the gates, at the entry of the city, at the coming in at the doors: unto you, o men, I call; and my voice is to the sons of man....I lead in the way of Righteousness, in the midst of the paths of judgement."

7. At the end of the Sabbath prayers are said with wine and spices, mourning the death of Sabbath or Shekinah. The spices are kept so that their aroma will last throughout the week until another Sabbath is reborn. Sabbath is the Alpha and Omega, the *"end of the beginning"* of

---

177. Ibid.
178. Ibid.

the seven days of creation and the *"beginning of the end."* [179] Through the last enactment, the death of Sabbath, we are redeemed to the on going cycle of creation and a new week is resurrected at sunset on the Saturday evening. In other words, by believing in Genesis 1 where we are made in the image of God and are therefore immortal, and by acknowledging the Spirit or feminine component of God, we have life everlasting and are saved from death through Wisdom. Proverbs 8:35:

"For who so findeth me findeth life..."

8:36:

"...all they that hate me love death." (or mortality. Gen2.)

Wisdom of Solomon 9:1,2,9 & 18:

"O God of my father, and Lord of mercy, who hast made all things with thy Word and ordained people through thy Wisdom...and Wisdom was with thee; which knoweth thy works, and was present when thou madest the world...and we were saved through Wisdom."

8. Hebrews pray that the peace of the Sabbath and the equality experienced within it, democracy, will in the future not just be lived out on one day, but throughout the rest of the week. Creation (Genesis 1), revelation (be fruitful and increase) and redemption, reclaiming another seven days (Sabbath) are the three in one. They also relate to the past, present and future, experienced on one day of the week which means

---

179. Ibid.

that we have a brief glimpse of eternity.[180] In Proverbs 6: 20 & 23 the balance between the commandments and the working of the law through democracy is again explored:

"Keep thy father's commandments, and forsake not the law of thy mother....For commandment is a lamp; and the law is the light;"

Politically speaking, the Shekinah is a symbol of racial and social tolerance where everyone is *"royalty"* so to speak and everyone is considered to be equal in the eyes of God. The whole of the Sabbath aims at equality and freedom and so, through Sabbath becoming part of our daily experience, we will be redeemed into a world of freedom and equality. In other words, we will be redeemed to Zion-the watchtower. Hence the reciting of Psalms 126:

"When the Lord returned us to Zion we were like dreamers....Our mouths filled with laughter and our tongues flowed with song."

This occurs when God and the divine presence, the Shekinah-Sabbath-Zion, are reunited. In Judaism and Christianity, the Shekinah or Holy Spirit will come to direct us throughout our lives every day of the week and she is the Spirit of Gen.1. Freedom and equality means not being subject to slavery or subservience and where male and female are both made in the image of the Supreme being and respected as such.

---

180. Pinchas H.Peli. "The Jewish Sabbath." Schocken Books. 1988.

What I would like the reader to note, is that the sequence of events in the Sabbath, runs parallel to the sequence of events of the Last Supper and coupled with the misnomer of the Passover and *"Hallel"* occurring on the night of the 14th of Nisan as Matthew's text suggests; the harvest festival on the 16th of Nisan as John's text suggests; and the Last supper on the night of the 19th of Nisan; implies that the authors who wrote a biographical account of these events were ignorant of Hebrew customs. The Greek authors who wrote them, even if they had been converted to Christianity, would not have practised Passover, Sabbath, Pentecost, the feast of Tabernacles or Rosh Hoshannah and therefore the reference to the *"Hallel"* would have made no sense to them neither would John's reference to the *"Omer."* But even more startling is the fact that between 70 A.D. and 300 A.D, the Gospels were edited, certain texts being deemed undesirable while others were retained, resulting in four distinct Gospels that do no always bare each other out. Even within the separate texts, we find editing anomalies. For example, consider John Chapter 14 during the Last Supper which ends with the words:

"...come, let us go!"

But following this statement comes chapter 15, where the group in the upper room appear not to have left as they did at the end of chapter 14. We are obviously looking at two separate incidence that have been so well glued together that it is difficult to find the truth in either. If the Last Supper was the Sabbath as this author believes it to have been, where men and women would have sat around one table, and that these men and women were Nazarenes in accordance with Numbers 6, then it is highly likely that some of the quotes mentioned in the Gospels would have been said by a woman. I believe that in John, we have two stories, one of a man and one of a woman. But the story about the woman has been edited and the words and actions attributed to her have been given a masculine gender under the name of *"Joshua,"* a name which a woman could have carried if she was an Essene, or *"Essa"* which in Arabic means *"Jesus,"*[181] and regarded as a *"Essaioi"* or a follower of Jesus. John begins chapter 15 with the words:

"I am the true vine...."

By comparing these words in the NT to the OT, it becomes obvious that they were quotes from the Old Testament which were familiar and easily recognisable by any Hebrew at the time, or they were said by a woman. In Ezekiel 19:10 he says:

"Thy mother is like a vine in thy blood, planted by the waters: she was fruitful and full of branches by reason of many waters. And she had strong rods for sceptres of them that bare rule...and her stature was exalted among the thick branches, and she appeared in her height with the multitude of her branches."

Proverbs 31:16:

"She considereth a field, and buyeth it: with the fruit of her hands she planteth a vineyard."

Song of Songs 8:12 Bride:

"My vineyard, which is mine, is before me: thou, O Solomon, must have a thousand, and those that keep the fruit thereof two hundred."

John 15:4 & 5:

---

181. Ahmed Osman. "The House of the Messiah." Grafton. 1993.

"Abide in me, and I in you. As the branch cannot bear fruit of itself, except it abide in the vine, no more can ye except ye abide in me. I am the vine, ye are the branches."

As with the Sabbath and the Shekinah, the symbolism used by John at the Last Supper in chapter 15, is feminine in origin. The vine is clearly a feminine symbol. If John 15 was said by a man, then he is quoting from the Old Testament and referring to the mother of all Israel, as opposed to referring to himself. If, however, John 15 was said by a woman, then she is referring to herself as this symbol.

John goes on to say in his First Epistle 5:9, that there are three witnesses on earth, these being the Spirit, the water and the blood and that these three agree in one. They relate to the Spirit being the bride of God and the blood and water of birth. The words *"No one sees the father except by me,"* if said by a woman instead of a man, relates to the birth of a child, whereby a new born baby will not see it's father's face, unless it is born of it's mother. Spiritually, we are reborn through the Holy Spirit or Shekinah before we can see the Kingdom of God. As such, this woman is the door through which all life comes and equates with Malkuth-Zion-Tau-the mark-and Shiloh which is a conduit for water. John 3:5:

"...Except a man be born of water and of the Spirit, he cannot enter into the kingdom of God."

In John 16:21 at the Last Supper it reads:

"A woman in labour is in pain because her time has come; but when her baby is born she forgets the anguish in her joy that a child has been born into the world."

When carrying a child, the baby is cushioned and protected by the waters of the womb. Hence, the mother becomes *"a living well."* Proverbs 18:4:

"…the well-spring of wisdom as a flowing brook."

Song of Songs 4:12:

"A garden inclosed is my sister, my spouse; a spring shut up, a fountain sealed."

In pre-historic religions the door was equated with the Goddess, as it is through women, or the door-way of the virginia that we are born into the world. In Proverbs 8:3 & 34 says:

"She crieth at the gates, at the entry to the city, at the coming in at doors…Blessed is the man that heareth me, watching daily at my gates, waiting at the posts of my doors."

Hence the words in John 10:9 refer to Wisdom as quoted by a man or were said by a female Nazarene who associated herself with this symbol:

"I am the door: by me if any person enter in, they shall be saved,…"

Proverbs 9:18:

"…and we were saved through wisdom."

What I propose is the following: The Gospels as we know them, were complied and edited by Constantine's Bishops at Nicea in 325 B.C., who had little to no real knowledge of Hebrew customs or the Old Testament due to the fact that Paul had eliminated all Hebrew elements within the early Christian church. They saw the Old Testament as insignificant and did not incorporate it into New Testament interpretation. The Last Supper was the Sabbath with it's message of the Shekinah, Holy Spirit or Wisdom, acknowledging the *"beloved"* by quoting from Proverbs and reading the Song of Songs in a Garden of Gethsemane, the Passover having occurred six days before with the singing of Hallel and the sacrificial lamb. The wedding ceremony and the Passover feast as well as the Sabbath have been superimposed over the crucifixion of one or a number of the Teachers of Righteousness, which I believe occurred at a later date.

I believe that the message of democracy through the Holy Spirit was not only a teaching, but was acted out by a woman, our biggest clue being the *"thirty pieces of silver"* payed to Judas, which was the price given in Leviticus for a woman who wanted to make a singular vow of a Nazarene. Lev. 27:4:

"And if it be a female, then thy estimation shall be thirty shekels…."

If Judas had betrayed a man, then the payment would have been fifty pieces of silver. Lev.27:3:

"…And thy estimation shall be of the male from twenty years old even unto sixty years old, even thy estimation shall be fifty shekels of silver, after the shekel of the sanctuary."

Through historical fact it is possible to track down this woman who symbolized democratic thinking, a philosophy that Herod Agrippa 1 clearly did not agree with to the extent that he set himself up as a dictator God. The Herod kings are the clue to the priestess hidden within our Gospels and the democracy that she advocated.

Chapter Nine.

The Bride

Herod Agrippa 1, the brother of Herodias, the son of Aristobulus and the grandson of Herod the Great, sought to become king of Judea throughout his life, a mission that he finally accomplished in 37 A.D. when Caligula became Emperor of Rome. He was hindered by Herod the Great's will which was written in favour of Herod's Samaritan wife, Malthake.

At the time the Levitical priesthood in Judea accepted Herod the Great, an Edomite descended from Esau (the twin brother of Jacob who had stolen his birthright in Genesis) because they hoped that his successor, the son of Mariamme 1, a Maccabean princess, descendent of the tribe of Levi through Judas Maccabeus, would restore this dynasty through the female line. Instead, Herod murdered Mariamme 1 and his son Aristobulus who would become king, and left the throne to his son Archelaus, a Samaritan through the female line of his wife Malthake. This was anathema to the Sadducees who neither associated with nor touched Samaritans. They would have resisted being led by a king whose mother was a Samaritan, as decent is always followed through the female line.

Malthake's son, Archelaus, went to Rome to plead for the title of king in 4 A.D., but was denied the monarchy by the Emperor Augustus and instead made ethnarch of Judea and Samaria. In 6 A.D. he was deposed and sent to Gaul, a situation which was no doubt, encouraged by the Sadducees. The title of king according to Herod the Great's will then fell to Malthake's second son, Herod Antipas who was given the tetrarch of Galilee and Perea, which was Jordan, the river flowing from the Sea of Galilee to the Dead sea. Herod Antipas was not made king or tetrarch of Judea or Samaria, a situation which would have suited the Sadducees. His half brother Philip, son of Herod's wife Cleopatra, was given the tetrarch of Trachonitis, Ithuraea, Gaulanitis, Auranitis and Baneas.[182]

HERODIAN FAMILY TREE.

Herod the Great.

m. Mariamme 1   m.Mariamme 11   m.Malthake   m.Cleopatra

I   I   I   I

Aristobulus   Herod (Philip)   Archelaus & Herod Antipas   Philip

I

I   m.Herodias/ daughter is Salome

Herod Agrippa 1   Herodias

I

Herod Agrippa 11   Bernice   Drusilla

---

182. O.Odelain and R.Seguineau. "Dictionary of Proper Names and Places in the Bible." Robert Hale. 1991.

Max Dimont's view of Herod Antipas is at variance to what we have been led to believe. According to this author, Herod Antipas was an exceptional ruler with a stable government and brought prosperity to the territories that he administered.[183] Burton Mack supports Dimont's views, adding that Galilee, the circuit of nations, known as *"the land of the Gentiles,"* during the time of the Gospels, prided itself on having no loyalty to foreign kings or the Gods that they worshipped.[184]

Herodias, the daughter of the murdered Aristobulus and granddaughter of Herod the Great, is said to have been married to Herod Philip, the half brother of Herod Antipas by Mariamme 11. But according to Robin Lane Fox, Josephus makes no mention of this marriage, he only mentions her marriage to Herod Antipas, which means that she might not have been previously married to anyone[185] and this in turn would put Salome's parentage under question. According to the synoptic Gospels, (Mat.14:3, Mark 6:17 & Luke 3:19) Antipas married *"his brother Philip's wife,"* the Gospel of Luke 3:1 implying that this Philip was the son of Cleopatra rather than Herod Philip, the son of Mariamme 11.

"Now in the fifteenth year of the reign of Tiberius Caesar, Pontius Pilate being governor of Judea, and Herod being tetrarch of Galilee, and his brother Philip tetrarch of Ituraea and of the region of Trachonitis,…

But Herod the tetrach, being reproved by him for Herodias his brother Philip's wife,… "

183. Max.I.Dimont. "Jews, God and History." Nal Penguin. 1962.

184. Burton Mack. "The Lost Gospel of Q." Harper Collins. 1994.

185. Robin Lane Fox. "The Unauthorized Version." Penguin. 1992.

Salome would therefore be this Philip's daughter, which makes sense when we consider that Herodias would have been approximately fourteen when Philip became tetrarch of Trachonitis in 4 B.C, a perfect age for marriage at that time. Philip died between 33 and 34 A.D [186] leaving Herodias a widow. According to Josephus, Herod Antipas married Herodias in 34 A.D., after the death of Herod Philip in 33–34 A.D., when she was in her late thirties or early forties,[187] which would mean that Salome was in her late twenties at the time of her father's death.

According to the synoptic Gospels, the Baptist accused Antipas of breaking the law by marrying *"his brother Philip's wife."* If this Philip was the tetrarch of Trachonitis rather than Herod Philip who was not included in Herod the Great's will, then Herod Antipas married his half brother's widow, Philip the son of Cleopatra.

According to Leviticus 18:16 and 20:21, a man may not have sexual relations with his brother's wife and thereby commit adulatory. Although the texts do not clearly state whether this includes a half brother with a different mother or a deceased sibling, theologians interpret it as such, though the issue could be open to debate.

"Thou shalt not uncover the nakedness of thy brother's wife: it is thy brother's nakedness."

"And if a man shall take his brother's wife, it is an unclean thing: he hath uncovered his brother's nakedness; they shall be childless."

---

186. O.Odelain and R. Seguineau. "Dictionary of Proper Names and Places in the Bible." Robert Hale. 1991. pg. 459.

187. Robin Lane Fox. "The Unauthorized Version." Penguin. 1992.

Deuteronomy 25:5–6 on the other hand, states that if the brother dies without an heir, which according to historical records was the case, Philip the son of Cleopatra dying in 33–34 A.D. without a male heir,[188] then according to the laws of a *"levirate marriage,"*[189] it is the duty of his brother to marry the widow.

"If brethren dwell together, and one of them die, and have no child, the wife of the dead shall not marry without unto a stranger: her husband's brother shall go in unto her, and take her to him to wife, and perform the duty of an husband's brother unto her."

In order to perform this duty, Antipas divorced the daughter of Aretas, as according to *"The Dead Seas Scrolls"* a man was only allowed to have one wife,[190] Deuteronomy, 24:1–2, stating that divorce was permissible under the law.

"When a man hath taken a wife, and married her, and it come to pass that she find no favour in his eyes, because he hath found some uncleanness in her: then let him write her a bill of divorcement, and give it in her hand, and send her out of his house. And when she is departed out of his house, she may go and be another man's wife."

The Gospels of Matthew and Mark do not denounce Antipas for divorcing his previous wife, but for marrying his *"brother Philip's wife,"* which according to the law, was permissible. This could be due to the fact that Antipas divorced the daughter of Aretas long before he

---

188. O.Odelain and R.Seguineau. "Dictionary of Proper Names and Places in the Bible." Robert Hale. 1991.

189. Louis Jacobs. "The Jewish Religion." Oxford University Press. 1995.

190. Damascus Document. History and Exhortation. V11

married Herodias, which could also imply that he did not divorce her in order to marry Herodias as he was already divorced.

As for Herodias's relationship with Antipas, according to Hebrew law, there is no injunction against their marriage. There is no law stating that you cannot marry your half brother's (Aristobulus, son of Mariamme 1) daughter, especially if you don't share the same mother or grandmother. The matrilineal line is twice removed with only the patrilineal line intact. According to Leviticus 18, an uncle can marry his niece,[191] Herodias being a half niece to Antipas. In our Gospels, however, Herodias and Antipas are believed to be condemned by the Baptist for marrying against the law, which if we take half brothers who have different mothers and the levarite law concerning widows into account, was not necessarily the case.

I suspect that the authors of Matthew and Mark, who much like Paul supported the Herodian camp under Herod Agrippa 1 and 11, and/or their later editors, sort to discredit Antipas and Herodias in order to achieve their own religious and political ends. Matthew and Mark tell the story of Herod and Herodias in the past tense and not in consecutive order, while Luke mentions Herod Antipas in consecutive order and admonishes him for putting the Baptist into prison. Luke 3:19 & 20:

---

191. Louis Jacobs. "The Jewish Religion." Oxford University Press. 1995.

"But Herod the tetrarch, being reproved by him for Herodias his brother Philip's wife, and for all the evils which Herod had done, Added yet this above all, that he shut up John in prison."

In this text his reference to Herodias is not explicit. For all we know, the Baptist could have reproved him for *not* marrying Herodias, his brother's wife, in accordance with levarite marriage. We only interpret it as him reproving them for marrying each other due to the quotations found in Matthew and Mark.

If anyone was guilty of sexual relations against the law, then it was Herod Agrippa 11, son of Herod Agrippa 1, grandson of Aristobulus, great grandson of Mariamme 1 and supporter of the Roman Empire, a convert of Paul who baptised him[192] and who had an incestuous relationship with his sister Bernice.[193] Acts 25:23, 26:28 & 30:

"...And on the morrow, when Agrippa was come, and Bernice, with great pomp, and was entered into the place of hearing, with the chief captains, and principal men of the city, at Festus commandment Paul was brought forth...Then Agrippa said unto Paul, Almost thou persuadest me to be a Christian....And when he had thus spoken, the king rose up, and the governor, and Bernice and they sat with them:...."

According to the Gospels, the Baptist was put to death shortly after Herod Antipas married Herodias, which historically gives us a date of 34 or 35 A.D. Such a discrepancy proves that from an historical point of

---

192. Barbara Thiering. "Jesus the Man." Doubleday.1992.

193. O.Odelain and R. Seguineau. "Dictionary of Proper Names and Places in the Bible." Robert Hale. 1991.

view, the Gospels are inaccurate. Within the Biblical texts, especially the
Gospel of John, the story of the Baptist and a *"Jesus"* could have been
superimposed over each other. It was the Baptist who was condemned
to death in 35 A.D. after Herodias married Antipas in 34 A.D.² when
Tiberius was Emperor of Rome, Pontius Pilate was procurator of Judea
and Caiaphas was High Priest. This date is important because:

1. Someone, who I believe to have been the Baptist, was put on trial
during the Passover of 35 A.D. by the Sadducees, Pontius Pilate and
Herod Antipas after he married Herodias in 34 A.D.

2. During a religious Hebrew festival in 35 A.D. Pontius Pilate
ordered the massacre of the Samaritans at Mount Gerizim, most probably to suppress an uprising that had occurred due to the rumour that
a *"King of Israel"* had entered Jerusalem;

3. During the Passover of 36 A.D. Caiaphas was replaced as high
priest by Jonathan, the son of Annas;

4. In the autumn of 36 A.D. Pontius Pilate was deposed and put to
death under the orders of Tiberius,[194] the Emperor who had denied
Herod Agrippa 1 the title of king.

In March 37 A.D. Tiberius died and Caligula took his place, giving
Herod Agrippa 1 what he had long sought after by giving him the title
"King of the Jews."[195] Agrippa 1 was educated at the Roman imperial
court after the execution of his father by Herod the Great. He was a
popular ruler amongst the Jews, not surprisingly as his grandmother

194. O.Odelain and R. Seguineau. "Dictionary of Proper Names and Places in the Bible."
Robert Hale. 1991.

195. Barbara Thiering. "Jesus the Man." Doubleday. 1992.

was Mariamme 1, the Maccabean princess. He was however, totally opposed to the Christians and persecuted them. Like the Sadducees, he was opposed to rule under a Samaritan, being Archelaus and later, Herod Antipas.

Herod Agrippa 1 achieved his aims in more ways than one and through his influence, the Samaritan line was removed from Israel, being the northern kingdoms of Galilee. Herod Antipas, a Samaritan by virtue of his matrilineal line, and his wife Herodias were then exiled to Lugdunum (Lyon in France) leaving Agrippa 1 as the sole heir of Herod the Great's kingdom. I suspect that it was through Archelaus and Herod Antipas that the French Merovingian dynasty arose, a dynasty that practised many Hebrew customs, one of which was growing their hair long in the manner of the Nazarenes.

I believe that the historic data, which at first contradicts the Gospels, can in fact, lead us to some understanding of the truth. Taking the historical data into account, I hope to prove below that the Baptist was put to death during Caiaphas's term in office when Pontius Pilate was in Jerusalem and Herod Antipas was in Samaria in 35 A.D., whilst our *"Jesus,"* instead of being crucified in 30 A.D. or even 35 A.D, was in fact crucified by Herod Agrippa 1 in 44 A.D. when he was approaching his fiftieth year. This would mean that he was born somewhere between 7 B.C. and 1 B.C. John 8:57:

"Then said the Jews unto him, Thou art not yet fifty years old, and hast thou seen Abraham."

If a Jesus was referred to as the *"King of Israel"* as John 1:49 and 12:13 suggests,

"...thou art the King of Israel..."

then Herod Agrippa, who held the title of *"King of the Jews"* given to him by Caligula in 37 A.D., would have seen Jesus as a political threat to his kingdom. A closer look at the Gospels also proves that a *"Jesus"* was still alive in 35 A.D. when Pilate ordered the massacre at Mount Gerizim,[196] where no doubt, both Samaritan and Galilean Hebrews had come to celebrate one of their Hebrew festivals. Pilate's actions would have been supported by Herod Agrippa 1. Luke 13:1 makes reference to this incident:

"There were present at that season some that told him of the Galileans, whose blood Pilate had mingled with their sacrifices."

In order to track down a female Essene, the bride of a Jesus and the embodiment of the Holy Spirit, I would like to take a closer look at the Gospel of John. His text is noticeably different from the synoptics. He does not give a Judaic genealogy for Joshua which is in keeping with his view that he was the *"King of Israel;"* his is considered to be more mystical and spiritual; he is not consecutive with the synoptic Gospels; and his text differs in seven important areas:

1. Although the Baptist's arrest is mentioned, the context in which John has put it could relate to the past, present or, as I believe, a future date. John 3:24.

"For John was not yet cast into prison."

2. John never once mentions the marriage of Antipas to Herodias.

3. In John 10:40, it appears that the Baptist is still alive just prior to Joshua's arrest by the temple priests.

---

196. O.Odelain and R.Seguineau. "Dictionary of Proper Names and Places in the Bible." Robert Hale. 1991.

"And went away again beyond Jordan into the place where John bap-tized; and there he abode..."

3. The Baptist's death and beheading is noticeably absent as it is in the Gospel of Luke.

4. But most important, the miraculous catch of a multitude of fish mentioned in Luke 5 which occurs at the beginning of the ministry:

"And it came to pass, that as the people pressed upon him to hear the word of God, he stood by the lake of Gennesaret...

And Simon answering said unto him, Master, we have toiled all night, and have taken nothing...And when they had done this, they inclosed a great multitude of fishes..."

Is placed by John in 21:1–10 AFTER the resurrection:

"After these things Jesus shewed himself again to the disciples at the lake of Gennesaret...Then Jesus saith unto them, Children, have ye any meat? They answered him no...They cast therefore, and now they were not able to draw it for the multitude of fishes...."

5. Unlike Matthew 10, Mark 3, Luke 6 and Acts 1:13, a list of the apostles is not given.

6. At the end of John's Gospel, AFTER the resurrection, 21:20:

"Lord, who is it that will betray you?"

implies that Jesus had not as yet been betrayed.

7. In John 21:25, he suggests that Joshua did many more things after the resurrection which he believes *"could not contain the books that should be written."*

John's Gospel, coupled with the trial of the two Joshua's, Barabbas being set free, suggests that a Joshua, an Essene Teacher of Righteousness was Baptised in approximately 30 A.D. in Bethany beyond the Jordan. During his three year probation period he returned to this area time and time again, having a close affiliation with the women who lived there who were most probably of the order of Asher led by the Bishopess Anna/ Hannah.[197]

In 35 A.D. a Joshua (taking into account that there could have been numerous Essenes who used the mitzvah name Joshua while giving a sermon) was anointed by a woman and both were arrested due to their unorthodox practices, the woman being thrown into jail, whilst a Jesus departs to a desert place and separates himself in the wilderness, a factor that is mentioned in the synoptic Gospels after the Baptist's arrest. Matthew 14:12–13, Mark 6:31–32.

I believe that the woman that we are searching for was the Baptist who lived in Bethany beyond the Jordan, in the House of the Goddess Anath and who was most probably the Bishopess Hannah of the order of Asher, the name John being a masculine derivative of the feminine form Hannah, both of which mean *"grace."*[198] In such a way Jeremiah's prophecy (31:22) was fulfilled and a woman either openly, or more likely, covertly due to the sexist climate at the time, *"played the part of a man."* Hannah was a prophetess who at times in the Gospels was referred to as *"Mary,"* an Essene initiation title that means *"prophetess."*[199] As such, Hannah was Joshua's cousin, of a priestly family, a Nazarene from birth who Baptised people in the name of the Holy Spirit, as Wisdom, who is a *"wellspring"* baptises us in Proverbs. It is my belief that Luke 7:35, refers to the Baptist, not

---

197. Barbara Thiering. "Jesus the Man." Doubleday.1992.

198. O.Odelain and R. Seguineau. "Dictionary of Proper Names and Places in the Bible." Robert Hale.1991.

199. Ibid.

only in the feminine gender, but also associates her with the embodiment of wisdom:

"For the Baptist came neither eating bread nor drinking wine; and ye say, there is a devil...
But wisdom is justified of all her children."

In Mark 1:14 & 2:18& 19, the disciples are fasting after the Baptist has been put into prison and ask why Jesus's disciples are not fasting. In answering, Jesus refers to himself as *"the bridegroom."*

"Now after that John was put in prison, Jesus came into Galilee, preaching the gospel of the kingdom of God...
And the disciples of the Baptist and of the Pharisees used to fast: and they come and say unto him, Why do the disciples of the Baptist and of the Pharisees fast, but thy disciples fast not?
And Jesus said unto them, Can the children of the bridechamber fast, while the bridegroom is with them? as long as they have the bridegroom with them, they cannot fast."

The inference is that unlike the bride, being the Baptist who is incarcerated, the bridegroom is still amongst them. Even if you do not agree with the femininity of the Baptist, this particular chapter and verse raises some questions. If Joshua refers to himself as the bridegroom, particularly at this point, then we must ask ourselves who is the bride that is no longer amongst them? By using the term *"bridegroom"* when the Baptist is in jail, implies that the bride is the Baptist, the High Priestess Hannah. At the end of the Gospel of John, Jesus leaves *"the beloved"* behind as he leaves the Baptist behind in the synoptic Gospels and he instructs Peter to *"follow me"* (John 21:22) as he does at the beginning of the synoptic Gospels in Matthew 4:19, Mark 1:17 and Luke 5:10.

John 13:1–20 is omitted in the synoptic Gospels where a Joshua washes the disciples feet as a *"Mary"* washed the feet of Jesus and anointed them in chapter 11. Also omitted is chapter 14 which deals with the speaker being *"One with the father"* and the speech in chapter 15, *"I am the true vine..."* the mother of all Israel in Ezekiel, which starts after the speaker in the previous chapter has said, *"...come let us go!"* In chapter 16 we have the lesson of the Holy Spirit, also not found in the synoptic Gospels.

I would like to suggest that the ministry of Joshua as found in the synoptic Gospels, which as I hope to prove below came after his anointing in 35 A.D., has been inserted with and superimposed over sections of the Baptist's life in 35 A.D. which are only found in the Gospel of John. The historic facts converging on the marriage of Herodias, Pilate's term of office and Caiaphas's period as High priest, suggest that the crucifixion of a Jesus did not take place during this period in history or in 30 A.D. and therefore makes the identification of such an individual within an historic context difficult. Large sections of the ministry, eg: healing a leper, choosing the twelve, the Sermon on the Mount, Herod Agrippa's fear that Jesus is John the Baptist resurrected, (Matt.14:1–2, Mark 6:14–29 Luke 9:7–9), Antipas's marriage to Herodias and the beheading of the Baptist have not been included in John's witness.

The overall picture, a bird's eye view, includes that of a person who baptises, resurrects, anoints and whose life is continuously being threatened by the orthodox priesthood. The crucifixion has possibly been pasted over the death of the Baptist, the beheading being absent in John and hence, the miraculous catch of fish which is found at the end of John's Gospel is found at the beginning of the synoptic Gospels in Matt. 4:18–22, Mark 1:16–20 and Luke 5:1–11.

In the Gnostic scriptures, the Pistis Sophia states:

"Maria the Magdalene with Iohannes the Virgin will become excelling all my disciples." [200]

In this text, John in the list of disciples is also referred to as *"the flower of virginity."* I do stand open to correction, but no where as far as I have discovered in the Old Testament, the Dead Sea Scrolls or in the Gospel of Thomas has a man ever been referred to as a virgin. A *"virgin"* in it's original Semitic sense of the word meant an independent woman not owned by a man and in Hebrew tradition would have been a holy q'deshah or prophetess, as the Bishopess Hannah of the order of Asher was considered to be.

Hannah, or John as we have come to know this person, offered Baptism to all converts. Taken in a Hebrew context, Baptism is no more and certainly no less than Mikveh, a ritual bath, considered by the Hebrew Zohar to contain the secret of life itself. Mikveh is thought to be only for women and relates to the seven days after menstruation. As a bath, it symbolizes the total immersion of the body within the uterine waters so that rebirth can occur, a ritual blessed by the Holy Spirit as it tells us in Proverbs 1:23 & 18:4 as well as in the Gospels. But this bath as the Baptist taught, was not only for women, but for all, men and Gentiles included.

In the first century A.D., Mikveh available to all as opposed to women, whereby the vessel of the body is cleansed and reborn in order

200. Jean Doresse. "The Secret Books of the Egyptian Gnostics." Inner Traditions International ,Ltd. 1986.

to receive the Holy Spirit, symbol the dove, would have been a revolutionary concept especially if taught by a woman *"who played the part of a man"* as Jeremiah 31 suggests, an incident that is linked with the return of the Joseph tribes, being Rachel's children and the firstborn being Ephraim as suggested in Matthew 2. This woman was no doubt denounced by the orthodox Sadducee priesthood.

As the feminine principle pours out the Holy Spirit in Proverbs so does Hannah, which we see in Joshua's baptism with the symbol of the dove. Another interpretation for the name Moses is *"drawn out of water"* (Shiloh). Joshua was drawn out of water (Shiloh) in Baptism. Moses was saved by the Pharaoh's daughter in Egypt, and so Joshua was most probably attended by another Mizraim, meaning Egypt, (the saviour comes from out of Egypt) at his Baptism. The dove of Anath appears over his head, and Mary-Mizraim-Miriam his mother, of the order of Asher, of the tribe of Ephraim at Bethany, the house of the Goddess Anath, proclaimed, *"this is my firstborn son in whom I am well pleased."* As Hannah gave her firstborn son, Samuel, of the tribe of Ephraim (1st born) to the Lord, so Mary, gives her firstborn son, Joshua, of the tribe of Ephraim (1st born) to the Lord. The Magnificat found in the New Testament, is a version of the Magnificat found in 1 Samuel 2:1-10 when Samuel's mother Hannah, dedicated him to the Lord.

Luke's Gospel is the only one that mentions a prophetess called Anna, who like the Baptist, *"spake of him to all them that looked for redemption."* (2:38) Her actions are similar to those of the Baptist who prepared the way of the Lord. Again I believe that the events found in our Gospels were repetitive and were acted out by numerous people instead of by an individual. In *"The Dead Sea Scrolls" "The Manual of Discipline"* reflects the Gospels and initiation taking place in the wilderness or desert coupled with enlightenment through the Holy Spirit which leads in righteousness and justice:

""In the wilderness prepare the way of the LORD; as it is written," In the wilderness prepare the way of the LORD; make straight in the desert a

highway for our God." This is the study of the law, as he commanded through Moses, to do according to all that has been revealed from time to time, and as the prophets revealed by his Holy Spirit."[201]

John 1:23:

"...I am the voice of one crying in the wilderness, Make straight the way of the Lord,..."

Hannah was born into a priestly family and her mother was Elisheba, meaning, *"the power of the sacred seventh"*[202] as in Proverbs 9:1:

"Wisdom hath builded her house, she hath hewn out her seven pillars..."

As a firstborn in accordance with Exodus 13:2 as opposed to Num.3:12, she is sanctified and devoted to God and a Nazarene from birth taking no wine or strong drink as it states in Numbers 6:2 that both men and women could be ordained as Nazarenes:

"Speak unto the children of Israel, and say unto them, When either man or woman shall separate themselves to vow a vow of a Nazarite, to separate themselves unto the Lord."

She dressed in camel's hair, Gimel on the Kabbala, which is the High Priestess and like the woman in Proverbs 31:17:

"She girdeth her loins with strength, and strengtheneth her arms..."

---

201. Millar Burrows. "The Dead Sea Scrolls." Secker and Warburg. 1956.

202. O.Odelain and R.Seguineau."Dictionary of Proper Names and Places in the Bible." Robert Hale. 1991.

She girds her loins in Matthew 3:4:

"...and a leathern girdle about the loins..."

Hannah can be likened to Rachel in Jeremiah 31:15:;

"...A voice was heard in Ramah, lamentation and bitter weeping; Rachel weeping..."

symbolized by the vine in Ezekiel 19:13 & 14:;

"...now she is planted in the wilderness...This is a lamentation..."

and the bride in Song of Songs 8:5:;

"Who is this that cometh up from the wilderness, leaning upon her beloved?..."

Was a voice crying out from the wilderness. John 1:23:;

"I am the voice of one crying in the wilderness..."

When asked who he is, Hannah denies being the Messiah, Elijah or the prophet. She only admits to being *"a voice crying out in the wilderness."* (John 1:20–23.) This confrontation between the Pharisees and Hannah occurs at Bethany, *"the house of the Goddess Anath."* (John 1:28) John says that this Bethany was beyond the Jordan which would place it near Qumram. Joshua was Baptised beyond the Jordan and so it appears that both the Baptism and the anointing with oil by a prophetess occurred in the same area. As the Bishopess, it could have been Hannah/Miriam who anointed Joshua with costly perfume made from pure oil of nard. Such an act would have been within her power. Here she is referred to as a *"Mary."*

If the woman was given power to anoint, then she is not some silly besotted girl kneeling on the floor in submission. Rather, she is acting as a conduit for the Holy Spirit or Binah on the Kabbala and is the equivalent of Isis in Egypt, anointing the firstborn. Through the acts of Baptism and the anointing, women regained their rightful position within the church. As in the Isis rituals where the Goddess not only has the power to resurrect Osiris but is the first to see the risen lord (compare John 11:45 & John 20:11–18) as well as to give birth to the new born child, so women regained this right. Through the Wisdom teachings came the belief in life after death, or like Osiris, the ability to be raised from the dead. Those who did not believe in an eschatological philosophy, also rejected the Wisdom teachings, eg. Proverbs 8:36 where Wisdom or the Holy Spirit says:

"But he that sinneth against me wrongeth his own soul: all they that hate me love death."

Barbara Thiering is of the opinion that all of the incidents within the Gospels occurred in the New Jerusalem, being Qumram.[203] The first chapter of John appears to confirm her views. *"Bethany beyond the Jordan,"* would not be Bethany near Jerusalem, which in effect places the whole Gospel story outside of the realms of Judah and rather within what was once the realm of the northern kingdom of Israel. Some scholars of the Dead Sea Scrolls are also of the opinion that the divisions between the Sadducees and the Essenes spoken of in the texts, refer to a split within the Qumram community itself. The orthodox remaining Sadducees whilst those who believed in an eschatological

---

203. Barbara Thiering. "Jesus the Man." Doubleday. 1992

philosophy, of spiritual resurrection after death, became known as the children of Zadok, descendants of Melchizedek, the priest-king of justice. Although these views change the geography and would no doubt put paid to the massive tourist industry in Jerusalem, I do not believe that this new evidence changes the essence of the story in any way.

Whether at Qumram or Jerusalem, one of Mary's sons, being an Essene-Joshua the Righteous was the beloved at the Last Supper during his marriage and had recently been anointed by Hannah. Through his marriage to a *"virgin daughter of Zion,"* there is a joining together of the order of Asher led by the Bishopess Hannah and a male Essene group creating the Hebrew (Christian) Zion-ist church. Hence the Lord, El, becomes a Mountain Dweller, Shaddai-Zion and upholds the Law within a democratic context. As John says:

"The Lord is found in Zion."

This marriage between a *"King of Israel"* and a prophetess who both resided within Herod Antipas's jurisdiction, occurred in 35 A.D. during which time Joshua's probation period came to an end and he was initiated with the anointing. This would suggest that up until this time, Joshua was not the leader of the group and according to the Gospel of John, the twelve disciples had as yet not been chosen.

Within the traditions of the Essene community we are missing a leader who was known as the Mebakker/Bishop or Overseer and one of his main functions was to act as treasurer.[204] In the Gospels it tells us

---

204. Eisenman & Wise. "The Dead Sea Scrolls Uncovered." Element. 1992.

that Judas was the treasurer because he carried the common purse and by this implication, was the leader of the group. John 12:6:

"This he said, not that he cared for the poor; but because he was a thief, and had the bag, and bare what was put therein."

Any person found guilty of breaking the Laws of Righteousness, was to be cursed at Pentecost due to the Community Rule, whereby:

"...the expellee is not to participate in the pure food of the Community any longer (or, according to another vocabulary circle, not to keep "table fellowship" any more), here one is not to "eat with him" (15). In the Community Rule, too, no one is to cooperate with him in "common purse" or "service"/"activity"/"ministry", here one is not to "keep company with him" in any way or "ask after his welfare." [205]

Is this not what occurred in the Biblical text about Judas? He did not join in the Last Supper, but left with the *"common purse"* (John 13:29–30) whilst Acts 1 verifies the fact that Judas was the Bishop and at Pentecost he was replaced.

"These all continued with one accord in prayer and supplication with the women, and Mary the mother of Jesus, and with his brethren...this scripture must needs have been fulfilled, which the Holy Spirit by the mouth of David spake before concerning Judas, which was guide to them that took Jesus....Now this man purchased a field with the reward of

---

205. Ibid.

iniquity; and falling headlong, he burst asunder in the midst, and all his
bowels gushed out....For it is written in the book of Psalms, Let his
habitation be desolate, and let no man dwell therein: and his bishopric let
another take....And they appointed two, Joseph called Barsabas, who was
surnamed Justus, and Matthais..."

If Judas was the groups Mebakker and treasurer, a Bishop who led them, then we must ask ourselves why he betrayed a Teacher of Righteousness and why his actions, in the end, caused the apostles to curse him from moving either to the left or the right of the law.

1. According to the Gospels, as treasurer he objected to a woman anointing Joshua with costly oil. If Jesus rode into Jerusalem on the Sunday, being the first day of the week, then the anointing with oil would have occurred the day before, on the Sabbath. Judas could have objected to the anointing due to the *"Damascus Document. History and Exhortation. X111"* which states:

"Let him not open a sealed vessel on the Sabbath. Let not a man take on him ointments to go out and come in on the Sabbath." [206]

2. Judas objected to James the less also known as Alpheus later James the Righteous, becoming an anointed high priest because of his small stature, which was considered to be a deformity according to the Levitical laws of purity.

---

206. Millar Burrows. "The Dead Sea Scrolls." Secker and Warburg. 1956.

3. He objected to the raising of Lazarus on the Day of Atonement in accordance Levitical practice where only the High Priest could exercise the ritual of Yom Kippur, an incident which will be explored in the last chapter of this book.

Whether Judas was the *"Wicked Priest"* spoken of in the Dead Sea Scrolls or not, the parallels between Judas and this person converge on the events in the Gospels. To quote from Millar Burrows in *"The Dead Sea Scrolls. Habakkuk commentary:"*

"This means the wicked priest, who persecuted the teacher of righteousness in order to confound him in the indignation of his wrath, wishing to banish him; and at the time of their festival of rest, the Day of Atonement, he appeared to them to confound them and to make them stumble on the day of fasting, their sabbath of rest." [207]

Millar Burrows goes on to add:

"Be all that as it may, something important undoubtedly happened on the Day of Atonement. What was it? Here again different scholars take widely divergent ways in their interpretations. Eiger supposes that the conflict between the teacher of righteousness and the wicked priest remained latent until it came to an open breach on the Day of Atonement, when the high priest revealed his real intentions. Either then or soon afterward the teacher of righteousness was arrested and brought to trial." [208]

---

207. Ibid.
208. Ibid.

In Burrows assessment of the Habakkuk commentary he says that it is not clear or even probable that the teacher was put to death at this time. Though it is clear that the wicked priest was punished:

"...the wicked priest, whom, for the wrong done to the teacher of right-eousness and the men of his party, God delivered into the hand of his ene-mies, afflicting him with a destroying scourge, in bitterness of soul, because he acted wickedly against the elect." [209]

The teacher on the other hand:

"...was exiled and pursued to the House of his exile." [210]

Which would have been Galilee, where as we have seen in the synoptic Gospels, Jesus returned after the Baptist's arrest.

In Christian circles and in Hebrew circles, the blame for the crucifixion has been laid at the door of the Romans due to the belief that the Jews, in accordance with their law, would not have hanged a person from a tree but rather stoned him to death. This is an inaccurate argument. According to Deuteronomy 21:22 & 23:

"And if a man have committed a sin worthy of death, and he be to be put to death, his body shall not remain all night upon the tree, but thou shalt in any wise bury him that day; (for he that is hanged is accursed of God;) that thy land be not defiled, which the Lord thy God giveth thee for an inheritance."

---

209. Ibid.
210. Ibid.

We have two stories that adhere to this law. The first the crucifixion where Joseph insists on burying the body before sunset in accordance with Deuteronomy, though the reason given is that it was the Sabbath and the second, the death of Judas who hung from a tree and was then taken down and buried. Taking the Essene tradition of the treasurer being the Bishop, superimposing it on the Gospels and then amalgamating the two stories, the situation could have gone as follows.

1. Judas, as Bishop, Mebakker and treasurer, objected to the raising of Lazarus and an eschatological philosophy, being life after death and split from the group as he was a supporter of orthodox Levitical Sadducee principles based on Gen.2. which advocated our mortality...

2. baptism and the anointing with holy oil from an alabaster jar by a woman, especially on the Sabbath; and...

3. the initiation of a stunted or deformed person, being James, to a High Priest.

4. He betrayed the group and one individual in particular, with a *"kiss."* (Luke 22:47, Matt. 26:48 & Mark 14:45.) If this had been a homosexual act instigated by Judas, then Judas himself would have been arrested according to Levitical law. The person who Judas kissed was the Baptist, the same woman who had anointed Jesus with Holy oil. The soldiers in turn, employed by the Sanhedrin, fell back in astonishment because they believed that this *"Jesus"* or Essene was a man, while at the same time, an unknown male figure, who was naked, escaped with a sheet wrapped around him.[211]

---

211. This naked person could only have been the bridegroom, the ceremony in the Garden of Gethsemane being a culmination of the wedding feast held on the Sabbath, where as we have seen above, like the Sabbath, was a celebration of the joining together of Zion to the Lord.

5. Through this betrayal, Judas upheld the Levitical laws of purity and inadvertently or deliberately brought about the death of the Baptist, therefore, according to Hebrew law, he had *"committed a sin worthy of death"* by *"causing the death of an innocent person."*

6. At Pentecost the apostles cursed him. He was scourged as was the *"wicked priest"* in the Habakkuk commentary and sentenced to hanging from a tree as decreed in Deuteronomy 21:22 & 23, a similar punishment to crucifixion.

7. According to the law of Deuteronomy, his body had to be buried before sunset.

In Leviticus 27, the *"firstborn"* being a person (male or female), an animal or the first fruits of the harvest is automatically considered to be *"devoted"* to God and by virtue of this law, may not be sold or redeemed. Such a person, male or female, from birth to death would be called a *"firstborn"* and like Samuel, in addition to this title could be a Nazarene from birth to death, growing their hair long, never cutting it and also abstaining from wine or strong drink. According to Leviticus 27 26–29, if a firstborn who is considered to be *"devoted"* from birth is sold or redeemed, then this person must be put to death by having their neck broken, as with the ass in Exodus 13:13.

It appears that the Baptist was a Nazarene and firstborn from the womb and did not take strong drink. The Baptist, by virtue of being the only child of Elisheba and born from the tribe of Aaron being a priestly family would have been regarded as a firstborn from birth and as such, would be *"devoted"* and a Nazarene. As it says in Numbers 6, both men and women could be Nazarenes. The Sanhedrin was threatened by the Baptist's followers who were male, female and Gentile.

After the anointing of a Joshua, Judas threw in his lot with the Sanhedrin and helped Caiaphas to bring about a scheme to bring her to trial and condemn her to death. Through the Levitical law he betrayed her. Being the leader, Bishop and treasurer of the group, he had the power to sell her, make a dedication on her behalf to the Sanhedrin, who valued this singular vow at *"thirty pieces of silver,"* the price for a singular vow made by a woman in Leviticus 27:4. By so doing and becoming a *"wicked priest"* he had broken the rule found in the *"Damascus Document. History and Exhortation. X:"*

"Any man who dedicates anything which is the property of the camp, according to the statutes of the Gentiles he must be put to death."

The High Priest's army then went to collect her by force and she is followed by another disciple, who went into the palace of the high priest (John 18:15). This could have been Theudas, Jesus Barabbas, who was set free. Again, Judas broke the community rule. *"Damascus Document. History and Exhortation.XX:"*

"Concerning the law of the free will offerings, a man shall not vow for the altar anything taken by force."

The Baptist is then asked *"are you the son of God?"* which by Old Testament interpretation means *"the firstborn"* being *"devoted"* and of a priestly family, which she was, her father being a priest and decedent of Aaron. When she answers yes, the priests tear their clothes as Jephtah did and as Jews do today when someone has died. According to Levitical law, the *"firstborn/devoted"* may not be sold in dedication. By breaking such a law, the Baptist had to be put to death. As Jephtah in Judges had inadvertently caused the death of his daughter so had Judas purposefully caused the death of the Baptist and her neck in accordance with Exodus 13:13 was to be broken. Leviticus 27:29:

"No human being thus devoted may be sold or redeemed; but must be put to death."

Under Roman occupation the Jews were forbidden to put a person to death and so the priests take the Baptist and Theudas, who was later released, to Pilate in 35 A.D. Pilate, realizing that the Baptist comes from Bethany beyond the Jordan, then hands her over to Herod Antipas who was the tetrarch of Galilee and Jordan. Antipas did not want to put the Baptist to death, as described in Matthew 14:5 and Luke, the only Gospel which says that Jesus was brought to Herod Antipas. Herod Antipas, in Luke's Gospel, was greatly pleased, a sentiment supported in Matthew 14:5. I believe that the Herod who vowed to put Jesus to death was Herod Agrippa 1, not Herod Antipas and secondly, I believe that the person who was brought to Herod Antipas in Luke 22:7–10 as in Matthew 14, was the Baptist.

"....and on learning that [she] belonged to Herod's jurisdiction Pilate remitted the case to him, for Herod Antipas was also in Jerusalem at that time. When Herod saw [her] he was greatly pleased; he had hear about [her] and had long been waiting to see [her] in the hope of witnessing some miracle. He questioned [her] at some length without getting any reply; but the chief priests and scribes appeared and pressed the case vigorously."

The *"case"* was that a firstborn/devoted, a Nazarene from a priestly family who took no strong drink or wine, could not be sold in a singular vow of dedication and Judas had sold her for *"thirty pieces of silver,"* the price given by the priests for a woman's singular vow to God. The punishment for such a crime imposed on the firstborn who was devoted to God, as in Judges, was to break her neck by beheading as Adah had been beheaded. Herod Antipas was forced by the Sadducees to behead the Baptist through the law.

The story of the Baptist includes that of Salome and her mother Herodias. Salome danced for Herod Antipas and as a reward could choose anything she wanted. On Herodias's instigation, she asked for the head of the Baptist. After receiving it, the Baptist's followers buried the body in a tomb.

Questions:
1) Was the Salome who went to the tomb with spices, the same person as the Salome who danced for Herod Antipas?
2) Why did Herodias ask for the Baptist's head?
3) Was the Baptist possibly decapitated earlier than the given time?
4) Could burial have occurred without the skull?
5) Did Herodias possibly ask for the Baptist's skull so that the body could be buried?
6) Or did she keep the skull as a religious talisman?

The followers of Jesus were Salome, Joanna the wife of Chuza who was Herod Antipas's stewart and Mary Magdalene. Magdalene means *"tower,"*[212] therefore we have Mary of the Tower. Herodias was a descendent of Herod the Great who had built the citadel of Herodium with it's four towers 12 km from Jerusalem. Within Herod's palace in Jerusalem, there was also a tower, known as Mariam, the Greek translation being Mary which was in effect the *"Mary Tower."*

Mary Magdalene, we are told, was a rich woman who supported the followers of Jesus, Mary, being a religious name meaning prophetess, rather than a circular name. She stood at the cross, attended the burial and bought spices for anointing the corpse. She was at the empty tomb, was the first to see the risen Christ and brought the Apostles the news of the resurrection. Prior to this, she is only mentioned twice before, in Mark 16:9 and Luke 8:2 as the woman from whom seven devils were

212. O.Odelain and R.Seguineau. "Dictionary of Proper names and Places in the Bible." Robert Hale. 1991.

cast out and is always linked to Joanna, the wife of Herod Antipas's stewart and Salome. As such, she has been ignonomously remembered throughout history as the sinner and prostitute.

The *seven devils* with which she has been tainted, are to my mind the equivalent of the seven deadly sins being anger, envy, gluttony, lust, pride, sloth and avarice. I don't know of one person who is not guilty of at least one of them which in effect would mean that if Mary Magdalene had had these devils or sins cast out of her, then she must have reached a degree of enlightenment or Christ consciousness similar to Jesus's own. Therefore, she should have been remembered throughout history as a saint rather than a sinner and as the Pistis Sophia states, "*Maria the Magdalene...will become excelling all my disciples,*" including the apostles.

I would like to propose that she was Herodias who was referred to as Mary of the tower, "*Magdalene*". That Herodias, her daughter Salome as well as her best friend Joanna, the wife of her husband's stewart were Essenes who followed Jesus during his three year probation (Mark 15:40 & 41 & Luke 8:2, 24:10). That it was Hannah, the name of a Bishopess of the order of Asher, who was sold by Judas to the priesthood for "*thirty pieces of silver*" (Lev.27:4) and who then, according to the law and the Sadducee priesthood, had to be beheaded because no devoted thing sanctified to God, ie: a firstborn or a Nazarene from birth, may be sold or redeemed, (bought back as is the firstborn to this day)[213] as was Adah, the only child and firstborn of her

---

213. Louis Jacobs. "The Jewish Religion." Oxford University Press. 1995.

father Jephthah who was put to death for the same reason by the priests in Judges 11.

That it was Mary Magdalene, the woman from the tower of Mariam-Mary in Herod's Palace who asked for Hannah's head after she had been beheaded. Salome who danced like a whore in order to get it and then wrapped it in a cloth. Mary the mother of James and Theudas, her sister Mary Zebedee the mother of James and John, Salome and her mother Mary Magdalene and Joanna, the wife of Chuza who went with anointment to bury the body of Hannah. Theudas, now known by the religious title of *"Joseph"* who buried the body in his own tomb, which could have been at Mount Gerizim, the cave of Machpelah. Herodias, who with Herod Antipas went to Lyon in France giving rise to the legends of the Magdalene who crossed the oceans and landed in Marseille, having in her possession the cloth and the holy skull and establishing a Hebrew-Christianity that was later wiped out in the South of France, the Languedoc during the Albigensian Crusade which massacred the Cathars and burnt them at the stake. The Albigensian heresy was a belief that a Jesus had married and had children.

The Baptist in true medieval style, could of course have been locked up in the tower of Mariam being pregnant with the *"King of Israel's"* child and then rescued and saved from beheading. Before Pilate's massacre of the innocents which was instigated by Herod 1, she could have escaped to the south of France with Joseph of Arimathea, who adopted her child and later, under the protection of Herodias and Antipas, her skull and cross bones were kept by the descendants of either this family or her own. If this was the case, then she too could have been known as *"Mary of the Tower,"* Magdalene.

Truth or fiction? Allegorical or based on fact? It appears that the Ephraimites/Samaritans who fled Palestine both prior to and after the fall of the temple in 70 A.D. went to Gaul, giving rise to the Merovingian dynasty, who like the Nazarenes had long hair which they never cut. This dynasty was brought to an end by Charlemagne who with the support of the Roman Catholic Pope, put many of them to death.

During the thirteenth century, both the large and thriving Jewish population as well as the Christian Cathars in the Languedoc in South western France were burnt at the stake as heretics and their wives were punished as witches. The Cathars worshipped a woman's skull which was known as *"Caput 58 Virgo,"* the head of the virgin, and appeared to pay more homage to the Baptist (Hannah?) than they did to Jesus.[214] Hugh Schonfield, who has studied the Essenes in depth stated:

"The Greek Sophia represents a female rather than a male, and we are not surprised to find in Templar hands, according to inquisition records, a casket surmounted by "a great head of gilded silver, most beautiful, and constituting the image of a woman." [215]

Much like Galilee under the governorship of Herod Antipas, the Languedoc was a wealthy and independent state. The nobles from the north plundered it's wealth, murdered it's people and under orders from Rome, the inquisition tried to put a stop to it's religious beliefs, both Cathar and Hebrew through terror and fear. The Cathars were believed to be heretics because the fundamental philosophies of their religion were a threat to Rome. They believed:

---

214. Dr.Anthony Harris."The Sacred Virgin and the Holy Whore." Sphere Books. Limited. 1988.

Michael Baigent, Richard Leigh & Henry Lincoln. "The Holy Blood and the Holy Grail."Corgi. 1983.

215. Hugh Schonfield. "The Essene Odyssey." Element Books Limited. 1984.

1) In the Dove as a symbol of the Holy Spirit, which was also a symbol of the Goddess in Greece.

2) In the children of light and the children of darkness, so often mentioned in the Dead Sea Scrolls.

3) In passive resistance, like Ghandi a thousand years after them.

4) In the concept of re-incarnation.

5) That the virgin birth was a fallacy.

6) In the feminine principle of God as well as the masculine and wore the equal sided cross. Hence, both men and women joined the priesthood and were known as Parfait and Parfaite respectively. They only joined the priesthood after leading an active life which entailed marriage and bringing up their children and then travelled around the country side administering to the poor and needy. It was from the Cathars that the troubadours originated, composing love songs that not only related to physical love between a man and a woman, but spiritual love between God and the Holy Spirit.

7) In astrology, to the extent that they wore a girdle, as did the Baptist and the woman in Proverbs 31, with a buckle designed in the sign for Pisces.

8) In direct knowledge of God, not knowledge passed down through the Bishops of the church and practised meditation.

9) In the Kabbala, through which they studied alchemy and herbalism and became knowledgeable in medicines and astronomy.

10) In a Jesus as a prophet, a mortal, who was crucified. They did not see the crucifixion as particularly relevant to their religion, refused to worship the Roman cross and rejected communion.

11) In a living resurrection ceremony for the individual as opposed to being saved through the crucifixion of a man.

12) In fellow worship in the home as opposed to in a church and did not pay the Parfaites tithe or taxes.

In the Middle Ages, there was a female Pope called Joan/John/Hannah in approximately 930 A.D. She managed to hide the truth of her sexuality until one day, whilst walking through the streets, she gave birth to a child and was subsequently murdered for *"playing the part of a man."*[216]

In the fourteenth century a woman called Joan/Joanna/Hannah d' Arc, meaning Joan of the Ark, or of the tribe of Aaron, *"played the part of a man"* and helped to bring about the end of the Hundred Year's War. She was eventually sold (thirty pieces of silver?) to the English; locked up in a tower (Magdalene?); given a trial by ordeal; and burnt to death at the stake not for her political actions, but for being a heretic.

Truth is surely stranger than fiction and the repetitiveness of the story, whether perpetuated by word of mouth, allegorical metaphors or by actual events never ceases to amaze me. All those fairy tales about a princess being locked up in a tower and then saved and freed by the prince, or the princess being put to sleep for a thousand years and then woken up by the kiss of a prince, could all be based on fact. *"France,"* incidently, means *"a free woman,"* whilst the most important church in this country is Notre Dame, Our Lady.

After the French Revolution when a democratic Republic was established, the church of La Madeleine was built in Paris. It looks more like a Greek Temple to Athena than it does a church and inadvertently celebrates the Goddess of Democracy where a woman stands on the altar, symbol of the Ark of the Covenant, and is raised up to heaven. The streets surrounding it form a pentagon, which in turn becomes a five pointed star, Esther who saved her people in the month of Adar, Purim, symbol of Venus, the morning and evening star, the apple of the Lord's

---

216. Dr.Anthony Harris."The Sacred Virgin and the Holy Whore." Sphere Books Limited.1988.

eye which when cut horizontally forms a five pointed star [Proverbs 7:2]. Symbolically, the Goddess of Democracy is within the pentagon whilst the most democratic country in the world, being the U.S.A is defended from the Pentagon. Is it any wonder that the French gave the U.S.A the Statue of Liberty which stands on Elis Island, an Island where the river Alpheus originated in ancient Arcadia. Poison's painting of *"The shepherds of Arcadia"* are led to The Ark of the Covenant by the Shepherdess.

Chapter Ten.

The Bridegroom

In 37 A.D. Herod Agrippa 1 was granted the title of king by Caligula. By 39 A.D. Herod Antipas had been exiled to France and his tetrarchy handed over to Herod Agrippa 1. By 40 B.C. Herod the Great's kingdom had been reconstituted under King Herod Agrippa 1 who began building the third wall of Jerusalem.[217]

During this same period, as this author believes, a man with the religious title of Jesus or an Essene, had completed his probation period in 35 A.D. and in accordance with Essene practice, had been anointed and had begun his missionary service throughout Galilee, Samaria and Judea while at the same time Herod Agrippa 1 became a cruel and obsessed man who was opposed to the Essenes and what was later to

217. O.Odelain and R.Seguineau. "Dictionary of Proper Names and Places in the Bible." Robert Hale Limited. 1991.

become known as the Christian movement. He vowed to kill *"a"* Joshua or Essene who many referred to as the *"King of Israel,"* a man who threatened Agrippa's position as *"King of the Jews."* He regarded Joshua as a revolutionary whose political philosophy (which was based on judges and councillors in a federated state of Israel) undermined the stability of his throne and was going to let nothing undermine his rule.

Herod Agrippa 1 clearly advocated an autocracy, seeing himself as a supreme god as related in Acts 12:21–22. Jesus on the other hand, although referred to by John as the *"King of Israel,"* deplored such a political and religious system as we have seen in John 10:34, where Jesus believed that scripture decreed that all who receive *"the word"* are *"Gods."*

But for Jesus, being *Gods* as he suggests, does not mean having dominion over others, but rather being of service to others. This is clearly expressed when James and John Zebedee requested to sit on his right and left hand side and agreed that in order to do this, they would have to drink from the same cup and experience the same baptism as Jesus. Mark 10:38,39 & 40:

> *"But Jesus said unto them, Ye know not what ye ask: can ye drink the cup that I drink of? and be baptized with the baptism that I am baptized with?*
>
> *And they said unto him, We can. And Jesus said unto them, Ye shall indeed drink of the cup that I drink of; and with the baptism that I am baptized with shall ye be baptized.*
>
> *But to sit on my right hand and on my left hand is not mine to give; but it shall be given to them for whom it is prepared."*

The response of the other disciples was jealously and indignation and in all probability they considered James and John to be *"thieves"* for attempting to steal a prime position in the New Kingdom. Unbeknown to them, James, John and Jesus were, as we will see below, not only discussing a priestly role, but political matters as well. Jesus reprimanded his disciples for their jealousy with these words in 12:42:

"You know that among the gentiles the recognized rulers lord it over their subjects, and make great their authority felt. It shall not be so with you; among you, whoever wants to be great must be your servant, and whoever wants to be first must be the slave of all. For the Son of Man did not come to be served but to serve, and to give his life as a ransom for many." [218]

A quote from the *"Manual of Discipline"* reflects this Gospel teaching:

"There shall be in the council of the community twelve men, and there shall be three priests who are perfect in all that has been revealed of the whole law, to practice truth and righteousness and justice and loyal love and walking humbly each with his neighbour..." [219]

By being allowed to share the same cup and the same baptism as Jesus, James and John were elevated to a position higher than the ten disciples, where it states that the council of the community which consists of ten, must have three priests. For example the *"Manual of Discipline"* states:

"In every place where there are ten men of the council of the community there shall not be absent from them a priest...This is the order for the session of the masters, each in position. The priests be seated first and the elders second....there shall be in the council of the community twelve men, and there shall be three priests...." [220]

The ten led by the three priests is reflected in Luke 10:41:

---

218. There are many politicians today, who could learn from this lesson, as well a governments who are voted in to serve the people, not the other way around. The only two men that I know of who have tried to live this Biblical passage in word and deed are Mahatma Ghandi and Nelson Mandela, two men incidently who experienced the greatest indignity of all. Apartheid in South Africa.

219. Millar Burrows. "The Dead Sea Scrolls." Secker and Warburg. 1956.

220. Ibid.

"And when the ten heard it, they began to be much displeased with James and John."

But what were the political matters that James, John and Jesus were discussing, other than elevation to the priesthood that the *"ten"* were so displeased about? In answering their objections, Jesus refers to the Son of Man giving his life as *"a ransom for many,"* and therein lies the clue.

In Acts 12:2, Herod Agrippa 1, now made king by Caligula, launched an attack on certain members of the church. In 44 A.D, James Zebedee, the brother of John the apostle, was arrested by Herod Agrippa 1 and martyred by Caspius Fadus.[221] By token of his name, it appears that as with all Teachers of Righteousness, he could have already become an anointed High Priest/Joseph and also possibly a Bishop, taking on the name James/Jacob/Israel after Jacob/Israel in the Old Testament. As such, he would have been one of the *"Messiahs"* of Israel and Aaron spoken of in the Dead Sea Scrolls.

In the Bible James Zebedee's death in Acts occurs *"during the festival of Unleavened bread,"* (12:3) *"The Passover,"* as the crucifixion in the Gospels occurs during *"The Passover."* The parallels between this story and the one found in the Gospels is uncanny. I suspect that the story in Acts and part of the Gospel story are in fact one and the same. Acts is believed to have been written in 63 A.D. and starts with the ascension at Pentecost; the replacing of Judas as Bishop; and the establishment of

---

221. Larousse. "Dictionary of Beliefs & Religions." Larousse. 1994.

the early church in Jerusalem. James Zebedee in turn was arrested by the Sanhedrin; handed over to Herod Agrippa 1; and martyred by Caspius Fadus where upon he was put to death by crucifixion. In Acts 12:19–23 Herod Agrippa 1 returned north after James Zebedee was put to death, after which he was assassinated for calling himself a god-emperor.[222]

Coupled with this parallel is the story of Peter who was also arrested. In the Gospels Peter follows Jesus to the Sanhedrin and then deserts him by sunrise. In Acts 12 Peter is arrested and imprisoned, but is set free by an *"angel."* Again I think we are talking about one event and I suspect that the angel was a cover up story told to the Apostles because Peter had denied knowledge of a Jesus three times. Or perhaps, he denied knowledge of *"three"* Essenes. As the historic dates and John 21:20 suggest, Jesus had been neither betrayed not denied in 35 A.D. during Pilate's governorship and Caiaphas's term as High Priest. But what of the events in Acts that took place in 44 A.D.?

In the order of session according to the Dead Sea Scrolls, it appears that James and John Zebedee were ordained as priests over and above the *"ten"* who resented their positions and called them *"thieves."* James and John were allowed to drink from the same cup and undergo the same Baptism that Jesus underwent. But what was meant by drinking from *"the same cup"* and what was this *"baptism?"* In the Garden of Gethsemane Jesus prays that this *"cup"* will be taken from him. In other words, the *"cup"* refers to his crucifixion. The *"cup"* and the *"baptism"*

---

222. Barbara Thiering. "Jesus the Man." Doubleday. 1992.

that Jesus refers to, is I believe, the fact that all three were about to be crucified for their actions. Hence James and John, knowing fully well what the result of their actions would be if they supported Jesus in all that he does:1) Request to sit on his right and the left hand side. 2) Drink from the same bitter cup. 3) Experience the same *"baptism of fire."* Although Jesus can promise them that they will be punished with crucifixion, he cannot promise them that they will all be crucified together, although the crucifixion story implies as much by referring to the two *"thieves."* Hence Jesus replies to the first request by saying in Mark 10:40:

"But to sit on my right hand and on my left hand is not mine to give: but it shall be given to them (their executioners) for whom it is prepared."

Contrary to the accepted orthodox view, John Zebedee was crucified alongside his brother James in 44 A.D.[223] The *"Dictionary of Beliefs and Religions"* concurs with this view. Earlier traditions relate how John Zebedee was put to death by Herod Agrippa 1 whilst the belief that he spent his last days in Ephesus is only concurrent with the 2nd century A.D.[224] This would explain the two *"thieves"* crucified alongside a *"Jesus,"* either being a simultaneous crucifixion or a symbolic retelling of the deaths of three men. So who was the third man?

In *"Jesus the Man"* Barbara Thiering implies on page 403 that Jesus had close associations with Paul and the Agrippa family. I cannot agree.

---

223. Gordon Thomas. "The Trial." Corgi. 1988.

224. Larousse. "Dictionary of Beliefs and Religions." Larousse. 1992.

I think that if Jesus associated with anyone, it was Herod Antipas who did not want to become king of Judea or Samaria and Galilee, whose mother was a Samaritan and whose wife was Herodias, who I suspect of being Mary Magdalene. Barbara Thiering does however identify another character, who to my mind, fits the requirements necessary for the *"third"* man. Namely Theudas, the brother of James the Righteous who was also known as James Alpheus in the Gospels.

Thiering says of Theudas that he was the head of the Egyptian Therapeutae [healers born out of Mizraim-Egypt] who were called the order of Ephraim. Therefore he *"came out of Egypt."* He was a leader of the moderate Alexandrian [Egyptian] group who tried to moderate between the opposing east and western viewpoints. In 1 A.D. he went with Joseph to the far country, identified as Qumram and spoken of as *"Egypt."* He was called *"Moloch, the king, the sceptre,"* and took on the name of Jacob, he was also called Barabbas. Thiering gives the Aramaic of *"Bar"* to be servant whilst Odelain and Seguineau give the Aramaic to be *"son"* not servant of the Father.[225] Either is correct in a religious context as Joshua was the *"son"* and the *"servant"* as he came to serve and not to make his authority felt. He chose to be an anointed Judge or High Priest as opposed to an anointed king in the vein of the Rehoboam the king of Judah, or Jeroboam the king of Israel, although the Gospel of John refers to him as such. Theudas was wanted by Pilate and arrested at the same time as the Baptist, but as the Jesus Barabbas, the son of Mary and Joseph, he was let go. It is my belief that the

---

225. O.Odelain and R. Seguineau. "Dictionary of Proper Names and Places in the Bible." Robert Hale Limited. 1991.

political matters discussed between Jesus and James and John Zebedee, the result of which would lead to all three giving their lives as a "*ransom for many*," was as follows:

The climax to Theudas's whole ministry was when he led an imagined "*entry to the Promised Land*" by commanding the waters of the Jordan to part as did Moses, in order to bring about the "*New Kingdom*" as Joshua had done centuries before. Not surprisingly he was executed for this act in 44 A.D[226] alongside two men namely James and John Zebedee, who chose to support him, drinking from the same "*cup*" and undergoing the same "*baptism*" which resulted in crucifixion for all three men. Hence a "*Jesus*" or Essene, being a follower of Joshua in the Old Testament, was put to death alongside two "*thieves*" who were placed on his right and his left hand side. These thieves in turn were also Essenes, or followers of Joshua in the Old Testament who had brought about the New Kingdom of Israel in the promised land.

In this light, Mark 10: 39 & 40 becomes perfectly understandable. Although Jesus could assure James and John that they would suffer the same fate as himself if they supported him in making such a political statement, he could not promise them that they would be on his right and left hand side. Historic accounts support my view that Theudas was the "*third man*." Robin Lane Fox states that although Josephus gave no details about a "*Jesus*" being put to death,[227] he does however elaborate

---

226. Barbara Thiering. "Jesus the Man." Doubleday. 1992.

227. Any references being considered to be insertions by modern scholars.

on Theudas, the brother of James the Righteous as well as the death of James Zebedee.[228]

One of the simplest questions that has plagued Christians for centuries, myself included, is *"who was Jesus?"* In spite of so much having been written about him, in spite of testimonies as to his existence, he has remained as illusive as ever, a half magical figure, some kind of fairy tale myth without a happy ending that we cannot come to grips with.

I suspect that the original Joshua/Jesus was an Old Testament figure, the same person referred to in Zechariah 3 & 6. I do however, also believe that a person or persons in the 1st century A.D. not only upheld his principles but that one of them could be the specific individual that we are looking for. A man who saw religion, sociology and politics as being holistically interwoven. He tried very hard to change our religious, psychological, social, economic and political views on life, advocating a *"polyarchy based on equality"* which was later rejected by Rome. Theudas was murdered for his beliefs by the Sanhedrin, Herod Agrippa 1 and the Roman Empire, which is not surprising considering the political climate of the time. When he decided to do what he did, James and John agreeing to join him, he must have known that he would surely be put to death for these actions.

---

228. Robin Lane Fox. "The Unauthorised Version." Penguin. 1992.

Today the Western world cannot conceive of anyone believing that democracy, equality and justice for all under the laws of liberty could ever be regarded as evil or socially destructive concepts. But in the 1st century A.D., such a view in a Judaic light where Judea was ruled by Herod Agrippa 1 and under Roman occupation would have been regarded as exactly that.

Theudas's symbolic entry into the New Kingdom, reflecting both Moses and Joshua was a political threat as he was trying to re-instate the Kingdom of Israel as Joshua had done before him in accordance with the prophecy found in Jeremiah 31 and Zechariah 3 & 6. Such a philosophy would have been anathema to Rome and to those who awaited a Davidic Messiah king. Those who later followed James the Righteous maintained and upheld the philosophies of Theudas. Hence it states in the Gnostic Gospels:

"The disciples said to Jesus, "We know that you will depart from us. Who is to be our leader?"

Jesus said to them, "wherever you are, you are to go to James the righteous, for whose sake heaven and earth came into being." [229]

On the other hand, there were those who followed Peter & Paul, maintaining that Jesus was from the tribe of Judah, thereby ensuring a political philosophy based on a hierarchal society led by an anointed king as Herod Agrippa 1 believed himself to be, his grandmother being

---

229. James M. Robinson. "The Nag Hammadi Library." Harper Collins. 1990.

Mariamme 1, descended from Judas Maccabees. Which raises the question: "*Who was Paul's Christ?*"

I believe that Judas was Paul's Christ, a Bishop through the Judaic line who was also given the name "*Joshua*" at circumcision and who through becoming cursed by hanging from a gibbet (Deu. 21: 22 & 23), redeemed believers from the Levitical laws of purity and unfortunately, due to the evolving events in the Pauline camp, the Mosaic Laws of Righteousness as well (Gal. 5:3 & 4). Paul believed that all authority should be under the High Priest of the Sanhedrin and Herod Agrippa 1, a descendent of the Levite Mariamme the daughter of Judas Maccabee, as opposed to the judges, the priests of Zadok who followed the laws of Righteousness (Romans 13:1). This obviously stands in direct opposition to the philosophies of James the Teacher of Righteousness.(James 1: 19–25)

Paul was largely influenced by Simon Peter and it was Peter who denied or betrayed Jesus three times. Judas Iscariot, we are told in John 12:2, was the son of Simon who I believe was Simon Peter, the name "*Peter*" being given to him in order to differentiate between himself and Simon, the brother of Jesus (Matt. 13:55). Both Peter and his son Judas not only betrayed Jesus but were the only ones in the Gospels referred to as being possessed by Satan. Luke 22:3:

"*Then Satan entered into Judas, who was called Iscariot.*"

Luke 22:31:

"*Simon, Simon, take heed: Satan has been given leave to sift all of you like wheat.*"

Matthew 4:8 & 9.

"*The devil took him next to a very high mountain, and showed him all the kingdoms of the world in their glory.*"

"All these," he said, "I will give you, if you will only fall down and do me honour."

But Jesus said, "Out of my sight Satan! Scripture says, "You shall honour the Lord your God and worship him alone."

Again we see a rejection of a monarchy or potentate in the interests of the Law of God. The parallel of Mat. 4:8 & 9 is found in Mark 8:32, 33 & 36:

"At this Peter took hold of him and began to rebuke him. But Jesus, turning and looking at his disciples, rebuked Peter.

"Out of my sight, Satan!" he said. "You think as men think, not as God thinks....For what shall it profit a man, if he shall gain the whole world, and lose his own soul?'

Later in Peter 2:13, 17 & 18, Peter, like Satan, encourages worship, honour and submission to potentates or *"masters"* rather than like Jesus who said, *"You shall honour the Lord your God and worship him alone."*

"Submit yourselves for the sake of authority, whether to the emperor as supreme (Caligula & later Claudius), or to governors as his deputies (Caspius Fadus)...Honour all men. Love the brotherhood. Fear God. Honour the king...(Herod Agrippa 1)."

Peter, I believe, is in fact advocating a servile philosophy in order that those in power can maintain and suppress all those beneath them, not adhering to the laws of justice, but to their own laws of suppression and subjugation. He goes on to say in 18:

"Servants, submit to your masters with all due respect, not only to those who are kind and forbearing, but even to those who are unjust."

This in turn means that they should not *"seek justice by way of the laws of righteousness"* and contradicts the laws of Moses whereby a wronged slave is entitled to recompense.

What I propose is that it was Simon Peter's son who *"hung from a tree,"* John 12:4:...

"Then saith one of his disciples, Judas Iscariot, Simon's (Peter's) son, which should betray him..."

...and in accordance with Deuteronomy 21: 22 & 23:

"And if a man have committed a sin worthy of death, and thou hang him on a tree:
His body shall not remain all night upon the tree, but thou shalt in any wise bury him that day; (for he that is hanged is accursed of God;)....

Simon Peter in turn, referred to as Simon the Cyrene, followed Judas to *"the gibbet."* After this act, Peter continued to praise Judas Iscariot and teach an autocratic religious belief that influenced Paul's beliefs. Hence, Jesus was given a Judaic descent to the tribe of Judah through David. Judas Iscariot and David are linked in Acts 1:16:

"My friends, the prophecy in scripture, which the Holy Spirit uttered concerning Judas through the mouth of David,...."

In Acts, 10:39 & 13: 29 Peter says of his saviour:

"They put him to death, hanging him on a gibbet;[230]...they took him down from the gibbet and laid him in a tomb."

---

230. A gibbet, unlike a cross is:gallows; a post or tree with an arm from which an executed criminal person is hung.

Mark, Luke and John make no mention of Judas hanging from a tree or gibbet, which to my mind is a strange omission. Surely the death of a betrayer would have been a noteworthy event? The only brief allusion to the death of Judas in the Gospels is found in Matthew 27:5:

"And he cast down the pieces of silver in the temple, and departed, and went and hanged himself."

In Acts 10:39 & 13:29 Peter does not say that his saviour was crucified but hung from a gibbet in accordance with Deuteronomy, whilst in the Habakkuk commentary it was the wicked priest, rather than the Teacher of Righteousness who was afflicted *"with a destroying scourge"* and was *"delivered into the hands of his enemies."*

The only *"treasurer"* mentioned in the Gospels was Judas and as treasurer, he would have been a Bishop in accordance with Essene practice. The only person referred to as a Bishop was Judas and Peter considered Judas as Bishop to be his saviour. Peter 2:24 & 25:

"Who his own self bare our sins in his body on the tree, that we, being dead to sins, should live unto righteousness: by whose stripes ye were healed. For ye were as sheep going astray; but are now returned unto the Shepherd and Bishop of your souls."

Jesus, on the other hand, was never referred to as a Bishop. The first mention of a Bishop in the New Testament comes in Acts and this Bishop is mentioned in relation to Judas. The first decision made in Acts by the Apostles, is the election of a new Bishop. One would have thought that Jesus was the Bishop, the leader who needed to be replaced, but instead in Acts 1:20, we are told that it is Judas who is replaced as leader.

In Mark 6:34 after the Baptist's death when Jesus goes to Galilee, he also makes a reference to a Shepherd, whom Peter refers to as Bishop, and his followers who are now lost after his death:

"*And when Jesus came out, saw much people, and was moved with compassion toward them, because they were as sheep not having a shepherd: and he began to teach them many things.*"

Both Judas and Simon Peter are referred to as Satan and of Satan Jesus has this to say in John 8:44.

"*He was a murderer from the beginning, and is not rooted in the truth; there is no truth in him. When he tells a lie he is speaking his own language, for he is a liar and the father of lies.*"

Due to the fact that Judas hung from a gibbet, he is a murderer whilst Simon Peter is guilty of lying by denying Jesus three times. As a murderer Judas could be the "*wicked priest*" whilst Peter and could be "*the man of the lie*" in the Habakkuk commentary. Peter behaved in a manner that Jesus would never have behaved. Instead of restoring sight, in Acts he makes a man blind and before that he murders Ananias and Sapphira in Acts 5. Peter rules through fear, Peter 2:17:

"*Fear God.*"

Acts 5:11.

"*And great fear came upon all the church, and upon as many as heard these things.*"

John on the other hand, advocates a diametrically opposed epistemology in 4:8 & 18:

"*He that loveth not knoweth not God; for God is love. . . .There is no fear in love; but perfect love casteth out fear: because fear hath torment. He that feareth is not made perfect in love.*"

After the Baptist was arrested, Theudas and his followers escaped and went first to Galilee and then up to Mount Gerizim for Pentecost.

During the community meal at Pentecost, Judas, *"the wicked priest,"* was cursed, possibly for betraying the Baptist and the Samaritans/Ephraimites as we will see later, as well as informing "the orthodox Sadducee priesthood, Herod Agrippa 1 and Pontius Pilate of the groups movements. Like Peter, he supported the emperor as supreme, the king and the governors. He then either hung himself from a tree or was hung from a tree in accordance with Deuteronomy. His story, the Baptist's story and Lazarus's story of being raised from the dead become intertwined. Acts, in turn, begins at this point, and in spite of a Jesus instructing Peter to *"follow me,"* as John suggests, he betrays them and with Paul throws in his lot in support of the now dead Judas. Acts 10:39:

"...whom they slew and hanged on a tree."

Acts 13:29:

"They took him down from the tree, and laid him in a sepulchre."

Later this *"hanging from a tree"* is put into the Roman context rather than the Hebrew, of being crucified. Herod Agrippa 1, who desired to be king in the mold of Herod the Great, hearing rumours about a *"King of Israel"* who had entered Jerusalem on a donkey at Passover, informed Pilate, who being afraid of insurrection, ordered the massacre of the Samaritans in 35 A.D., later known as *"the massacre of the innocents"* by King Herod. Pontius Pilate was sent back to Rome for this crime in the Autumn of 36 A.D. after Caiaphas had been deposed at the Passover and replaced by Jonathan. As we can see from the dating, three passovers as given in the Gospels could not have taken place between the Baptist's arrest in 35 A.D. and the deposing of Pilate and Caiaphas in 36 A.D .

If there is any value in the Biblical crucifixion, it is this. The allegorical metaphors used state that the Romans crucified *"the firstborn of God."* The Samaritans believe that they are the direct descendants of Ephraim, being *"the firstborn"* in accordance with Genesis, Jeremiah and James 1:18. Hence, the historic facts are that the massacre of the innocents, the firstborn sons and the Joshuas (plural), or Essene Nazarenes, were put to death by Pilate. Pilate was supported in this act by Herod Agrippa 1 and Joseph Caiaphas, a Levitical priest.

The synoptic Gospels appear to pick up the story from here, whilst the resurrection of Lazarus, the death of the Baptizer and a Bishop/Mebakkar hanged from a tree have been superimposed over the deaths of Theudas, James and John Zebedee. Hence the historic dates do not tally with the Biblical text. The story of the miraculous catch of fish in John which is placed at the end of his text is placed by Matthew at the beginning of his as well as Simon Peter being instructed to *"follow me."* John does not give a list of disciples and makes no mention of Mary and Joseph fleeing to Egypt, which appears to have occurred simultaneously with the Samaritan massacre in 35 A.D., where I believe, Johanna the Baptist being a Mary and wife of Jesus, escaped with Joseph of Arimathea who later married her and adopted her child.

I suspect that our *"Jesus"* in the Gospels is an amalgamation of the lives of four people. The Baptist told in John whilst the story of John Zebedee and Theudas are told in either/or Matthew and Mark. Taking Josephus's histories and Thiering's research into account, I would go so far as to pose the possibility that Theudas is the central figure that we are looking for. Because the Bible is a religious and symbolic work, the history of the time was interwoven with Joshua's philosophies giving us a New Testament Gospel that runs like a parable. The story of Joseph and a Mary being one example where we saw above that it was a parable of the age as related through Cabalistic studies, the mysteries of the kingdom of heaven.

The last of the four characters could be James the Righteous related in the Gospel of Luke. He refers to the anointing with holy oil from an alabaster jar by a woman as early as chapter 7:37. In chapter 13:1 we can, miraculously enough, pin point an historic date when he makes a reference to the massacre of the innocents at Mount Gerizim by Pilate in 35 A.D...

"There were present at that season some that told him of the Galilaens, whose blood Pilate had mingled with their sacrifices."

According to Josephus in his Antiquities XV111. 85–87:

"...a claimant to be the Taheb appeared among the Samaritans about the same time as Jesus was manifesting himself as Messiah. The Samaritans streamed towards Mt.Gerizim where this Taheb promised to reveal to them the sacred vessels of the Tabernacle which Moses had buried there. Pontius Pilate sent his troops against them and killed many, taking others prisoners who were afterwards executed." [231]

Besides Luke's mention of this incident, all three of the synoptic Gospels refer to a *"Jesus"* ascending a mountain in Samaria after the Baptist's death where three Tabernacles are made for Joshua, Moses and Elias. (Matt. 17. 1–13, Mark 9 2–13 and Luke 9 28–36.) The Gospel of John, however, makes no mention of this incident at all.

---

231. Hugh Schonfield. "The Essene Odyssey." Element Books Limited. 1984.

After a long period spent in Samaria between chapters 9 and 19, Luke finally has James return to Jerusalem through Jericho, the city that Joshua conquered in order to enter the Promised Land. His last speeches refer to the prediction of the fall of the temple in 70 A.D. and his accurate descriptions suggest that the writer and biographer of James the Righteous, witnessed the event. Under the orders of the High Priest Anan, James who at this time was the leader of the church, was stoned to death in 62 A.D.

Besides all three men possibly having the mitzvah name *"Joshua"* or being known by the Arabic equivalent *"Essa"* giving rise to the Essenes, the sequence of their many other names would have been subject to change and therefore no one person would retain the same name from birth to death, which for our purposes causes confusion.

In Africa, this custom is still prevalent. A name is given at birth, another at puberty during initiation into manhood or womanhood and yet another later on when marriage takes place. Coupled with their own traditions is a new one whereby they also have a European name used for general purposes but not used in their private lives.

To my mind, Theudas, James and John Zebedee as well as James the Righteous could all have used the circumcision name Joshua when advocating Ephraimite philosophies whilst giving a sermon in a synagogue or temple. The *"three"* who were crucified at exactly or roughly the same time, were Theudas, James Zebedee and John Zebedee.

The High Temple priests persecuted these men for the simple reason that they had embraced Zion, a mountain, believing that a leader's duty, a judge and a holder of the law was to serve and not to lord it over people by making their *"authority felt."* They were fulfilling the philosophies of Joshua in the Old Testament who had set up a *"New Kingdom"* consisting of a democratic federal state within Israel, in opposition to the Judaism that Ezra had instituted under a High Priest when the Jews returned from Babylon. But worse than this, they prayed in a grove of trees in the Garden of Gethsemane, thereby bringing the sacred pillar, the Ashtaroth, the tent of meeting or democracy to Jerusalem and thereby living as Joshua lived in the Old Testament and fulfilling Isaiah 49:22 in accordance with Proverbs 2:18:

"Thus saith the Lord God, Behold I will lift up mine hand to the Gentiles, and set up my standard to the people: and they shall bring thy sons in their arms, and thy daughters shall be carried upon their shoulders."

"She is a tree of life to them that lay hold upon her: and happy is every one that retaineth her."

The two last and final objections that the High Priests had regarding these Messiahs, was that through the rituals carried out in Numbers 6, they were ordaining all classes of people, both male and female, to be firstborn named Israel/Jacob under the Nazarite priesthood which the Sadducee Levitical priesthood would have condemned in terms of Numbers 3:41 and 8:18. What is more, they were teaching a theology that advocated atonement for sins, sacrifice for the people of Israel, spiritual rebirth and an eschatological philosophy of resurrection from the grave rejected at the beginning of the ministry as seen in Matthew 3:4 where we have been led to believe that a resurrection had not as yet occurred. Which raises the question: was a Jesus literally and figuratively raised from the dead, or was this a spiritual philosophy whereby being raised from the dead had nothing to do with a bodily resurrection but was a living resurrection?

Although many authors, Barbara Theiring included, have postulated that Jesus survived the cross due to the fact that there would not have been a flow of blood and water when the soldier pierced his side with a sword if he was dead, and in this instance I would say that it was Theudas who survived, I believe that the real message of resurrection lies in Hebrew ritual, as all answers lie in the original Hebrew, of the celebration of Yom Kippur.

Chapter Eleven.

Yom Kippur and the Nazarene

The Gnostic Gospel of Philip:
"Those who say that the lord died first and (then) rose up are in error,
for he rose up first and (then) died."[232]

Yom Kippur takes place at the end of Rosh HaShannah, the Hebrew New Year, in the seventh month of Tishri. Rosh HaShannah is known as *"The Days of Judgement"* or *"The Days of Awe."* It is the only celebration that is considered to be as Holy as the Sabbath. *"Rosh"* means head and *"HaShannah"* means year. As Sabbath is the bride of the Lord, so is HaShannah, and the bridegroom and the bride, God and the Spirit, the Lord and Zion are reunited.

---

232. James M.Robinson. "The Nag Hammadi Library." The Gospel of Philip. Harper Collins. 1990.

Being New Year, it too, like the Sabbath is the Alpha and Omega, *"the end of the beginning"* and the *"beginning of the end."* Once again, as occurs in the Sabbath, the world is redeemed to another cycle with the gathering of the harvest. The Lord with his scythe goes through the fields on Judgement Day with the onset of winter when everything dies. It is an ongoing, timeless process where the past, present and future stand still in eternity and not something that we have to wait for. In other words, *"Judgement Day"* comes once a year and the living dead arise from their graves in a living resurrection, which brings us to Yom Kippur, the Day of Atonement.

In Judea during the first century A.D., the high priest entered the *"holy of holies"* in a white robe. This robe symbolized purity and the grave and the high priest went through a symbolic death to save all of Israel. He stayed there for a twenty-four hour period, fasting and making sacrifice for the people. At the end of Yom Kippur/Day of Atonement, he emerged and the people were considered to be spiritually reborn *through him.* Hence, through this act sins were atoned for, sacrifice was made for the whole of Israel and this resulted in resurrection from the grave, the white robe being cast aside. Such practices are not only traced to Egyptian initiation rites where priests and priestesses entered the realm of the dead like Osiris, and were then resurrected, but to Jacob's sons atoning for the *apparent* death of Joseph and his miraculous *resurrection* when he is reunited with his father in Egypt.

Today there is no High Priest and there is no temple. Any devout Hebrew is permitted to fast for a twenty-four hour period (the same amount of time that Jesus is said to have spent in the tomb), dress in grave clothes, ask for atonement from sins, be redeemed, resurrected and reborn *through their own efforts.* The psychological effect that a yearly enactment of this ritual has on people, is that if they practice it throughout a life time, when they do in fact die, they will not fear the passing, because like Yom Kippur and the seasons, they know that they will be reborn to a new life through the Holy Spirit or our right brain spirituality. It also alleviates any guilt that one might feel over things done in the past year, leaving you free to dump all the psychological garbage that weighs you down and then you will be able to live for the moment with a clear heart and open mind.

According to Hebrew tradition and Revelation, the book of life is opened on Rosh HaShannah, the *"Days of Judgement"* and closed on Yom Kippur when your fate will be sealed for the coming year. God forgives all sins against himself during this time but any sins against our neighbours we have to ask them for forgiveness as well as forgiving ourselves for the things that we have done. Yom Kippur is the only festival that is not based on a natural or agricultural event or an historic event, though I believe that it was a ritual kept from Egyptian times. Up until the first century A.D., Yom Kippur was the prerogative of the elect, the High Priest of the Temple, preferably a Levite and no mere mortal was allowed to enact this judgement and resurrection. Thereafter, due to the Essenes it became the privilege of all the people of Israel who attained personal salvation as opposed to going through a priest.

It follows that if Joshua was advocating an *"anointing"* for all then he would also have advocated this spiritual rebirth from the grave for all after the *"Days of Judgement"* on *"The Day of Atonement."* John 3:3–10:

"Except a man be born again, he cannot see the kingdom of God...so is every one that is born of the Spirit...Marvel not that I said unto thee, Ye must be born again...Nicodemus answered and said unto him, How can these things be? Jesus answered and said unto him, Art thou a teacher of Israel, and knowest not these things?"

As a teacher of Israel, Nicodemus was expected to know of the ritual of the Day of Atonement (Yom Kippur) and was chastised by Jesus for his ignorance. It appears that within the Essene community a split occurred between two groups and a movement associated with *"the end of days"* began to take form. At Qumram, an eschatological doctrine of resurrection [Matt.3:4] began to emerge and in turn, created a split within the priesthood. Those who agreed with this philosophy based their arguments on Gen.1 seeing themselves as immortal and made in the image of God, while those who did not based their arguments on Gen.2. seeing themselves as mortal, made from clay and denied the fruit from the tree of everlasting life.

According to Eisenman and Wise, this split is mentioned in the Damascus Document whereby *"the eschatological activity of "the sons of Zadok....in the last days"* is condemned and referred to as *"the Wicked."* To quote 4Q397–399, lines 13, 14, 15 and 33 and taking into consideration that the *"end of time"* and the *"end of days"* could have referred to as what is known today as Rosh HaShannah, the Days of Judgement:

"It shall come to pass that when all these things come upon you in the End of Days, the blessing and the curse that I have set before you, and you call them to mind, and return to me with all your heart at the End of Time, then you will live Once again. Then you will rejoice at the End of Time, when you find some of our words were true. Thus, it will be reckoned to you as Righteousness your having done what is Upright and Good before Him, for your own Good and for that of Israel."

I suspect that an Essene's resurrection on the Day of Atonement or Yom Kippur occurred six months before the Baptist was arrested at Passover and was the true Christian story of being reborn. Being associated with Yom Kippur, it is available to all generations on a yearly basis for all time. Because it is a personal, individual and direct experience, we can, each and every one of us be redeemed and resurrected to a new life during the *"Day of Atonement"* after we have been judged, which makes sense of the Gospel words, *"God is the God of the Living, not the dead."* (see Proverbs 8:36)

The resurrection on the Day of Atonement is not to be mixed up with Judas hanging from a gibbet or James, John and Theudas's crucifixion in 44 A.D. and certainly had nothing to do with an Adonis figure nailed to the cross. Alternatively, I believe that the raising of Lazarus gives us the true story of death and resurrection and is in keeping with the Hebrew practice of Yom Kippur.

Joseph Caiaphas, who was the High Priest during 34/35 A.D. heard about the raising of Lazarus, his rebirth through the Spirit and symbolic death and resurrection. He was aware of the ritual and had just carried it out himself when he heard of what went on in Bethany. He says in John 11:49–51, that the Pharisees know nothing at all. It was expedient for the High Priest to make a symbolic sacrifice of death on the Day of Atonement/Yom Kippur so that the whole nation should not perish. From then on, the orthodox Jews vow to put a Jesus to death for exercising the ritual and for playing the role of a High Priest. Caiaphas also warns them that by this act, the Essenes will gather together in one the children of God that were scattered abroad being the Lost Tribes of Israel, thereby fulfilling Jeremiah's prophecy that Ephraim would gather the nations and re-establish the New Kingdom as well as Isaiah's prophecy that a standard would be lifted up to the nations. He tells them that if they let this happen, then the Romans will come and take away their place and their nation.

Lazarus's actions were in keeping with Yom Kippur, for Martha, an Essene, says in John 11:24:

"I know that he shall rise again in the resurrection at the last day."

The *"resurrection at the last day"* is not the later Catholic view of the one and only *"Day of Judgement."* This resurrection is Yom Kippur that ends the Hebrew New Year of Rosh HaShannah, the *"Days of Judgement."* It appears that Lazarus, as the Gospels tell us, had fallen asleep, which a *"Jesus"* first says he has. But then a Jesus on the way to the tomb becomes afraid that he is in fact dead.

Lazarus was not a disciple and this story is only mentioned in the Gospel of John, although Luke makes reference to it as a parable long after the anointing with holy oil. So who was he? The name *"Lazarus"* is the Greek form of the Hebrew *"Ezer."* There were two Ezers in the Old Testament, one being the son of Ephraim and the other the son of Joshua.[233] Symbolically Lazarus represents the descendants of Ephraim and Joshua (the firstborn), the Kingdom of Israel being raised from the dead where *"all classes of people,"* both male and female could be reborn through the Spirit at Yom Kippur.

I believe that the story could possibly go as follows. During Rosh HaShannah of 34 A.D., Joshua went to Cana in Galilee where the first wedding celebration between Hannah and himself took place as related in John 2. According to Barbara Thiering, the Essenes had two wedding ceremonies. One in September which co-insides with Rosh HaShannah and one in March that co-insides with the Passover.[234]

The celebration of Rosh HaShannah is both God's creation of the world, Genesis 1, God and the Spirit who moves across the waters, as well as the end with the judgement of the world where we have the holy marriage. As occurs at Sabbath, the bride, the Shekinah is welcomed:

"This is the day the world was called into existence. This is the day He causeth all creatures to stand in judgement."

---

233. O.Odelain and R.Seguineau. "Dictionary of Proper Names and Places in the Bible." Robert Hale Limited.1991.

234. Barbara Thiering. "Jesus the Man." Doubleday. 1992.

It is both the beginning and the end and a new year is established. Hence the new Jerusalem comes down with the twelve foundations of the twelve months and the four walls of the seasons. Rev. 19:5, 9 & 10:

"And I heard what sounded like a vast throng..." Hallelujah! The Lord our God, sovereign over all, has entered on his reign! Let us rejoice and shout for joy and pay homage to him, for the wedding day of the Lamb has come! His bride has made herself ready, and she has been given fine linen, shining and clean, to wear...Happy are those who are invited to the wedding banquet of the Lamb!..."

Rev. 20:13:

"Everyone was judged on the records of their deeds."

The cycle of the beginning and the end is again set in motion. 22:13:

"I am Alpha and Omega, the first and the last, the beginning and the end."

In the New Testament Joshua says, *"Though you are dead, yet shall you live."* The spiritually dead, after passing through the judgement of Rosh HaShannah (Rev.20:13) then go through the rebirth of Yom Kippur (Rev. 22:13). They dress in grave clothes, enter the synagogue for a twenty-four hour period and are then resurrected as only the High Priest Caiaphas was permitted to do in Biblical times.

On the Day of Atonement an Essene went up to Gethsemane near Bethany where he entered a cave for a twenty-four hour period, dressed in a white robe with his head wrapped in a cloth as of a turban, being grave clothes and a symbol of purity. Rev. 22:14:

"Happy are those who wash their robes clean."

The ritual, being resurrection into the new year of Zion is associated with the tree of everlasting life spoken of in Proverbs and denied to Adam and Eve in Gen.2. Rev.22:14:

"They shall be free to eat from the tree of life and may enter the city by the gates."

As it says in John 3:3–8, Lazarus was reborn of the Spirit and could therefore enter the Kingdom of Heaven. Thereafter, a *"Mary"* gives testimony as to what has occurred in John 11:45:

"Then many of the Jews which came to Mary (the baptist) and had seen the things which Jesus did, believed on him."

Miraculously enough, the one thing that has remained in Christianity is that it was only the women who testified to the resurrection and women who spread the news, as in the ancient rites where Isis raised Osiris from the dead. Those who thought that he was dead, instead of asleep, as the story of Lazarus states, cannot believe that he has come out of the tomb and want evidence. In the Gospels this evidence is given by Jesus showing the marks on his hands, but these marks are the symbols of the Holy Spirit, Zion, not marks made by nails. Isaiah says in 49:14–16, that the Lord will not forget his bride, the Holy Spirit, because:

"But Zion said, The Lord hath forsaken me, and my Lord hath forgotten me. Can a woman forget her sucking child, that she should not have compassion on the son of her womb? yea, they may forget, yet will I not forget thee. Behold, I have graven thee upon the palms of my hands."

Saint Francis of Assisi was never crucified and yet he too, had these stigmata on his hands, symbol of Zion, the Holy Spirit, as did Saint Catherine of Seine. There are up to twenty stigmatics alive today. Stigmata is caused by altered states of awareness whilst in meditation or deep prayer and is a type of self hypnosis whereby we connect with the subconscious mind and the feminine right brain which governs our spirituality. It is interesting to note that there are more female stigmatics than male.

At the Passover festival the second wedding celebration was performed. After this marriage we have the Baptist's arrest in 35 A.D. and the initiation of a man who was to become a Nazarene. The rules of a Nazarene as we have already discussed, was that they were not to take wine or strong drink; that they were to separate themselves from others, becoming the penitents of Israel in the desert; that they were initiated after eight days with the sacrificial lamb, unleavened bread and holy oil; and lastly that they were to have their heads shaved. The same sequence of initiation is found in the Gospels.

1) No longer drink the fruit of the vine. Mark 14:25:

"Verily I say unto you, I will drink no more the fruit of the vine, until that day that I drink it new in the kingdom of God."

2) Mary Magdalene is only mentioned twice in the Gospels. Once as the woman from whom seven daemons were cast out and once at the tomb. If she was Herodias, as I suspect, then she went to find Jesus in the Garden of Gethsemane after the Baptist's arrest, but he warns her not to touch him in accordance with the laws laid down for Nazarenes, who were not allowed to have physical contact with anyone until the Nazarene ceremony was completed. John 20:17:

"....Touch me not; for I am not yet ascended to my Father: but go to my brethren, and say unto them, I ascend unto my Father, and your Father; and to my God, and your God."

3) They were to separate themselves apart from others. Jesus separates himself into the desert as all the penitents of Israel did and tells his disciples to meet him in Galilee. Matthew 14:13:

"...he departed thence by ship into a desert place apart."

4) They became Nazarenes after eight days. John 20:26:

"And after eight days...then came Jesus..."...who John says did many
more things thereafter.

5) Neither Mary Magdalene nor the disciples at first recognized him.
This could be that as an initiated Nazarene, he had had his head shaved.

The above evidence in conjunction with Hebrew practice, suggests
that Jesus either raised an Essene in accordance with Yom Kippur, or
was raised himself at the Hebrew New Year, teaching his followers that
all people can be Spiritually raised from the dead in a living resurrection during the *"Days of Judgement"* and the *"Day of Atonement."* The
shroud or grave clothes were a symbol which was cast aside after this
initiation ceremony.[235]

According to Essene practice, these ceremonies co-insided with a
holy marriage ceremony, as recorded in Revelation, of which there were
two. One in September at the New Year which takes place in the seventh
month of Tishri, and one in March during the Passover which takes
place during the first month of Nisan. The Passover ceremony in turn,
included the anointing after a three year probation period and the rituals necessary, which include those of the Passover (See Num.6) in
order to become a Nazarene.

Due to these ceremonies, Jesus *"rose up first and (then)..."* died when
he was crucified in 44 A.D.

Zechariah 3:

---

235. This shroud is still used in Freemasonry where the initiate is covered in a shroud and
also goes through a symbolic death and resurrection.

"And he shewed me Joshua the high priest standing before the angel of the Lord, and Satan standing at his right hand to resist him.

And the Lord said unto Satan, The Lord rebuke thee, O Satan; even the Lord that hath chosen Jerusalem rebuke thee: is not this a brand plucked out of the fire?

Now Joshua was clothed with filthy garments, and stood before the angel.

And he answered and spake unto those that stood before him, saying, Take away the filthy garments from him. And unto him he said, Behold I have caused thine iniquity to pass from thee, and I will clothe thee with change of raiment.

And I said, Let them set a fair mitre upon his head. So they set a fair mitre upon his head, and clothed him with garments. And the angel of the Lord stood by.

And the angel of the Lord protested unto Joshua, saying,

Thus saith the Lord of hosts; If thou wilt walk in my ways, and if thou wilt keep my charge, then thou shalt also judge my house, and shalt keep my courts, and I will give thee places to walk among these that stand by.

Hear now, O Joshua the high priest, thou, and thy fellows that sit before thee: for they are men wondered at: for behold, I will bring forth my servant the BRANCH.

For behold the stone that I have laid before Joshua; upon one stone shall be seven eyes: behold, I will engrave the graving thereof, saith the Lord of hosts, and I will remove the iniquity of that land in one day.

In that day, saith the Lord of hosts, shall ye call every person your neighbour under the vine and under the fig tree."

Epilogue

This is our ancient past. But what of the last two thousand years and what of our future? It is my belief that throughout the last two thousand years, the descendants of the Essenes, of Joseph, Ephraim and Joshua, have never lost sight of their convictions and have strived to bring about a democratic world with freedom, justice and equality for all. But who were these people and who are they today?

Many will speculate that they fled to the south of France where their descendants became the Cathars and the Knights Templar and after the Inquisition and the death of Jaques de Molay re-established themselves in Scotland and became what was later known as the Fraternity of the Freemasons. This may well prove to be the case. Of their former residence in Provence and the Languedoc, I am more certain, of their later involvement with the Freemasons I am not so sure for the simple reason that Freemasonary is a Brotherhood which precludes, in most cases, the involvement of women.

But whoever this group proves to be in the end, I believe that we owe them a great debt, for without this secret society, the majority of the world's population would be subjected to tyranny under megalomaniacs who seek to rule the world through divine right, physical might or monetary manipulation as opposed to serving it.

If there is a Messiah, or direct descendent of Joshua, and if this person should make him or herself known, I doubt very much if he or she would take any kind of pontifical role or accept the throne of any country, let alone the throne of the world. If anything, he or she and their followers will remain hidden, steering history from the background instead of seeking the glory, fame and especially the power that so many leaders have sought to have over others in the past.

Of the twentieth century leaders who have embraced the philosophies that I have expounded on in the above text, three come to mind and these three in turn saw their roles in international politics not as one of power and authority, but one of service to their nation and the world at large.I believe that it is towards their lives that we should look for guidance in the future, for each of them walked in the footsteps of Joshua. Ghandi, Mandela and the Dalai Lama.

Bibliography

Andrew,Richard & Schellenberger, Paul. *"The Tomb of God."* Little Brown and Company. 1996.

Ashe, Geoffrey. *"The Virgin."* Arkana. 1988.

Baigent, Michael; Leigh,Richard & Lincoln,Henry. *"The Holy Blood and the Holy Grail."* Corgi. 1983.

Baigent, Michael; Leigh,Richard & Lincoln,Henry. *"The Messianic Legacy."* Corgi. 1987.

Baigent, Michael & Leigh, Richard.*"TheTemple and the Lodge."* Corgi. 1990.

Baigent, Michael & Leigh,Richard *"The Dead Sea Scrolls Deception."* Corgi. 1992.

Berg, S, Philip.Dr. *"The Kabbalah Connection."* Research Centre of Kabbalah-Jerusalem. New York. 1983.

Burrows, Millar.*"The Dead Sea Scrolls."* Secker & Warburg. 1956.

Cook, Edward. *"Solving The Mysteries of the Dead Sea Scrolls."* Zondervan Publishing House. 1994.

Collins, Andrew. *"From the Ashes of Angels."* Michael Joseph Ltd. 1996.

Collins, William Sons & Company LTD. *"Holy Bible."* King James Version. 1947.

Dimont, Max. *"Jews, God and History."* Signet. 1962.

Doresse, Jean. *"The Secret Books of the Egyptian Gnostics."* Inner Traditions Ltd. 1986.

Durdin-Robertson, Lawrence. *"The Year of the Goddess."* The Aquarian Press. 1990.

Eisenman, Robert & Wise, Michael. *"The Dead Sea Scrolls Uncovered."* Element. 1992.

Fasold, David. *"Noah's Ark."* Sidgwick and Jackson Limited. 1990.

Fiorenza, Schussler, Elizabeth. *"But She Said."* Beacon Press. 1992.

Fox, Lane, Robin. *"The Unauthorized Version."* Penguin. 1992.

Gardner, Laurence. *"Bloodline of the Holy Grail."* Element. 1996.

Glatzer, Nahum. *"The Passover Haggadah."* Schocken Books. 1989.

Graves, Robert. *"Hebrew Myths: The Book of Genesis."* Arena. 1989.

Gurney, O.R. *"The Hittites."* Penguin Books. 1990.

Halevi, Shimon Ben Z=Ev. *"the way of Kabbalah."* Gateway Books. 1991.

Hamlyn, Paul. *"Art Treasures of the World."* Paul Hamlyn Ltd. 1964.

Hancock, Graham. *"The Sign and the Seal."* Mandarin.1993

Harris, Anthony. *"The Sacred Virgin and the Holy Whore."* Sphere Books Limited. 1988.

Harver Publishing Inc.*"Webster Universal Dictionary."* 1968.

Jacobs, Louis. *"The Jewish Religion."* Oxford University Press. 1995.

'Johnson, Buffie. *"L'ady of the Beasts."* HarperCollins. 1990.

Jones, Steve. *"In the Blood. God, Genes and Destiny."* HarperCollins. 1996.

Jordan, Michael. *"Gods of the Earth."* Bantam Press. 1992.

Knight, Christopher and Lomas, Robert. *"The Hiram Key."* Century. 1996.

Knight, Christopher and Lomas, Robert. *"The Second Messiah."* Century. 1997.

Kolatch, Alfred. *"The Jewish Book of Why."* Jonathan David Publishers Inc. 1994.

Larousse. *"Dictionary of Beliefs and Religions."* Larousse. 1994.

Burton L.Mack. *"The Lost Gospel of Q."* HarperCollins. 1994.

Macrone, Michael. *"Brush up your Bible."* HarperCollins. 1994.

McCarta, Robertson, Verlag, Nelles. *"Egypt."* Nelles Verlag. 1991.

Osman, Ahmed. *"The House of the Messiah."* Grafton. 1992. Odelain, O and Seguineau, R. *"Dictionary of Proper Names and Places in the Bible."* Robert Hale Limited. 1991.

Oxford University Press. Cambridge University Press."*The Revised English Bible."* 1989.

Peach, Emily. *"Tarot for Tomorrow."* The Aquarian Press. 1988.

Redgrove, Peter. *"The Black Goddess."* Paladin Grafton Books. 1989.

Robinson, James. *"The Nag Hammadi Library."* HarperCollins. 1990.

Robinson, John. *"Born in Blood."* Arrow. 1993.

Rogerson, John."*Atlas of the Bible."* Phaidon Press Limited. 1989.

Rohl, David. *"A Test of Time. The Bible-From Myth to History."* Century. 1995.

Rosenberg, David and Bloom, Harold. *"The Book of J."* Grove Weidenfeld. 1990.

Schonfield, Hugh. *"The Essene Odyssey."* Element. 1984.

Silberman, Asher, Neil. *"The Hidden Scrolls."* Mandarin. 1996.

Smith, Morton. *"The Secret Gospel."* The Dawn Horse Press. 1984.

Smoot, George and Davidson, Keay. *"Wrinkles in Time. The Imprint of Creation."* Little Brown & Company. 1993.

Spong, Shelby, John. *"Born of A Woman."* HarperCollins. 1992.

Struik."*The World's Religions."* Struik. 1989.

Thiering, Barbara. *"Jesus The Man."* Doubleday. 1992.

Thomas, Gordon. *"The Trial."* Corgi. 1988.

Wilson, Ian. *"Jesus the Evidence."* Pan Books. 1985.

Zalewski, Pat. *"The Kabbalah of the Golden Dawn."* Liewellyn Publications. 1993.

Szekely, Bordeaux, Edmond. *"The Gospel of the Essenes."* C.W.Daniel Co, Ltd. 1988.